Disclosing Church

From 2006 to 2011, researchers at Heythrop College and the Oxford Centre for Ecclesiology and Practical Theology (OxCEPT, Ripon College Cuddesdon) worked on a theological and action research project: 'Action Research – Church and Society' (ARCS). 2010 saw the publication of *Talking About God in Practice: Theological Action Research and Practical Theology* (SCM), which presented in an accessible way the work of ARCS and its developing methodology. This turned out to be a landmark study in the praxis of Anglican and Catholic ecclesiology in the United Kingdom, showing how theology in these differing contexts interacted with the way in which clergy and congregations lived out their religious convictions. This book is a direct follow-up to that significant work, authored by one of the original researchers, providing a systematic analysis of the impact of the 'theological action research' methodology and its implications for a contemporary ecclesiology.

The book presents an ecclesiology generated from church practice, drawing on scholarship in the field as well as the results of the theological action research undertaken. It achieves this by including real scenarios alongside the academic discourse. This combination allows the author to tease out the complex relationship between the theory and the reality of church.

Addressing the need for a more developed theological and methodological account of the ARCS project, this is a book that will be of interest to scholars desiring more information not only on Western-lived religion but ecclesiology and theology more generally too.

Clare Watkins is Reader in Ecclesiology and Practical Theology at the University of Roehampton, UK, having previously worked as Vice Principal of the Margaret Beaufort Institute, Cambridge. She has researched, taught and published in a range of areas across ecclesiology and sacramental theology, with particular interests in lay vocation, marriage and family and the practical living of ecclesial life 'in ordinary'. Her publications reflect this, including: *Living Baptism: Called out of the Ordinary* (2006) and *Talking About God in Practice: Theological Action Research and Practical Theology* (2010). She is the Director of the Theology and Action Research Network (TARN), based at the University of Roehampton.

Explorations in Practical, Pastoral and Empirical Theology
Series Editors: Leslie J. Francis, Jeff Astley, Martyn Percy and Nicola Slee

Theological reflection on the church's practice is now recognised as a significant element in theological studies in the academy and seminary. Routledge's series in practical, pastoral and empirical theology seeks to foster this resurgence of interest and encourage new developments in practical and applied aspects of theology worldwide. This timely series draws together a wide range of disciplinary approaches and empirical studies to embrace contemporary developments including: the expansion of research in empirical theology, psychological theology, ministry studies, public theology, Christian education and faith development; key issues of contemporary society such as health, ethics and the environment; and more traditional areas of concern such as pastoral care and counselling.

Women Choosing Silence
Relationality and Transformation in Spiritual Practice
Alison Woolley

Ecclesial Leadership as Friendship
Chloe Lynch

Poetry, Practical Theology and Reflective Practice
Mark Pryce

Tragedies and Christian Congregations
The Practical Theology of Trauma
Edited by Megan Warner, Christopher Southgate, Carla A. Grosch-Miller and Hilary Ison

Disclosing Church
An Ecclesiology Learned from Conversations in Practice
Clare Watkins

For more information and a full list of titles in the series, please visit: www.routledge.com/religion/series/APPETHEO

Disclosing Church

An Ecclesiology Learned from Conversations in Practice

Clare Watkins

Routledge
Taylor & Francis Group
LONDON AND NEW YORK

First published 2020
by Routledge
2 Park Square, Milton Park, Abingdon, Oxon OX14 4RN

and by Routledge
605 Third Avenue, New York, NY 10017

Routledge is an imprint of the Taylor & Francis Group, an informa business

First issued in paperback 2021

Publisher's Note
The publisher has gone to great lengths to ensure the quality of this reprint but points out that some imperfections in the original copies may be apparent.

British Library Cataloguing-in-Publication Data
A catalogue record for this book is available from the British Library

Library of Congress Cataloging-in-Publication Data
A catalog record for this book has been requested

ISBN 13: 978-1-138-30774-2 (hbk)
ISBN 13: 978-1-03-223786-2 (pbk)
ISBN 13: 978-1-315-14253-1 (ebk)

DOI: 10.4324/9781315142531

Typeset in Sabon
by Apex CoVantage, LLC

To Guy, Christopher, Michael, Alice and Stephen – my family – my loving of whom not only delays my writing but also teaches me the wisdom and joy of attending to God's presence in the ordinary and everyday.

And to Digby – 1948–2018 – who taught me much about the 'adventure of holiness' which has kept me going.

Contents

Preface

A word to the reader

This book makes a significant and original contribution to the burgeoning field of practical theology, and that of practical or ethnographic ecclesiology in particular, by articulating learning from the theological action research work carried out by the Action Research Church and Society (ARCS) team from 2006–2011. It has been a difficult and slow piece of writing to undertake for a number of reasons: the amount of time taken over the research and its organisation; the move from group to sole authorship; the usual constraints of writing and researching whilst juggling the demands of an increasingly busy academic world and the realities of family; and of just *living*. But above all, I believe the central difficulty in writing has concerned a proper difficulty: that of the complexity of writing theologically in ways which are authentically integrated with real life practices whilst not colluding with any assumption that 'theology' and 'practice' are in any way separate or dis-integrated. Here the work of writing has become fraught with the need to witness truthfully to the one-ness of theology and practice. This challenge shapes all that follows, as the possibility for practice-based ecclesiology – the discernment of 'church' from faith-full living and attentive, multi-voiced conversation – is explored and demonstrated in written, book form, with all the limitations implied. It is perhaps for these reasons that the result is a slightly odd-looking book – as a quick glance at the contents page will illustrate. Before the reader gets down to their study of the text, a word of explanation about its unusual structure is helpful.

One of the original research team's claims is that, all too often, theologians' attempts to integrate theology with practice remain unable to achieve *both* an authentic witness to the complex detail of practice itself *and* a coherent and substantial theological account of the realities of faith. Such attempts will tend either to 'flatten' the realities of practice through the (apparent) coherence of our theology or lose theological potency and confidence in the face of the sheer complexity of data from practice. The challenge is: how are we to locate practice and theology in our text – which must have a beginning, middle and end – without implying and actualising a privileged position for one of our different sources, or 'voices', over the rest? How can something as linear as a *book* reflect the comings and goings of conversations across differences of practice, intellect, faith tradition and education or disciplinary background?

On one level, a book can only be a book. However, the original research team designed this book in such a way as to attempt to subvert the linear reading of the text so as to better embody a commitment to conversational methods of generating theology. To this end, after the foundational chapters 1–4, chapters 5–11 each engage with a number of 'accounts of practice', which are interspersed between the chapters of contextual and theological thought and discussion. Whilst readers are invited to engage with this structure in the way that most appeals to them, I would also encourage readers to read the texts of chapters 5–11, with their interleaving Accounts of Practice, as presented. This may be difficult; but in the end, it will make greater sense of the conversational dynamics as the different case study voices join in. For all its non-linear unorthodoxy, I believe this design of the book best replicates the conversational methods by which data has been gathered and discerned, and the meta-analysis taken place. I hope readers from their varied starting places – the academy, church practice, outreach work and practical theology in its various guises – will each discover fruitful ways in which to engage with the text.

For, in the end, all that follows is only ever a contribution to an on-going conversation. This book and its underpinning research do have some significant learning and insight to share, but the nature of such learning is non-definitive and non-prescriptive. Rather, it seeks to open up fresh thinking, speaking and listening amongst all of us whose practices (including academic practice) seek to discern more deeply what God is doing in the world.

Clare Watkins, *2019*

Acknowledgements

As discussed in the early chapters of his book, this study depends on the work carried out by a team of researchers from 2006 to 2011. Indeed, it is an essential quality of the methods and theological epistemology embodied in this work that real-life conversation, teamwork and relationships are part of the process. For this reason, I acknowledge with deep gratitude the friendship, scholarship and insightful conversation of my ARCS co-researchers: Dr. James Sweeney CP; Dr. Helen Cameron; Dr. Deborah Bhatti (now Ross), and Revd. Catherine (Cath) Duce. In addition, a special thanks must go to Cath for her early collation of materials for the writing of the Accounts of Practice; her skill and dedication in honouring this data as real gift has been invaluable to this book's task. Helen, too, has been a significant help both in bringing her expertise to bear especially for the themes of chapters 5 and 6, and for her careful, critical reading of the manuscript as it came into being. Thank you!

I am grateful for the generous research leave provision and support of this work from the University of Roehampton. In particular, the on-going encouragement of the Susanna Wesley Foundation and its funding of subsequent theological action research projects has helped develop and deepen this approach.

Thanks, too, to Dr. James Butler for his helpful reading of the early drafts and his comments and for the encouragement from Professor Pete Ward, and the Ecclesiology and Ethnography network generally, over my years of working with theological action research.

To the many research students, church practitioners and colleagues who have shown so lively an interest in theological action research and its 'four voices' framework I am also indebted. We never realised this would all 'take off' in the way that it has, and these conversations, critiques, challenges and affirmations over the years have shaped this book and its thinking.

Josh Wells and his co-workers at Routledge have shown extraordinary patience and a commitment to this project which has kept me going.

Acknowledgements 2

The data – what was gifted and its givers

The Acknowledgements of this book must include, in a particular and highlighted way, the insights, wisdom and gifts shared by those practitioners who were our co-workers in the theological action research projects. Everything has depended on their lived theologies and their willingness to share in conversation with us about them.

All the data referred to in this work is the fruit of empirical research, co-designed with practitioners, and carried out, in the main, by ARCS team members. It was carried out under the oversight of the Ethics Committee of Heythrop College, University of London, who approved methods and documentation. All respondents to the research have been anonymised. Where names are used, these are not the real names of participants. Data is co-owned by the ARCS research project and each particular practice group in relation to their own data.

The nature of the research meant that we have not anonymised specific churches, dioceses or other organisations. However, it is important to note that a considerable amount of time has elapsed – in some cases, over a decade, since this research was carried out. Most of those involved in leadership of the projects will have moved on, and a number of the practitioner groups no longer exist. In particular, the Westminster Agency for Evangelisation has been closed; and the change of episcopal leadership in Portsmouth diocese, and the accompanying loss of many of the lay staff with whom we worked, makes this diocese a somewhat different location from what it was in our work.

Overall, the approach taken to our 'data' was true to its name: something given, gifted, by those whose work in faith-full practices both humbled and taught our own academic theological practices. I have worked to make sure its discussion and recording in this book is respectful, truthful and indicative of a spirit of continued listening and reflecting on these gifts, which I hope will also shape the reader's engagement with what will always be an inadequate textual account of deeply human, interruptive and alive conversations-in-practice.

1 Disclosing church

Attending to people, attending to the Spirit

"There are only two problems with the Church: the first is people, and the second is the Holy Spirit". In the last 20 years or so of teaching ecclesiology to undergraduates, this sentence has always found its way into the opening lecture. I never plan for this to happen; I've been saying it too long, too frequently and am slightly embarrassed to find it popping up again. The persistence of the assertion is, however, significant: it seeks to express, memorably and uncompromisingly, the nature of the church as that mysterious, practical reality of diverse men, women and children living together 'in the Spirit'. At the same time, it makes clear that this beautiful pneumatological presence among peoples, lived out in particular and varied contexts, is always, and of necessity, problematic. It is a statement which underpins everything in this book and the research upon which it depends.

Formally, what follows is a work of ecclesiology – the theology of church – and much of this opening chapter will be concerned to locate the current study in the wider fields of contemporary ecclesiology and in the practical theology which increasingly characterises it.[1] However, the work behind this book also represents a more fundamental struggle: to explore what happens to our reading and practice of 'church' when we allow the voices and experiences of faith-full[2] people – including those who might be seen as on the edges of church – to shape our thinking as authentic witnesses to the working of the Holy Spirit in the world. It may well be that people and the Holy Spirit are the only problems with the church, but they are also, together, her most central reality and beating heart. To enquire of the Spirit among people, and of people in the light of the Spirit, is to do the kind of ecclesiology which can be seen as 'disclosing church'.

'Disclosing church' is an ecclesiological practice that has been born out of more than a decade of practice-based theological research, together with many more years of engagement with ecclesiology.[3] It is an approach born of a conviction that there is a specific contribution to be made to the understanding of church which depends upon a renewal of thought through engagement with the church's 'everyday'. Such engagement can offer some fresh perspectives on what seem to have become perennial difficulties for our own time in speaking about, and being, authentically and effectively, church.

In this introductory chapter something of the context of contemporary ecclesiology will be outlined, so as to demonstrate what it is to which this book's argument and methods are responding. In particular, current approaches to the perennial ecclesiological dynamic of practical-and-transcendent, human-and-divine, and so forth will be indicated, before addressing some of the more fundamental questions that such approaches share with practical theology more widely. Through this overview of these broad contemporary fields, a set of ecclesiological questions emerges, both topical in their particularity to our present context, and perennial to the traditional theological struggles to articulate church, which have been with Christians from the beginning. This confluence of questions sets out the difficulties – practical and theological – to which this book, and the research which underpins it, responds.

Church concrete, church mystical: the classic tension in contemporary key

The ecclesiological challenge of articulating the sense in which the church can be understood as both 'human and divine', both institution and of the Spirit, is perennial. It is just such a tension that underpins St. Paul's image of the Body of Christ in writing to the Christians in Corinth[4] and that shapes a number of other New Testament images of church.[5] The nature of the church as the community of the Spirit can be seen as one of the fundamental things at stake through the Protestant Reformation of the sixteenth century: is the Spirit unfailingly identified – even 'possessed' – by the institutional church? Or does the Spirit transcend all organisations and structures, even those of church?[6] In the twentieth century, these questions emerged in new ways, whether through the radical Protestantism of Brunner's argument that 'true church' – being an entirely spiritual reality – has nothing to do with 'institution'[7] or through the long hard debates of the Fathers of the Second Vatican Council, which resulted in a formulation of church as one reality made up of divine and human elements, analogous to the mystery of the incarnation.[8] The church has always presented itself to Christians as both a very human community and a reality in the world which, in some way or another, communicates God's presence to its members, and to the whole human family.[9]

It is not surprising, then, that contemporary ecclesiology is patterned by the same inherent and proper ecclesiological tensions. However, in our own time, shaped by modern understandings of what is 'real', and of a certain materialism and pragmatism in the West, there can be traced a growing preoccupation with church as a concrete, organised, social reality. Indeed, theologians themselves increasingly prefer accounts of church which deal with practical (which is to say largely empirical) sources, rather than systematic, 'purely theological' sources.[10] Such tendencies have not been without their critics. For example, Gary Badcock's work of 2009 sets out explicitly to correct what he perceives as this imbalance of sources, commenting:

> the preference for a practical theology over a systematic (and particularly a dogmatic) treatment of the *doctrine* of the church has in fact been commonplace in theological thought for quite a long time. Books in ecclesiology today belong, mostly as a matter of course, to the genre of practical or applied theology.[11]

The shift in ecclesiology toward practical theological methods has been problematic, even as it has given fresh energy to ecclesiology. So, Paul Avis, a leading British ecclesiologist, in recognising this empirical turn, rightly questions any tendency to overstate the 'theoretical' nature of traditional ecclesiology over and against any naive adoption of ethnographic and other empirical approaches, which fails to recognise that these, too, are heavily theorised.[12] There are some recent fine examples of more integrated approaches to a practice-based ecclesiology – for example, the work of Pete Ward[13] and (from a quite different tradition) Neil Ormerod.[14] Nonetheless, the fundamental struggle, identified by Healy and Badcock, to find ways of integrated speaking of the church, with both theological precision and continuity as well as contemporary, practice-informed authenticity, remains. Ecclesiology's turn to practice and the empirical is problematic methodologically as well as theologically.

The present book speaks directly into these debates, and in particular, seeks to offer an alternative in increasingly polarised accounts of church through a particular practice of attending to the various voices of church experience, culture, the academy and church traditions as – together and distinctly – theological authorities. In order to demonstrate more clearly what the issues are here, I will briefly explore the work of one writer, whose work has been key in the ecclesiological turn to the practical, and in the identifying of the problems that attend it: Nicholas Healy.

In what has become a highly influential work, written at the turn of the millennium, Nicholas Healy comments on contemporary ecclesiology: "In general, ecclesiology in our period has become highly systematic and theoretical, focused more upon discerning the right things to think about the church rather than orientated to the living, rather messy, confused and confusing body that the church's actuality is".[15] Whilst this work is now well over 15 years old, and Healy's own position has shifted somewhat, as we shall see, we begin here because of the ways in which this comment, and Healy's response to it, describes with particular clarity a contemporary identification of the perennial ecclesiological challenge: that of the integral nature of church as 'both human and divine'.

It is significant that Healy's work of 2000[16] begins with an account of what the problem with contemporary ecclesiology is: that it fails to take full account of the lived realities of church, and tends, rather, to abstract doctrinal approaches, which Healy describes as 'blueprint ecclesiologies'.[17] We are left, he argues, with a repeated 'two-fold construal' of church, which separates the concrete from the doctrinal, and which tends to privilege what is 'heavenly' over what is 'earthly', leading to an undue authority being given the purely theological over the practical.[18] Such a separation of the 'ideal' church from its practised reality is not only inauthentic, but – according to Healy – dangerous, in so far as it disables Christians from speaking of the realities of sin at work in church life.[19]

Healy's concern throughout is to explore ways of doing ecclesiology which enable an integrative holding together of the eschatological reality of Church as 'of the Kingdom', with the realities of ecclesial living. He calls for an ecclesiology rooted in "theological reflection on the church ... [which is] ... from the very outset a matter of practical rather than theoretical reasoning".[20] Significantly, he recognises such integrated ecclesiological thinking as characteristic of ecclesiologies of the pre-modern era, and it is the search to speak in continuity with that tradition, in our own time, that shapes his argument. This leads Healy to develop his own approach using a reading of von Balthasar's theology in which the 'theodramatic horizon' enables a way of thinking theologically, which encourages connectivity and the integration of divine and human.[21]

Some of the most influential observations of Healy's work come at the end of his book, when he speaks about the contributions that might be made to such an integrative, eschatologically conditioned ecclesiology from the disciplines of history, sociology and ethnography.[22] Here, Healy's work has been greeted as an encouragement to more practical theological ecclesiological approaches – approaches which, since the publication of *Church, World and the Christian Life*, have developed into a sizable body of literature, and a strong voice in the fields of both practical theology and ecclesiology.[23] It is, broadly speaking, a vision for a practice-based ecclesiology that is shared in this book's argument and research processes. Certainly the work done in congregational studies and in ethnographic studies have produced pictures of the complexities, joys and challenges of lived church which are invaluable in holding before the systematic theologian certain unavoidable realities. The voices of the Church 'on the ground' are being heard and documented, and reflected upon, as the 'ordinary theology' that they might be.[24] However, it can also be seen that this productive period in what might be called 'practical ecclesiology' raises a new set of questions for us.

The response of practical theology: a new set of questions

The ecclesiological turn to the practical is closely related to the development of the field of practical theology more generally. Indeed, the research reflected in this book clearly locates itself in that field.[25] It is by turning to practical theological thinking here that we can begin to explore more clearly the specific challenges of doing a theology of church in a practice-based way.

Whilst some vivid and important work has been done in disclosing church practices through ethnographic approaches,[26] inspired, at least in part, by Healy's critique of 'blueprint ecclesiology', there continues a struggle with the perennial question: what is the relation of the *practices* described to the *theology or doctrine* of church? The difficulty is one of how we are to speak *theologically* into the often delicate places of Christian practice in ways which are neither imperialist or unduly corrective nor simply ineffectual. If the theological response to an ethnographic study of church is heard as 'correcting' the complex reality described, we can end up all too easily with another blueprint ecclesiology, albeit one decorated with a few examples from practice. On the other hand, the failure to bring practical data into an integrative relationship with the longer tradition can simply lead us to generate more and more data, information and stories without any way of discerning their significance (if any). Paradoxically, practical theological approaches can, in this way, contribute to the separation of practice and theology in church in that they simply offer the *opposite* to an abstract blueprint in a description of practice.

Part of the problem here is with the methods of much practical theology and their influence on practice-based ecclesiology. In particular, methods of 'theological reflection'[27] require some scrutiny. It is common for practical theologians to employ social science methods in gathering empirical data about practice to inform their theology. The research underpinning the present book employs such methods. Such articulation of practices is something of an advance in that it aims to give voice and a certain authority to practice within the doing of theology. However, the real challenge arises when, faced with a great deal of data, the theologian is called to respond to it *theologically*. A sociological description of a particular congregation may be painstakingly carried out, for example, according to established social sciences principles, and a vivid, truthful and lively description of that congregation's life may result. Is this, on its own, theology? Certainly not in any traditional sense, for all that it may give us a good and interesting account of church life. It is here that 'theological reflection' often makes an entry as a raft of approaches and processes which, ostensibly, allows the researcher to read this data 'theologically'. Unsurprisingly, this is extremely difficult to do[28] and often results in rather weak theological accounts of practice, or (less frequently) an inappropriately critical theological judgment on practice.

The struggle to enable empirical research to be thoroughly theological is something that Nicholas Healy himself has become increasingly aware of in the years following *Church, World and the Christian Life*. In a paper of 2010,[29] Healy identifies what is, for him, at the heart of this difficulty: ethnographic studies of church are, by their very nature, particular, detailed, contextual; doctrine is, of its nature, tending towards universal, abstract articulation. In practice, the move from concrete, particular detail to doctrinal or systematic theology is all but impossible:

> the ethnographic view undermines the notion that ... [what is observed can] ... constitute the church as a 'community' or moral person in a sufficiently rich and consistent way to work as a principle for theological or ecclesiological method. There is simply too much, materially, that is not shared. Indeed, the worldwide church ... when considered with a focus on detail, particularity and the exceptional, is arguably little more than a congeries of diverse forms of life, languages and meanings of the word 'God'. *We cannot, then, start with the church as it exists; everything slips through our fingers unless we cement and shape according to our agenda, our construal of Christianity and our formation within our particular world.*[30]

By the end of this book, I will have argued and demonstrated that such a stark statement of the admittedly complex relationship between particular practices of church – and theological and doctrinal articulations about church – is not the only option. Theological action research, and its theological implications, offer accounts of both ecclesiology and theology more widely, which find authoritative place both for contextual particularities and for doctrine and systematic theology. However, in Healy's account, and in much practical ecclesiology to date, the difficulty of relating the two perspectives of the concrete and the theological remains. The tendency then is for modern ecclesiologists to fall into two camps – one simply committed to the particular, detailed, contextual manifestations of church and the other committed to speaking doctrinally and normatively of church as a mystery of faith. In different ways, both presuppose a blueprint mentality.[31]

This specifically ecclesiological problem reflects the general difficulty with all 'practical theology' – theologies which aim to take as a key source empirical data from concrete realities and practices. Practical theology is a field characterised by the tensions surrounding practice and articulation, case study data and theological accounts.[32] The field of pastoral/practical theology is also, like much ethnographic or 'concrete' ecclesiology, committedly interdisciplinary in its approach,[33] leading to questions of how different perspectives on realities should be related to one another. These fundamental tenets of the discipline have led to its being characterised by its working within certain 'polarities', or 'creative tensions',[34] between experience and doctrine, past and present, the theological and the sociological and so forth. This has, in turn, presented *correlation* as a central theme in practical theology.[35]

There are important questions to be asked of practical theology concerning the centrality of correlational method.[36] In particular, it is a method which necessarily assumes a starting place of separation: that theology and practice, past and present, are presented as separate, and so in need of correlating or bringing into bilateral conversation. There is – as a matter of contextual reality – some truth in this, of course. However, the danger is that correlational methods come to depend on an assumption of separation, and so – ironically – perpetuate the very thing they are designed to overcome. This book and the research that underpins it is intentionally *non-correlational* (though perhaps not *anti-correlational*) in approach, believing that more integrated methodologies such as our own better reflect the fundamentals of Christian theological tradition, and better equip us to make whole-theology articulations of the work of God's Spirit in the world as it is.

After all, insofar as the contemporary problem with ecclesiology, and practical theology, is the perennial one of the 'things of heaven' and 'the things of earth' – of the Church's identity as in the world and not of it (John xvii 14–18), – then it is simply a *proper* difficulty and so not to be resolved so much as worked with or responded to. As Healy is aware, and Roger Haight makes clear,[37] it is precisely this tension of eschatologically conditioned living that characterises the pre-modern ecclesiologies of Augustine, Aquinas and Calvin.[38] It seems to me that both these earlier western theologians, and those like Denys the Areopagite in the East,[39] are able to draw on a framework of philosophical assumptions – largely neo-platonic – which facilitates a language for describing the admixture of 'heavenly' and 'earthly' in the lived reality of church.

So it is not the problem that is new but rather the context for our ecclesiological reflections – and this makes all the difference. We can no longer, in late modernity, adopt the same philosophical and socio-cultural assumptions of the pre-modern Church. What we need to find is a way of speaking of the actual Church, which holds that earthly-heavenly tension in faithful continuity with the longer tradition and in ways authentic to the epistemological assumptions of our own time. Contemporary ecclesiologies have helped us identify afresh the nature of the 'problem with Church'. What remains problematic is the way in which the question might be constructively and creatively responded to. Neither practical theological approaches nor doctrinal approaches, on their own, seem, as yet, to have developed the necessary vision or methodologies which can do for our own late modern context what Augustine or Denys did for theirs.

The question of church today: a first response

The present book, and the research that lies behind it, locates itself centrally within the problematics of contemporary ecclesiology outlined so far. Whilst not wanting to claim that we have 'the answer' to the bifurcation of faith-full speech about, and practice of, church, the researchers who carried out the original work do believe that the specific methods and processes with which we have worked should be presented as positive and integrative responses to the challenges of ecclesiology today. In setting out in the rest of this chapter the shape of this book, I will make some general and fundamental observations that will illustrate how it responds to contemporary thinking about and living of Church.[40]

The main weight of this book as an exercise in an integrated, practice-based ecclesiology, building on the theological action research of the ARCS project,[41] is to be found in the seven chapters and seven accounts of practice presented in Parts II and III. Part I (chapters 2–4) sets the narrative and methodological contexts of the research that has enabled this constructive ecclesiology. Chapter 2's brief account of that research goes beyond the short description given in the 2010 volume[42] in order to reflect more deeply on the significance of the ARCS team, its make-up and ways of working. In addition, this chapter sets out the developments in the theological action research methodology pioneered by the ARCS team since the publishing of that first book. It is this methodology which is taken up at more length in chapters 3 and 4. Drawing on more recent developments, and the considerable exposure, use, affirmation and criticism received for theological action research and its framework of the four voices of theology, these chapters give a more scholarly and critical attention to these approaches than that offered in 2010. Chapter 3 reflects on theological action research and its relation with wider action research discourse so as to surface the epistemology and account of theology implicit in this methodology. In a similar manner, aimed at deepening and giving more precision to the ARCS approach, chapter 4 devotes some much-needed attention to that four voices framework which has gathered so much support and been so widely employed (though variously) since 2010. Here, the suggestion that the four voices stands as a diagrammatically embodied account of a 'practical fundamental theology' is presented for further discussion.

Parts II and III are structured through the interleaving of chapters presenting our constructive, practice-based ecclesiological insights with 'accounts of practice'. These latter (labeled A-G) present the reader with significant learning points from seven of the original ARCS projects, upon which the ecclesiological insights argued for in the chapters are drawn. These Accounts – whilst not full case studies – witness both to the work and vision of the co-researchers with whom ARCS worked, and to those insights gained through the participative theological action research undertaken. Their learning points are the fruits of a conversational practice in which the 'four voices of theology' have been engaged with by academics and practitioners together, and insights concerning church gained thereby. Together, the ARCS team with our co-researchers, identified the 'epiphanic moments' of learning through the research conversations, which I have here written up to act as an on-going and inter-penetrating reference for the substantial chapters of Parts II and III. The accounts of practice are not especially connected to the chapters either side of them, though they have been ordered according to some resonances with the wider text. Rather, the seven accounts of practice as a whole act as the primary resource for the seven chapters which draw on the data across the accounts as most relevant.

Each of the practices described here worked with the ARCS team on their own, co-designed, theological action research project, each with its own integrity and specific learning. This is reflected in the rather different types of text and data that is referenced in the various Accounts of Practice. In this way, each might stand alone and, indeed, be written up more fully in terms of specific ecclesial learning.[43] However, as theological practitioners, the ARCS team themselves undertook something of a 'meta-reading' of the learning that had been evidenced across all the individual projects so as to see what might be learnt more widely for a practice engaged ecclesiology. Not many – perhaps not any – of the 'epiphanic moments' disclose earth-shatteringly new insights into the nature of church. That is not in the nature of disclosures that, by their nature, take place in the corners of church life which are particular, generally small and often hidden (and for that reason, arguably, central theologically!). Their purpose is rather different. In the first instance, the disclosures serve the practitioners themselves, enabling new insights and learning, often leading to renewed or changed practice. Subsequently – and this is the focus of the present book – through the research team's meta-reading, the disclosures also inform our wider understanding of church, in so far as they witness to what the Holy Spirit is already doing in church life, and so contribute to our developing understanding of ecclesiology for our own time and contexts.

It is this latter informing of an authentic 'whole-church' ecclesiological instinct that is the purpose of chapters 5–11. Chapters 5 and 6 are primarily concerned with the context for our research partners, as they seek to explore first the geographical settings (chapter 5) and then the organisational patterning (chapter 6) of the various agencies and ecclesial bodies involved. From here there are five chapters devoted to specifically ecclesiological themes, as read and renewed through theological action research with the ARCS Practices described (A-G). These chapters, taking their lead from the experience and embodied theologies of the practitioners with whom we worked, represent key areas of learning, concern and transformation: mission and evangelisation (chapter 7); the identity of church (chapter 8); sacrament and sacramentality (chapter 9); orders and ordering the church (chapter 10); tradition, normativity and creativity (chapter 11). In each case, building on the research conversations and learning, the voices of practice will be presented, and brought into relation with selected and briefly described normative and academic accounts, so as to 'disclose' an aspect of church in a renewed, and authentic ('whole-church') light.

The three short chapters of Part IV interrogate my claim that this book demonstrates the ways in which theological action research has the potential to make possible deep and lasting renewal not only of church practices but of ecclesiology, both in its academic, and more ecclesial or pastoral iterations. It is proposed that the approach of the project described in this volume, and its developments in the work of various scholars over the last decade, has, at its heart, a fundamental account of both ecclesiology (chapter 12) and theology more widely (chapter 13) which is of especial importance for the late modern church and its academy. Finally, the possibility of 'an Ecclesiology of Epiphanies' is opened up, as an ecclesiology which involves authoritatively the voices and insights of ordinary faith-full practice (chapter 14). The reader is invited to challenge and question the claims of the book, and, in particular, its positing of an renewed integrated fundamental account of both ecclesiology and theology as essentially practice-engaged.

A postscript: on the structure of this book and its significance

This book's preface – 'A word to the reader' – alerts the person picking this book up to the rather unusual structure of the text. This note sets out the reasons for this shaping of the text around chapters and accounts of practice, and makes some suggestions as to how different readers might navigate the sections; but at the end of this introductory chapter, it is worth noting that such a structure has theological significance. The concern has been to find a creative way in which both the proper complexity of practices and the systematising tendencies of theology and its related reflections can be authentically articulated and their inter-relation demonstrated. More than this, the very nature of our work insists that we are not only presenting 'accounts of practice', but are – at the same time – presenting accounts of embodied theologies, which exist in dynamic relation with other 'voices' of theology. The structure reflects the methods and thinking outlined in this introduction and detailed in Part I of what follows.

In particular, reflection on the 'correlation culture' of much practical theology described in this chapter, along with Healy's critique of much ethnographic ecclesiology, suggest that what is needed above all is an approach which enables an integrative *process* in relation to practices. If – classically – correlation begins with an assumption of separated realities requiring (re) connection, then the processes of theological action research attempt, rather, to begin with an assumption of coherence, in which theology is consistently held to be a complex, many-faceted reality expressed in practices and words together. As such a 'Rubik's cube' reality, this whole-theology cannot simply be set down in the form of a linear 'argument', but must of necessity be shaped by a 'coming and going', which unsettles the reader. The 'conversations' take place in a continuous movement between practices and intellectual and faith reflections.

In deciding to present our material in this way, the research team intentions were – unashamedly – to disrupt the reader's expectations. We are not, however, seeking to obscure, but rather to illuminate, in ways true to the realities presented. My hope is that this interpenetrating, perichoretic, coming-and-going of the main body of this book will enable a sharing in something of the adventure of theological action research as we discovered and celebrated it in ARCS, and as I have joyfully done and continue to do since.

Notes

1 This recognised empirical turn is nicely summarized by Paul Avis, "Ecclesiology and Ethnography: An Unresolved Relationship." *Ecclesiology* 14 (2018): 322–337. He describes late modern ecclesiology, compared to that of modernity 'as a more realistic, modest, chastened and self-critical ecclesiology emerged. It is an ecclesiology that is undertaken in a more tentative, exploratory, realistic and reflexive way. It does not disdain empirical studies of the church. It looks for a voice that is persuasive, yet practical; visionary, yet not utopian'. 326.

2 I use this language throughout rather than that of 'faithful' as this latter term begs the question, 'faithful to what/whom?', suggesting faith as simply equivalent to belief or religious identity. The term 'faith-full' refers, rather, to the dynamic of faith as a living relationship with and in God, as formative of the person and their practices.

3 In particular, the research team responsible for the original research included the present author, and Helen Cameron, whose previous works reflect this ecclesiological concern: Clare Watkins, "Organizing the People of God. Social Science Theories of Organization in Ecclesiology." *Theological Studies* 52 (1991): 689–711; "Collaborators, Informers and Secret Service. Some Thoughts on the Theologies of Laity and Ministry Since Vatican II." *New Blackfriars* (May 1993): 263–279; "Organization and Management: The Church as a Special Case." *Modern Theology* (October 1993): 369–384; "Objecting to *koinonia*. Why Communion Isn't the Answer." *Louvain Studies* 28 (2003); "Texts and Practices: An Ecclesiology of *Traditio* for Pastoral Theology." James Sweeney et al. eds. *Keeping Faith in Practice* (SCM, 2010); Helen Cameron, *Studying Local Churches* (SCM, 2005); *Resourcing Mission: Practical Theology for Changing Churches* (SCM, 2009); *Studying Local Churches: A Handbook* (with Philip Richter and Douglas Davies, SCM, 2011).

4 I Cor. 12:12–31.

5 For example, the image of the vine in John 15:1–8; or the 'living stones' of I Peter 2:4–5. In such image, the essential elements of structures and life are held together intractably.

6 This is vividly portrayed in the correspondence between the reformer John Calvin and Cardinal Sadolet, for example. John C. Olin ed., *A Reformation Debate: Sadoleto's Letter to the Genevans and Calvin's Reply* (Harper & Row, 1966).

7 Emil Brunner, *The Misunderstanding of the Church* (trans. Harold Knight, Lutterworth Press, 2003. Orig. German *Das Missverstaendnis der Kirche* 1951).

8 Second Vatican Council, Dogmatic Constitution on the Church, *Lumen Gentium*, 7–8. So: "the society structured with hierarchical organs and the Mystical Body of Christ, are not to be considered as two realities, nor are the visible assembly and the spiritual community, nor the earthly Church and the Church enriched with heavenly things; rather they form one complex reality which coalesces from a divine and a human element." Available at: http://www.vatican.va/archive/hist_councils/ii_vatican_council/documents/vat-ii_const_19641121_lumen-gentium_en.html.

9 This is amply described in Roger Haight's scholarly *Christian Community in History Volume 1. Historical Ecclesiology* (Continuum, 2004). Note in particular 417–423 with its naming of perennial tensions for ecclesiology.

10 For example: Harald Hegstad, *The Real Church: An Ecclesiology of the Visible* (Pickwick Publications, 2013); Johannes A. van der Ven, *Ecclesiology in Context* (Eerdmans, 1996). The fascinating work carried out through the Ecclesiology and Ethnography Network is particularly important and influential here: Pete Ward ed., *Perspectives on Ecclesiology and Ethnography* (Eerdmans, 2012); Christian Scharen, *Explorations in Ecclesiology and Ethnography* (Eerdmans, 2012); www.ecclesiologyandethnography.com.

11 Gary Badcock, *The House Where God Lives: Renewing the Doctrine of the Church for Today* (Eerdmans, 2009): 3.

12 Avis, op. cit. In particular, Avis' assessment that the contrasts between (traditional) ecclesiology as 'abstract', 'theoretical' and ethnography as 'descriptive', 'practical' are too clearly draw is important and resonates well with the present work's more integrative approach.

13 Pete Ward, *Liquid Ecclesiology: The Gospel and the Church* (Brill, 2017).

14 Neil Ormerod, *Re-visioning the Church: An Experiment in Systematic Historical Ecclesiology* (Fortress Press, 2014).

15 Nicholas Healy, *Church, World and the Christian Life: Practical Prophetic Ecclesiology* (CUP, 2000): 3.

16 For a more detailed account of Healy's work in relation to my own, see: Clare Watkins, "Practising Ecclesiology: From Product to Process." *Ecclesial Practices* 2 (2015): 23–29.

17 Healy, *Church, World and the Christian Life*, op. cit. 25ff.

18 Ibid. 26, 36–38.

19 Ibid. 37.

20 Ibid. 46.

21 Ibid. 52–76.

22 Ibid. 154ff.

23 Most notably, the work done by the Ecclesiology and Ethnography Network, op. cit. n.10. Pete Ward ed. and Chris Scharen ed. Further information can be found at: www.ecclesiologyandethnography.net, and in the related journal *Ecclesial Practices* (Brill).

24 For more on 'ordinary theology', see: Jeff Astley, *Ordinary Theology: Looking, Listening and Learning in Theology* (Ashgate, 2002); and Jeff Astley and Leslie J. Francis eds. *Exploring Ordinary Theology: Everyday Christian Believing and the Church* (Ashgate, 2013).

25 See Helen Cameron, Deborah Bhatti, Catherine Duce, James Sweeney, and Clare Watkins, *Talking About God in Practice: Theological Action Research and Practical Theology* (SCM, 2010): esp Chapter 2.

26 Outstanding here, to my mind is: Mary McClintock Fulkerson, *Places of Redemption: Theology for a Worldly Church* (OUP, 2010).

27 This term has gained central currency in practical theology and is supported by a substantial literature. For example: Patricia O'Connell Killeen and John de Beer, *The Art of Theological Reflection* (Crossroad, 1994); Elaine Graham, Heather Walton, and Frances Ward, *Theological Reflection: Methods* (SCM, 2005); and *Theological Reflection: Sources* (SCM, 2007); Judith Thompson et al., *SCM Study Guide to Theological Reflection* (SCM, 2008). All too often, however, the methods proposed return to a more or less correlative approach of 'theology' and practice, as if they were different and separate realities. See Clare Watkins, "An Argument for *Non-correlational* Approaches in a Catholic Practical Theology." *Cahiers Internationaux de Theologie Pratique. Actes no. 8* (March 2016): 141–158. Available at: www.pastoralis.org/CITP-Actes-no-8-Groupe-Santiago.

28 A difficulty well-recognised and responded to by Stephen Pattison, "Some Straw for the Bricks: A Basic Introduction to Theological Reflection." *Contact* 99, no.1

(1989): 2–9. My own conviction is that this approach, helpful as it is, is still too reliant on an assumption of dichotomies requiring correlative methods for it to be theologically integrated in a thorough-going way. See: Watkins, "An Argument for *Non-correlational* Approaches in a Catholic Practical Theology." Op. cit. n.27.

29 Nicholas Healy, "Ecclesiology, Ethnography and God: An Interplay of Reality Descriptions." Pete Ward ed. *Perspectives on Ecclesiology and Ethnography* (Eerdmans, 2012): 182–199.

30 Ibid. 189. My emphases.

31 In its largely historical / narrative approach to church, Roger Haight's important three-volume work is, perhaps, a notable exception to this contemporary tendency. Indeed, Haight is insistent that the tension of the ideal and the actual is essential to ecclesiology: "Deliberately building this tensions into ecclesiological self-understanding itself offers the only chance of success in this project." Haight, vol. II: *Ecclesial Existence: Christian Community in History* (Continuum, 2008): 40. For all that, it should be noted that Haight's work maintains the tension *in principle*, without the particular challenges and gifts of working with empirical practice based research into church. Pete Ward's more recent *Liquid Ecclesiology* (Brill, 2017) comes closer to a more integrated account of church, and shares in much in common with the present book's approach. More will be said of this later.

32 These are most recently and compellingly set out in the volume edited by Joyce Ann Mercer and Bonnie Miller-McLemore, *Conundrums in Practical Theology* (Brill, 2016).

33 For helpful discussions of this see, for example: Paul Fiddes, "Ecclesiology and Ethnography: Two Disciplines, Two Worlds?" P. Ward ed. *Perspectives on Ecclesiology and Ethnography* (Eerdmans, 2012): 13–35; and Ormerod, op. cit. 31–59.

34 As classically and influentially described by Stephen Pattison and James Woodward, *The Blackwell Reader in Practical and Pastoral Theology* (Wiley Blackwell, 2008): 15.

35 Elaine Graham's important work *Transforming Practice: Pastoral Theology in an Age of Uncertainty* (Wipf and Stock, 2002) can be understood as a rigorous search for how the practical theologian can work with such polarities with integrity. Significantly, Graham draws on the seminal work of Don Browning, and his 'revised correlational method'. Don Browning, *A Fundamental Practical Theology* (Augsburg Fortress, 1959).

36 Interesting accounts and critiques can be found in Paul Ballard's article: "Can Theology Be Practical." David Willows and John Swinton eds. *Spiritual Dimensions of Pastoral Care: Practical Theology in a Multidisciplinary Context* (Jessica Kingsley, 2000): 27–35. Here we also find an account of the Catholic theologian Matthew Lamb's typology of practice and theology. See also Watkins, "Texts and Practices," op. cit., 163–178.

37 Haight, op. cit.

38 Healy, *Church, World and Christian Life*, op. cit. 55–59.

39 Sarah Coakley and Charles M. Stang eds. Rethinking Dionysius the Areopagite (Wiley-Blackwell, 2009).

40 In what follows, reference will be made to the earlier volume co-authored by the original research team: Cameron et al., *Talking About God in Practice*, op. cit. This earlier volume was our first setting out of the methods and some of the preliminary findings of theological action research, upon which the present volume seeks to elaborate with more detailed accounts and appropriately complexified reflection.

41 For more explanation of ARCS – Action Research Church and Society – see chapter 2 below.
42 Cameron et al., *Talking About God in Practice*, op. cit. 1–2.
43 An example of this would be Clare Watkins and Bridget Shepherd, "The Challenge of 'Fresh Expressions' to Ecclesiology. Reflections From the Practice of Messy Church." *Ecclesial Practices* 1 (2014): 92–110.

Part I

The project

'Action Research – Church and Society' (ARCS)

Rationale for Part I

The ecclesiology set out in this book is largely generated by the work done through the Action Research Church and Society (ARCS) project between 2006 and 2010. The ARCS Project was unusual in that it was undertaken by an academic team working with practitioner teams in 12 different organisations in a period of four years. In this long period of working in close, participative and interdisciplinary teams, the academic researchers generated both a new methodology and a fresh approach to theological engagement with practice, as well as considerable data about church life in London. The following three chapters (Part I) not only serve as a summary introduction to the project, which is described in more detail in *Talking about God in Practice*,[1] but they also develop the methodological thinking of that earlier book, and describe learning and work in the field subsequent to 2010. As such, these chapters form the theological and methodological basis for the constructive work of practical ecclesiology carried out in Parts II and III of the book.

To serve this purpose, chapter 2 outlines the origins and development of the project and introduces the research team. Chapter 3 summarises the theological action research methodology developed by the project and described in the earlier book and responds to criticism of and developments in the method to date. Chapter 4 sets out the four voices approach to reflecting theologically on the ARCS data and offers a more enriched and theologically substantial account of this approach.

Note

1 Helen Cameron, Deborah Bhatti, Catherine Duce, James Sweeney, and Clare Watkins, *Talking About God in Practice: Theological Action Research and Practical Theology* (SCM, 2010).

2 The ARCS project

Reflections on a research community and its practices

The story of the ARCS project

The outline facts about the research project upon whose data this book depends are set out in *Talking About God in Practice*.[1] In what follows, something more of this story is told, not only so as to give the necessary background information to readers unfamiliar with the project but also as a way of reflecting in more detail on the significance of, and learning from, the research experience. In particular, and in response to some helpful criticism of theological action research,[2] I aim in this 'thicker' telling of the research story to surface something of the particular contexts and approaches of the original researchers, their practices as they developed, and the learning that ensued. In keeping with the best practices of ethnography,[3] action research,[4] and practical theology,[5] the account of the research must begin with reflection on the position, context and person of the researcher, recognising her or him as a proper element in the research process and data. In the case of theological action research, the well-recognised challenges faced here are further complexified by that commitment to working as a research *team* which characterised the projects under discussion.

A collaboration between research centres

The Action Research-Church and Society (ARCS) project, which ran between 2006–2010, was funded by the Higher Education Innovation Fund (HEIF).[6] Institutionally, this was a collaborative project between the Pastoral and Social Studies Department of Heythrop College, University of London and the Oxford Centre for Ecclesiology and Practical Theology, Ripon College Cuddesdon.[7] There are a number of points worth noting here. Both institutions were placed, in particular ways, at that crucial locus for practical theology: the interface of the academy and the pastoral realities of church. As a college of the University of London Heythrop was,[8] at the same time, a Jesuit foundation, part of whose on-going theological work was concerned with the equipping of both Jesuits in Formation and diocesan seminary students for ministry in the Catholic Church. In addition, many lay people from across ecclesial traditions benefitted from the Jesuit teaching of both theology and philosophy at undergraduate and, especially, Masters levels, which modelled an approach in which academic rigour, pastoral wisdom and experience, and cultural, multi-disciplinary learning were integrated. Ripon College Cuddesdon is a Church of England Theological College, with close ties to the University of Oxford, and – through Common Awards – Durham University. Here again, there was a holding together of the academic and ministerial, nurtured further by those students for ordained ministry who, as residents, share in a life of liturgy and fellowship. The Oxford Centre for Ecclesiology and Practical Theology (OxCEPT) at Ripon College Cuddesdon was set up with the specific purpose "to serve the life and mission of the church by attending to God's work in the world in order to develop faithful and reflective practice".[9] OxCEPT's first Director, Helen Cameron, recognised this purpose as having a strong affinity with the concerns of the ARCS project as it was established in 2006 at Heythrop. Both college Centres were motivated by concerns with the realities of lived faith in today's world, with attention to practices, ecclesial realities, theological traditions and sociological insights being central. Above all, their research was understood as a form of intentional service to the churches.

A collaboration between researchers

Reflecting back now, it is this sense of the two Centres' commitment to serving Christian life through their work which presents itself as most significant. In both cases, there were, of course, academic requirements to fulfill, and institutional pressures which required response; but overwhelmingly, the researchers involved were each shaped by a sense of personal vocation in relation to the practices with which we worked. As a Passionist priest, Dr. James Sweeney had long experience of working in Christian ministry with those considered to be 'on the margins', and had developed a strong research interest in questions of justice and Catholic Social Teaching.[10] His monastic training and priestly ministry, combined with a theological and sociology of religion academic training, shaped his way of thinking about the research and engaging with our practitioner co-researchers. In a similar way, Dr. Helen Cameron's committed living of Christian faith within a Salvation Army context, integrated with her academic expertise in practical theology and empirical study of church and faith practice, brought to the team clear and strong insights about social realities and a deep concern for justice, politics and faith together with expertise and experience in designing research based on empirical methods.[11]

The similarities between these two core members of the research team also served to highlight certain differences, as the Salvationist and Catholic ways of Christian faith challenged and illuminated each other. The gifts and struggles here will become clearer as the exploration of our research deepens. The ecumenical dynamic of the team is, in fact, a central feature of the research, and brings to the forefront the significance of conversational, multi-voiced theological reflection on the data. It was added to by the appointment of Ms. Catherine Duce (now Revd.) as our Research Assistant, following on from Dr. Deborah Bhatti, who assisted the early parts of the project. Cath's deeply Anglican formation and commitment, shaped intellectually by a background in geography and theology, as well as by a commitment to ecumenical engagement with Catholics, brought their own gifts of attentiveness and understanding to the data and the ensuing conversations.[12] In both our Research Assistants, we were blessed to have younger perspectives, from early career theologians who had a close engagement with church life, Catholic and Anglican, as well as considerable spiritual maturity and vocational sense.

I cannot reflect on questions of positionality and reflexivity on behalf of these colleagues of mine; we each have our own stories and personal experiences.[13] In shifting here, however, to the first-person singular, I will begin to identify not only my own academic and faith provenance, as I have done concerning other team members, but also to speak more personally about the experience and processes of the research, suggesting their formative place in my thinking, believing and practice. I contributed to the team from an orthodox, though not uncritical, Catholic faith shaped by studies in theology and specifically Catholic theology, all carried out in largely Anglican academic environments. At the same time, any academic career I might have pretensions to had been shaped by significant family commitments and by a strong sense of vocation to pastoral service in my church – a vocational sense not easily framed within the organisational life of the Roman Catholic Church. This all meant that I shared, in a different way again, something of the pastoral commitment and personal vocation lived through an academic professional life seen in the other core members of the team; but in fact, our similarities and differences cut across our relationships in different ways. I am now conscious of how it was not only my common Catholic faith and practice that opened up a 'familial' conversation with Jim (James Sweeney) but also my definitively lay status that opened up another kind of kindred connection with Helen. It became clear, as we faithfully attended with pastoral concern and care to our data from the church practices in front of us, that our ecclesial positionalities were complex and variously interconnected. Not only did our different confessions – Catholic, Salvationist and Anglican – situate us differently in relation to this close ecclesial work but also our 'church location' as cleric or lay, male or female, married or single, parent or childless, came into play – often taking us off guard with the awareness of being so differently located. In the substantive chapters of this book (chapters 5–11), something of the role played by these team realities can be glimpsed.[14]

From collaborative research to 'intellectual friendship'

I observed earlier that there is for this book a particular challenge in 'writing the researchers on to the page' in the way proper to practical theology and its interdisciplinary conversation partners, given that the research was carried out by a *team*. As observed in the co-authored book of 2010: "The term 'team' is not used lightly in that we are unable to say which of us should be credited with any particular part of what we have developed".[15] In an academic culture which prizes and rewards the individual researcher, from PhD to the increasingly assessed 'outputs' of university academic staff, our commitment to the realities of team research has been difficult to explain and, sometimes, gain respect for – despite the common-place recognition of the power of team research in natural and social sciences. Indeed, whilst the present volume is singly authored, and the thinking and overall argument my own and not always in agreement with other members of the team, it will be clear from the introduction and references through the text that the research on which the volume depends was forged in this unique, long-lasting and particular research team.

Much might be reflected on in this regard. In this early chapter, I want simply to refer to something which is, nonetheless, rather complex: the development of a particular kind of real, deep friendship which made the work possible and fruitful in the ways that it has been. There is a good deal written on friendship in a Christian theological context; in terms of the ARCS team, I want to characterise our relationships as 'intellectual friendship'. By this, I mean a kind of mutual affection, knowledge of each other, and of ourselves in the light of the others that was always concerned not with relationships *per se* but with a common purpose of faith and service. Our friendships are 'intellectual' not because they were lacking in any warmth or humour – far from it! Rather, the qualifier of 'intellectual' serves to remind us of that most human of qualities according to Aquinas: that *intellectus* which "implies a certain intimate knowing" of things as they really are, a human engagement with realities as given by God. "Intellective knowledge penetrates as far as the essence of a thing, its objective interest being ... what a thing really is".[16] It was through the committed and shared practice of such intellectual knowing of realities that the particular kind of friendship of the ARCS team members developed.

As commented on in the team's earlier book,[17] the forging of such friendship, whilst centred on the work in which we were all engaged in similar vocationally committed ways, was shaped by rather more 'ordinary' human practices: long gatherings around tables heaped with often muddled papers, notes, tea and coffee cups, and substantial amounts of chocolate-based comestibles. There was weariness and impatience with one another, periods of ill-health, frustrations and tensions over finance and work loads, but there was more often laughter, banter, prayer and meals together, and what I now recognise as unusual levels of trust, honesty and shared ownership. I believe we were modeling an approach to theological, practice-based and participative research that is rare and much needed for the future of theology if it is to be of service to the realities of church and faith-full living.

A collaboration with practitioners

From the beginning, the theological action research which the ARCS team developed was committed to *participative* action research.[18] More will be said about this in the next chapter. Here I simply flag it up so as to recognise, from the start, that not only was the work underpinning this book never simply that of a single researcher but also neither was it solely the project of an academic team. Above all, the particular project research design, data and, most importantly, the interpretation of the data, depended on active participation of the many practitioner-theologians with whom we worked. In all, the ARCS research project was involved in participative research with 14 church groups of various kinds and to varying extents.[19] In this book, seven of those will be presented in some detail (Accounts of Practice A-G), selected for the depth and fruitfulness of the work carried out, and so as to reflect something of the variety of practice types and faith traditions involved.

There are a number of important points for reflection at this stage of our narrative account of ARCS. First, not all of the practitioner groups had the same kind of experience working with the ARCS project, as our methods and methodological understanding became more developed and nuanced as we gained experience. There is a certain unevenness in the Accounts of Practice which witnesses to this. As I have frequently borne witness, "we were making it up as we went along"![20] To say this is not to suggest we lacked care or rigour; rather, it indicates the intentional, formative and on-going reflective nature of this research. In a manner appropriate to action research, team members themselves engaged in on-going reflection on the practices of the research itself, so as to improve and deepen our understanding of it. So, for example, the practice of practitioner and ARCS research groups ('insider' and 'outsider' teams) reflecting separately on data, and then sharing reflections for mutual challenge and learning, was something arrived at some way in to the research period. At the same time, and as our second point for reflection, I would note that stress was always laid on the ownership of the practitioner researchers of the research question and design. Whilst the ARCS project had its own over-arching research concern – the study of church outreach projects in relation to practice and theology – it was essential that the practitioner group identified the questions *they* wanted to ask of their own practice in line with their hoped for outcomes of the research for that practice. Appendices 2 and 3 of *Talking About God in Practice*[21] clearly set out the *procedures* for these early conversations around research design; it must also be recognised that this was often a delicate stage requiring sometimes lengthy processes of getting to know and understand each other, building trust and a common vision and enabling the beginnings of something like that 'intellectual friendship' which characterised the team itself. It is no coincidence that the more the team itself grew in these charisms of friendship and hospitality, the more easily these gifts were shared with our co-researchers in the practitioner groups.

It should be said that this participative research, so enjoyable in many ways, was not without its difficulties. There were, inevitably, asymmetries in theological understanding and expertise, as well as concomitant asymmetries in power. For some practitioners, even the mention of 'theology' was unthinkable in relation to the work they did and those with whom they worked; and the ARCS team members were often divided on how to respond to this and similar tensions. My own tendency – to want to push people to more theological language and concepts – was regularly kept in check by Helen's more properly action research commitment to handing over language, research questions and subsequent learning more wholeheartedly to the practitioner groups themselves. For other groups – notably those working with a tight ecclesiastical structure – there was a reluctance to question and challenge aspects of their work or mandate, which was at odds with the culture of honesty and free questioning developed in the ARCS team and required by academic research more generally.[22] In every case, relationships had to be built, attended to and nurtured for the most fruitful research to be co-operatively designed and worked through. In all honestly, despite a general level of success in this participative work, we were not always as successful as we would have liked to have been, suggesting some important learning about the time and personal qualities required by anyone involved in theological action research of this kind.

One concept that I found helpful in my own thinking about the participatory emphasis of our work is something I named 'the ethnography of faith'. It is well recognised that action research, and participative action research in particular, is concerned to break down the 'researcher-researched paradigm'.[23] As theological action researchers, we are not researching someone else's faithful practice or embodied theology from some quasi-objective, 'academic' distance; rather, we are accompanying them and facilitating their own journey of research and theological discernment and seeking to learn ourselves from their practice, wisdom and challenges. There are very good theological reasons for such a choice of approach as we will see in the next chapter; but, above all, it spoke to me of the tangible experience we had in the ARCS team of 'being on the same side' as those with whom we worked. We shared a commitment to ecclesial mission, even when our ecclesiologies or preferred methods might differ, a passion for embodying the Gospel in today's world, and a love for our shared Christian faith and the people we were called to serve. These bonds of faith and Christian vocation could not admit of a researcher-researched relationship, but rather drew us – even when we disagreed – into a deep ethnographic connection, constituted, I suggest, by our one-ness in Christ and His Spirit. This is 'the ethnography of faith'.

An on-going story

The Accounts of Practice which make up the empirical data from which the constructive ecclesiology of this book is drawn were all initiatives participating in the ARCS project. However, it is also important to note that the ending of the ARCS project in 2011 is not really the end of the theological action research story. Indeed, much of the mature reflection on our learning through ARCS has come via continuing theological action research work carried out by a widening network of scholars and doctoral researchers since the publication of *Talking About God in Practice* in 2010. At the end of this chapter, I want briefly to mention a few of the more significant of these and indicate how they have helped with the writing of this book some seven years after the ARCS project formally finished.

Two important initiatives saw their early beginnings in the closing months of the ARCS project. The first of these was a capacity-building project in which the ARCS team members worked as mentors with five church groups, enabling them to develop their own theological action research projects within their practice groups. Three of the initiatives worked with in this phase – CAFOD, London Jesuit Volunteers (LJV), and a Pastoral Area from the Roman Catholic Diocese of Portsmouth – already had experience of work with the ARCS team. Two others – the Centre for Youth Ministry (CYM)[24] and a small Methodist and Anglican team looking at lay ministry in rural churches in Oxfordshire – were new to the process.

Our experience of mentoring these groups – providing initial training and on-going support through the process, culminating in a sharing of outcomes in June 2011 – was enlightening in a number of ways. An early learning in the process, sparked by the very first training day for participants, is just how deeply ingrained and hard to shift the 'researcher-researched paradigm' is for many. It was clear that it can be quite hard to 'sell' the conversational, pedagogical research processes of theological action research to leaders and managers who want, ahead of time, to have a clear idea of the outcomes and their material benefits. The CYM team reported on the time and care needed simply to get the 'insider team' involved and committed and the frustrations along the way. The outsider team lead talked of being 'nervous the whole way through', reflecting the sense of a lack of control over the process. Even then, one participant refused to respond to the creative and reflective questionnaire as "it's not proper research". The crucial aspect of having *time* – not just for activity and data collection, but also for the development of trust, understanding and reflection – was stressed by all involved. Flexibility, being realistic and trusting the expertise and wisdom of participants were key themes.

Around the same time as the capacity-building projects were underway, an unexpected development came through an approach from an action researcher at Middlesex University, David Adams, who was interested in developing a network of theologians, action researchers and others interested in looking at the ways in which theology and action research could work together and be understood as mutually illuminating disciplines. The Theology and Action Research Network (TARN) began to meet and plan seminars and is now established at the University of Roehampton.[25] Of particular significance for the maturing of the ideas of the theological action research methodology has been the ways in which this network has enabled a deepening of understanding and appreciation of the varieties of action research itself. The fundamental epistemological insight of action research as a 'different way of knowing',[26] and as an approach (or rather set of approaches) which has resonances with spiritual disciplines of the Christian tradition,[27] have been two of the most significant learning points from this Network and will be clearly seen as enriching the account of theological action research offered in the next chapter. At the same time, TARN has enabled and nurtured the increasing currency of theological action research among practical theological researchers at a variety of levels.

Two other[28] national and large-scale projects should be mentioned as examples of how the use of theological action research has been extended in recent years: the *Visions for Educational Leadership* project carried out at Heythrop (2012–2014) in collaboration with the Catholic Education Service of England and Wales; and the *Catholic Marriage Care Ltd.* research, which was based at the University of Roehampton (2015–2016). Details and papers relating to these projects can be found on the TARN website;[29] there is not adequate room to describe them here. What is worth noting, however, is the way in which these two projects have deepened the understanding of theological action research. In the first, the sheer scale of the research, involving some 70 respondents across seven dioceses and multiple stakeholders, caused the university-based research team[30] to think about how the theological action research principles of on-going conversation, participation and practitioner ownership could be maintained. One important response to this quandary – never entirely resolved, I suspect – was the bringing together of research findings at a two-day colloquium for as many of those involved in the research as possible. This gathering was shaped by facilitating in-depth conversations around the research data presented (and so somewhat interpreted) by the university research team. This proved an enormously useful way of enhancing participation from a range of practitioners and church people, and became a feature of the Marriage Care project later.

Learning from the Marriage Care project for theological action research focused more on how to develop and sustain the methodology beyond the ARCS team. At this stage, all members of the original ARCS project, other than myself, had moved on to other work, leaving me with a task of pulling together a completely new team, sharing with them the ways and 'culture' of theological action research, and trying to develop that 'intellectual friendship' which I have described above as characteristic of the ARCS team. In part, this was achieved through developing 'training' materials for team members; but, more importantly, it highlighted the need for discerning where the necessary 'intellectual friendships' might grow, and finding ways of fostering such friendships as a part of the research work itself. Building on existing professional relationships, and including reflective, prayerful and social activities in our meetings proved crucial. Just as with the capacity-building project, we learnt the value of spending considerable time on building teams through simply talking, growing in trust and getting to know each other. The time needed for this is precious and essential and needs to be written into research plans.

Honouring the theological action research experiences

At the end of the capacity-building project's final reflection day in June 2011, participants were asked to send in evaluations of their experience. Some of these have been reflected in the brief account above of what we needed to learn; there was also specific enthusiasm for theological action research as "a tool which could bring about an organic and natural renewal of life throughout the church of all denominations and at all levels".[31] At the same time, a certain 'fragility' was recognised in the struggles experienced and the demands on energy, time and support. One participant wrote very clearly their hope for what would happen next:

> What I am hoping for, I think, is a means by which ARCS as the co-creators of TAR [theological action research], who have nurtured carefully through its infancy and adolescence, could now take on a role analogous to that of parents whose children have finally left home: still available for advice and support and the occasional bail-out if things go wrong, but essentially letting go and enabling TAR to take on a life of its own.

The analogy is not perfect; theological action research is merely an approach, a methodology, and has no personal qualities! But the instinct is a good one, and one which, for the last seven or so years, we have followed. In taking up the story again now, I do so with something of the accumulated experience and perspective of a grandparent (to pursue the analogy). The task ahead is one of honouring the fruits and gifts of that off-spring of theological action research, as it has worked among people of faith and practice. In the end, the measure of the approach's success is to be seen in the extent to which the faithful practices it has accompanied and explored can become the forces of renewal of church and ecclesiology that they are meant to be.

Notes

1 Helen Cameron, Deborah Bhatti, Catherine Duce, James Sweeney, and Clare Watkins, *Talking About God in Practice: Theological Action Research and Practical Theology* (SCM, 2010): 1–2.
2 Elaine Graham, "Is Practical Theology a Form of 'Action Research'?" *International Journal of Practical Theology* 17, no.1 (2013): 148–178. See particularly 169: " . . it would appear the whilst there is some attention to the subjectivity or positionality of the researcher in these studies, most of them stop short of any kind of first person reflexivity . . . the researcher is more off, than on, the page."
3 The widely recognised significance of the work of the sociologist and anthropologist Pierre Bordieu has been accessibly set out specifically for a practical theological audience by Christian Scharen, *Fieldwork in Theology: Exploring the Social Context of God's Work in the World* (Baker Academic, 2015).
4 One helpful action research account of the complexities of this question can be found in Sonia Ospina et al., "Taking the Action Turn: Lessons From Bringing Participation to Qualitative Research." Peter Reason and Hilary Bradbury eds. *The Sage Handbook of Action Research* (2nd ed., Sage, 2013): 420–434.
5 Widely discussed in practical theology, the issue is given a striking and focused treatment in Jaco S. Dreyer, "Knowledge, Subjectivity, (De)Coloniality, and the Conundrum of Reflexivity." Joyce Ann Mercer and Bonnie Miller-McLemore eds. *Conundrums in Practical Theology* (Brill, 2016): 90–109.
6 At the time of the research, all Higher Education Institutions funded by HEFCE (Higher Education Funding Council for England) were eligible for these Innovation Fund grants, which supported "a broad range of knowledge-based interactions between the universities and the wider world, which result in benefits to the economy and society." See: http://re.ukri.org/knowledge-exchange/the-higher-education-innovation-fund-heif/ (Accessed: March 2019). For the period of the research, the Heythrop College HEIF allocation was awarded to the ARCS project, under the directorship of James Sweeney, then Senior Lecturer at Heythrop College.
7 This collaborative partnership shaped the project after its first year when it was solely based at Heythrop College.
8 Sadly, Heythrop College closed in 2018.
9 www.rcc.ac.uk/study-centre/research. Accessed August 2019. Further information about the Centre can be found here.
10 For example, James Sweeney et al. eds., *Keeping Faith in Practice: Aspects of Catholic Pastoral Theology* (SCM, 2010); Kenneth Medhurst and James Sweeney, "Public Theology and Changing Social Values." *Studies in Christian Ethics* 1, no.2 (2004): 118–133; James Sweeney, "Faith in Culture." *New Blackfriars* 94 (March 2013): 148–159.
11 For example, Helen Cameron, *Theological Reflection for Human Flourishing: Pastoral Practice and Public Theology* (SCM, 2013); *Resourcing Mission: Practical Theology for Changing Churches* (SCM, 2010).
12 An example of Cath's work can be found here: Catherine Duce, "Church-based Work With the Homeless: A Theological Exploration of the Practices of Hospitality." *Practical Theology* 6, no.1 (2013): 87–103.
13 Something of this is captured in a recording of a 2017 TARN Conference in which the ARCS team (other than Deborah Bhatti, now working in the US) re-gathered to speak about the research. See: https://theologyandactionresearch.net/2017/11/08/theological-action-research-influence-impact-and-iterations-event/ for link to footage. Accessed August 2019.
14 An example of this published soon after the end of the ARCS project can be found in Clare Watkins and Helen Cameron, "Epiphanic Sacramentality: An

Example of Practical Ecclesiology Revisioning Theological Understanding." Christian B. Scharen ed. *Explorations in Ecclesiology and Ethnography* (Eerdmans, 2012): 71–89.

15 Cameron et al., *Talking About God in Practice*, op. cit. 1.

16 Thomas Aquinas *Summa Theologiae* 2a2ae 8.1.

17 Cameron et al., *Talking About God in Practice*, op. cit. 4.

18 Ibid. 34ff.

19 A full list can be found in *Talking About God in Practice*, op. cit. Appendix 1, 156–159.

20 See footage referenced in note 13 above.

21 Cameron et. al., op. cit. 160, and 161–162.

22 An example of this is to be found in Account of Practice B, Westminster Agency for Evangelisation.

23 See, for example, Davydd J. Greenwood and Morten Levin, *Introduction to Action Research: Social Research for Social Change* (Sage, 2007): 53.

24 Aspects of this work were later written up by Nick Shepherd, "Action Research as Professional Development." *Journal of Adult Theological Education* 9, no.2 (2012): 21–138.

25 See www.theologyandactionresearch.net.

26 The title of the TARN October 2017 Conference. See: https://theologyandactionresearch.net/a-different-way-of-knowing/. Accessed August 2019.

27 The Network has been especially indebted to the involvement of Dr. David Coghlan, the Jesuit action researcher, for whose ideas see his: "Seeking God on All Things: Ignatian Spirituality as Action Research." *The Way* 43, no.1 (2004): 97–108; and "Towards a Spirituality of Academic Work: Lessons Form Action Research." *Human Development* 27, no.2 (2006): 38–41.

28 At the time of writing, two further national large-scale theological action research projects are underway with leadership from the author, one looking at collaborative learning in British Methodism and another exploring instances of Catholic-Methodist collaboration in social justice projects. These will be completed in 2020, and reports posted on the TARN website. In addition, there have been a number of smaller, consultative projects with congregations, groups and projects eager to work with theological action research.

29 For the VfEL project, see: https://theologyandactionresearch.net/visions-for-educational-leadership/. For the Marriage Care project see: https://theologyandactionresearch.net/publications-and-reports/marriage-care-project-major-themes/. Accessed August 2019.

30 At this stage, made up of the present author, James Sweeney and Margaret Buck, assisted by our research administrator, Robert Ivermee.

31 Anonymous evaluation, 28th June 2011.

3 Theological action research

Whilst the ARCS project was underway, an important book in practical theology was published, which was to become highly influential in the field. John Swinton and Harriet Mowat's *Practical Theology and Qualitative Research*[1] has not only provided invaluable wisdom and theological thoughtfulness about the use of qualitative research methods in theologies concerned with practice but also named in a particular way the idea that "Practical Theology is fundamentally *action* research".[2] This assertion, which is discussed in a few pages in the final chapter of their book, has sparked a debate and the development of varying approaches to action research in practical theology, in which theological action research, as envisaged by the ARCS team, has had its part to play.[3] In these discussions, theological action research has not been without its critics;[4] and in this chapter, some of those more critical accounts will be engaged and clarifying responses given, as well as setting out a more constructive account of the *theological* nature of the action research approach of the ARCS project. First, however, it will be useful to give a brief account of 'theological action research' itself.[5]

Processes and characteristics: a summary[6]

Talking About God in Practice presents action research as a response to some of the problems identified in practical theological work.[7] In doing this, the emphasis is on participative forms of action research, which are characterised by partnership, on-going process, conversational approaches and the generation of knowledge in a particular 'way of knowing'.[8] As such, action research insights and practices are recognised as mitigating the tendency to perpetuate the researcher-researched paradigm of much practical theological work, and as creating a more appropriately grounded, contextual set of methods in which practice-embedded knowledge of practitioners is given its proper place and authority. These fundamental action research commitments are embodied in the practical methods used in theological action research and described in *Talking About God in Practice*. In particular, the detailed appendices demonstrate how research questions are developed through sometimes lengthy processes of meetings and conversation, and attentiveness to the concerns and experience of practitioners. In this way the research is co-designed.[9] Perhaps even more significant is the attention given to the practitioners' own reading of and reflection on the data gathered and its essential place in any learning from the research process.[10] Such learning is formative of new understanding and action for all participants, local practitioners and the theological practitioners of the ARCS team.

At the same time, the ARCS team were aware of not simply 'using' action research as a tool for a practical theology project. Rather, we were developing a specific approach of 'theological action research' which is characterised not only by its learning from and work with action research approaches but also by its especially *theological* commitments to a fundamental theology of revelation.[11] More will be said about this in chapter 4 below. Here it is enough simply to be reminded of those 'five characteristics' of theological action research identified in the 2010 book: being theological 'all the way through'; theology in four voices (operant, espoused, formal and normative); disclosing theology through conversational method; formative of transformation of practice; and formative of transformation in theology.[12] In discussing theological action research, it is crucial to remember that this is primarily a *theological* approach – indeed, an approach which itself embodies a theology, as we shall see in the next chapter.

Whether emphasising the theological or the action research components of theological action research, what remains central is the *practice* of *conversation*. Whilst conversation is a term much-used in theology – and especially practical theology and 'theological reflection' – all too often, it seems to refer to a conceptual conversation rather than the messy, interruptive comings and goings of actual people talking to each other.[13] Theological action research, however, as described in *Talking About God in Practice*, is forged in just such real-life conversations: the sometimes confused and halting conversations as we get to know each other;[14] the conversations struggling for practical clarity and wisdom in the co-designing of the research;[15] the opening up of conversation among respondents through the co-designed qualitative research methods; and, most complexly and profoundly, in the conversations of reflection on the data received.[16] The theological moment – the 'disclosure' of theological insight – is born out of this careful work of conversation.

Drawing attention to these participative features of theological action research goes some way to responding to criticisms that the processes used in theological action research are not so much those of action research as 'consultancy'.[17] It perhaps also hints at the ways in which the particularly *theological* nature of the ARCS research was based on a growing recognition that the doing of theology, in its articulated, academy-based forms, is, itself a practice. As the ARCS team worked together, not only did we grow in our understanding of that 'ethnography of faith' which involved us in heartfelt – even intimate – ways in the work of our practitioner co-researchers;[18] but we also learnt that we, too, were developing our practices as theologians and academics. The action research processes impacted on our own contributions to ecclesiology as 'actions' subject to change through the learning generated by the research. The learning and reflections of what was called the 'outsider team'[19] in *Talking About God in Practice* are, I would argue, fruits of action research in the realm of the 'intellectual action' of theology. This book is something of a testimony to that aspect of our work.

The significance of action research as an interdisciplinary partner

Whilst this chapter does not aim to give a detailed and exhaustive account of the highly varied and complex field of 'action research',[20] it is worth noting some of the features of this research approach which made it especially appropriate for the ARCS team and which have presented themselves positively to the wider practical theological discourse.

Prior to the establishment of the ARCS research, James Sweeney and myself had already been working with practices in Roman Catholic Evangelisation using qualitative research methods. The suggestion to take up a more action research approach came from Jim, and was initially motivated by a strong sense of wanting not so much to research the practices of others as to work with practitioners as co-researchers, positioning ourselves as far as possible as co-workers, of a particular kind, in a common ecclesial concern for the work of the church in and for the world. The action research emphases on participation and collaboration were primary attractors for us. On further exploration of action research approaches, the emphasis on 'action' became clearer and presented itself to us as a good fit for our own commitment to the kind of ecclesial theology that makes a difference in practice.[21] Neither Jim, nor myself nor the team members that joined us identified simply as 'academics'; each in their own ways were committed to the living, active traditions and practices of faith. Such a fundamental conviction of the ecclesial – and so practical and action-expressed – nature of theology meant that we were not content simply to carry out ecclesiological conversation in abstract cerebral ways which might struggle to relate to the realities on the ground.

In this way we were discovering action research through a similar process as that described by Swinton and Mowat: the realisation that qualitative research in general enables a clearer attentiveness to "fascinating worlds of meaning", in all their lived complexity,[22] is welcomed by practical theologians, who, at the same time, recognise their commitment not only to knowing things but to a way of knowing that enables "more faithful" living and action. It is this logic which leads to the now much-discussed statement that "Practical Theology is fundamentally *action* research".[23]

This simple assertion left as it is calls for some qualification, as we shall see; indeed, Swinton and Mowat themselves make clear the distinctiveness of the specifically *theological* use of action research approaches, which will be discussed in the next section. Here, I would simply note the difficulty of referring to 'action research' as a single methodology or approach. Action researchers themselves recognise the wide variety of ways in which 'action research' is carried out, with a clear recognition that the term refers not so much to a single methodology as to "a family of approaches".[24] This does, of course, make any critiques of practical theology 'as' action research, or of particular theological use of action research, problematic – "there can never be one 'right way' of doing action research".[25] For the contributors to the most recent edition of the *Sage Handbook of Action Research*, there are, nonetheless recognisable characteristics of any action research undertaking: not only does it necessarily require the clear positioning and personal transparency of the researcher (as discussed in chapter 2 above), but it also seeks to generate a new kind of knowing, which somewhat challenges the modern 'Western mindset' with its valuing of positivist accounts of knowledge. Reason and Bradbury sum this up in identifying three fundamental purposes for action research in all its variety:

> The first purpose is to bring an action dimension back to the overly quietist tradition of knowledge generation which has developed in the modern era. The second is to expand the hold over knowledge held traditionally by universities and the institutes of 'higher learning', ... [thirdly] to contribute to the ongoing revisioning of the Western mindset – to add impetus to the movement away from a modernist world view based on a positivist philosophy and a value system dominated by economic progress, toward emerging perspectives which share a 'post-modern' sentiment.[26]

The chapters of this substantial *Handbook* are witness to the wide variety of ways in which these core commitments can be adhered to through a variety of action research practices. They are purposes which, in a specifically theological way, also lie at the heart of theological action research.

Participation, the central importance of 'action', a certain flexibility of process – all these things attracted the first ARCS researchers to action research; but the just-quoted paragraph from Peter Reason and Hilary Bradbury also names another, perhaps deeper resonance between action research's epistemological concerns and the commitments of the ARCS team and of many practice-concerned theologians. For, if the values of modernist epistemologies have been costly for practical expertise and wisdom, and more humanly-embodied, multi-faceted accounts of what is true and valuable, then this is a cost especially keenly felt by theology as 'faith seeking understanding'. Faith is, after all, precisely one of those human, complex, mysterious realities in which truth as personally and communally held is referred beyond what can be known by rational investigation. Modern ways of knowing have, because of this, struggled to speak of 'faith' as a way of *knowing*, tending to consider it rather in purely phenomenological terms. To endeavour, as practical theologians, to enquire of Christian practice as a source of theology, is to place ourselves in that reaction against modern epistemological assumptions and seek another way of knowing. This instinct is one shared between practical theology and action research.[27]

One of the ways in which the resonance of epistemological commitments of action research and practical theology can be recognised is through the growing attentiveness to 'spirituality' among action researchers themselves. This is described by both Elaine Graham[28] and Jason Boyd,[29] and comes to a particular and unusually integrated account in the work of the Jesuit action researcher David Coghlan.[30] Like Boyd,[31] I recognise in Coghlan's work a distinctive account of the resonances between Ignatian discernment and certain approaches in action research which draws particular attention to the ways in which 'knowing' is always orientated to taking the next step, and is seen as emergent from attentiveness to everyday practice.[32] Indeed, the wider traditions of Christian accompaniment, spiritual direction, and discernment relate well to the epistemological commitments of action research, with its emphasis on contextual and personal emergent knowing as informative of actions. Action research seems unusual among social science approaches to the empirical for its instinct toward the mysterious, non-quantifiable dynamics of human knowing, lending itself well to a research process such as ours, which aims to be, first and foremost, 'theological'.

From 'action research' to 'theological action research'

In describing our methodology as 'theological *action research*', the ARCS team were making clear not only a commitment to practice, but also to a practitioner led and participatory process of reflection on practices, with a view to learning more about them, seeing them afresh, and renewing understanding and practice itself. This much we would hold in common with action researchers more generally. However, in describing our processes as '*theological* action research', we are witnessing to a number of crucial convictions which shape the way we work. These convictions are summarised in the account of theological action research's 'five characteristics', referred to above. To finish this chapter, I now offer some further reflection on the fundamentals signified by these characteristics and, in conversation with Swinton and Mowat, give a clearer account of the significance of the qualifier 'theological' for theological action research.

Central to these fundamentals is the commitment to understanding practices as themselves 'bearers of theology'; indeed, practices of the faithful are regarded as themselves embodied examples of 'faith seeking understanding'.

It is for this reason that theological action research's first characteristic is named as being 'theological all the way through'; and this particular understanding of practice also informs the development of the four voices of theology (characteristic 2). This distinctive understanding of practice as faith seeking understanding means that, whilst theological action research shares with practical theology the concern to 'place practice first', it also militates against any simply correlative method which puts 'pure practice' first and then introduces it to 'theology' through some method of reflection.[33] Rather, the professed understanding and actual practices of those concretely living Church – their 'espoused' and 'operant' theologies – are recognised as intrinsically theological voices from the outset. Like all theology, although in a particular and sometimes more muddled way, these voices are mediated through particularities and personalities, and are also the bearers of various kinds of brokenness. They are voices to be attended to and *discerned.*

With this fundamental starting place, the challenge that faces theological action research is how practice is to be 'read' and enabled as an effective theological authority. The four voices of theology framework summarises the theological action research response to this challenge, whilst the participative, action research approaches involved in our methods and described earlier in this chapter describe a distinctive approach to communal discernment as a research practice. The 'four voices' are the focus of the next chapter's discussions, and so will not be treated here. Rather, the way for that discussion will be paved by some concluding thoughts on what distinguishes theological action research from action research as such.

In clarifying these thoughts, it is helpful to engage with Swinton and Mowat's account of practical theology as action research. I described above how Swinton and Mowat – in what might be considered a surprising, last-minute move – developed their thinking around the need for qualitative methods in practical theology toward the assertion that practical theology is a form of 'action research'. They recognise that practical theology is not merely interested in seeing the complexity and detail of realities but is ultimately committed to *action.*[34] The authors go on to qualify the identification of practical theology as action research by describing the ways in which practical theology "presents as a quite specific form of action research with a particular understanding of the nature and purpose of action".[35] For them, the uniqueness of any practical theology action research lies specifically in the desire to bring about change in practice "in the hope that they [Christian practitioners] will move closer towards faithfulness".[36] This is important, because it makes clear that, unlike social science action research, the theological action researcher is not simply concerned with problem-solving.[37] However, it also raises an immediate question: 'faithfulness to what/whom?', to be quickly followed by the question of discernment: 'how do we recognise change toward this faithfulness?' In an implicit way the vexed question of normativity – how things 'ought' to be – begins to raise its head.

In part, Swinton and Mowat respond to these issues through identifying a distinctive *telos* for practical theology, which differentiates it from (other) action research:

> In other words, unlike the social sciences, there is an end or *telos* that transcends all particular forms of action in practical theology. This *telos* constitutes the primary purpose and meaning of human life and the eschatological horizon of the practical theological enterprise. For the practical theologian action is not merely pragmatic, or problem-solving, though there can be elements of this. For the practical theologian action always has a goal of interacting with situations and challenging practices in order that individuals and communities can be enabled to remain faithful to God and participate in God's mission.[38]

It is the eschatological framing of practical theology, shaped by the story of redemption in Jesus, that makes all the difference to how practical theology 'uses' empirical approaches and sets it apart from other action research. The question of how any 'content' for the *telos* might be established, and by whom, is left unanswered, suggesting the need for a more integral ecclesiology through which some sense of normative or communally held understandings might operate to give the *telos* some clear shared meaning.

That being said, I am broadly in sympathy with Swinton and Mowat's approach, and recognise in it something of what I would want to say about a characteristically *theological* action research. Elaine Graham's criticism[39] – that Swinton and Mowat here undermine their claim to practical theology's being action research, owing to the privileged position given to theological knowledge, and the resultant limits set on the change that might be enabled – highlights the significance of the *theological* as a qualifier in the present book's approach. In fact, both for Swinton and Mowat and proponents of theological action research, there is an authentic sense in which the formative authority of theology as human understanding illumined by divine revelation remains properly unresolved in relation to practice. Theological action research, unlike action research, is – simply – *theological.* This is to say, with Swinton and Mowat, that it is characterised by faith as a way of knowing, based on the given authority of divine revelation. That revelation is, itself, always contextually mediated and interpreted; it is no simple, fixed or self-evident thing. But, in principle, this commitment to theology as essentially based in divine revelation militates against any sense of a theological use of action research which remains simply at the level of human problem-solving, change and notions of success.

Indeed, as a proponent of theological action research, I would go somewhat further than Swinton and Mowat. The core conviction of theological action research – that practices are bearers of theology – is based on a prior fundamental theological belief in the activity of God in the world. This is made clear in *Talking About God in Practice* when we cite at length

Catholic teaching on Divine revelation in support of our position.[40] Such a position, with its attendant pneumatology and theology of grace, suggests not so much that we are concerned simply with human practice, change and agency *as such*; but it also, more boldly demonstrates our ultimate concern with the discernment of God's agency within these human practices. The primary 'actor' for theological action research is God, as Trinity, in which the life and thinking of church participates.

If that sounds overly grand and ridiculous to a social scientist (and to many practical theologians, I suspect), I want again to position the claim plainly in the longer tradition of Anselm's 'faith seeking understanding'. What is foundational is the assumption that we share with pre-modern (and so the majority of) Christian theology that we can know something about what God is doing because God reveals Godself to us and desires to be known. The pursuit of this (impossible) knowledge – which is, as God's knowing, integrally practical-and-theoretical[41] – is the purpose of theology as faith seeking understanding. Insofar as theological action research stands in continuity with that tradition, I think we can be bold enough to say that what we're trying to do is to discern divine agency in action. Indeed, Swinton and Mowat also hint at such a position when they complement their account of practical theology as action research, with a parallel account of the discipline as worship,[42] and refer to the ways in which qualitative research can open the practical theologian to the voices and dynamics of "the divine drama".[43] This sense of divine and human agency as both active realities for practical theology is also suggested in their use of language of "God's own redemptive practices", and the recognition of human living as "an important locus for the work of the Spirit".[44]

It may be concluded that, in part, the understanding of *theological* action research needs to take full account of the radical significance of the qualifier 'theological'. In particular, this makes clear the nature of the 'action' to which the research refers – God's action, mediated through the broken but graced practices of the women and men who seek to serve God in following Jesus, prompted by the Holy Spirit. It is fundamentally an approach which seeks to understand *God's* agency in actions, and so enable – not problem-solving or change towards some pre-designed goal – but an appropriate human response within a particular personal, faith and cultural context. I am not unaware either of the outrageous boldness of this claim, nor the complexity which must attend it. It is to the further nuancing of this position, through attentiveness to its proper complexity, that I will now turn through an exploration of that second characteristic of theological action research: the four voices of theology.

Notes

1 John Swinton and Harriet Mowat, *Practical Theology and Qualitative Research* (SCM, 2006).

2 Ibid. 255.

3 As well as the specifically theological action research literature noted in chapter 2 above, see: Elaine Graham, "Is Practical Theology a Form of 'Action Research'?" *International Journal of Practical Theology* 17, no.1 (2013): 148–178; Elizabeth Conde Frazier, "Participatory Action Research." Bonnie Miller McLemore ed. *The Wiley Blackwell Companion to Practical Theology* (Wiley-Blackwell, 2013): 234–243; Jason Boyd, *The Naked Preacher: Action Research and a Practice of Preaching* (SCM, 2018); Nick Shepherd, "Action Research as Professional Development." *Journal of Adult Theological Education* 9, no.2 (2012): 21–138. Theological action research has been specifically engaged with in a number of recent significant publications in practical theology: Pete Ward, *Introducing Practical Theology: Mission, Ministry, and the Life of the Church* (Baker Academic, 2017): 60–62; Zoe Bennett, Elaine Graham, Stephen Pattison, and Heather Walton, *Invitation to Research in Practical Theology* (Routledge, 2018): 92–93; Courtney T. Goto, *Taking on Practical Theology: The Idolization of Context and the Hope of Community* (Brill, 2018): 171–180.

4 So particularly Elaine Graham as cited in footnote 3. See also Gary O'Neill and Liz Shercliff, *Straw for the Bricks: Theological Reflection in Practice* (SCM, 2018): 155–160, although much of the criticism here seems built on a limited and flawed understanding of theological action research, as explained in later footnotes to this chapter.

5 *Talking About God in Practice* gives a detailed and practical account of the methods involved in theological action research, and these will not be repeated here. A certain familiarity with that earlier text and its account will be presumed.

6 This chapter assumes some prior knowledge of the practices of theological action research, as set out in Helen Cameron, Deborah Bhatti, Catherine Duce, James Sweeney, and Clare Watkins, *Talking About God in Practice: Theological Action Research and Practical Theology* (SCM, 2010). However, it may be useful to refer to the Appendix of the present volume which outlines the processes of theological action research.

7 Op. cit. chapter 3.

8 Ibid. 36.

9 Op. cit. appendices 2–5. This, and the following footnote, suggest that Gary O'Neill's criticism that the practitioners have 'no control' is based on a misunderstanding of the theological action research processes as described in *Talking About God*, and evidenced in subsequent theological action research publications, of which he appears unaware. Gary O'Neill and Liz Shercliff, *Straw for the Bricks: Theological Reflection in Practice* (SCM, 2018): 158–159.

10 See op. cit. appendices 11–12. The significance of this grounded learning can be more readily seen in some publications following *Talking About God in Practice.* For example, Clare Watkins and Helen Cameron, "Epiphanic Sacramentality: An Example of Practical Ecclesiology Revisioning Theological Understanding." Christian B. Scharen ed. *Explorations in Ecclesiology and Ethnography* (Eerdmans, 2012): 71–89; Clare Watkins, and Bridget Shepherd, "The Challenge of 'Fresh Expressions' to Ecclesiology. Reflections From the Practice of Messy Church." *Ecclesial Practices* 1 (2014): 92–110.

11 Cameron et al., *Talking About God in Practice*, 51–52.

12 Ibid. 51–60.

13 A highly influential example of this can be found in Stephen Pattison, "Some Straw for the Bricks: A Basic Introduction to Theological Reflection." *Contact*, 99, no.1 (1989): 2–9, where he writes: "... the model I want to commend as a starting point for theological reflection is that of the critical conversation. The basic idea here is that the student should imagine herself as being involved in a

three way conversation between a) her own ideas, beliefs, feelings, perceptions and assumptions, b) the beliefs, assumptions and perceptions provided by the Christian tradition (including the Bible) and c) the contemporary situation which is being examined" (4). Whilst there is some resonance between this and theological action research's account of the four voices of theology (see chapter 4), nonetheless this does not take us out of the realm of individual thinking about things, into the real messiness of human conversation as such.

14 *Talking About God*, appendices 2–3.

15 Working towards the agreed 'Remit Document'. See ibid. appendix 4.

16 Represented in the methods by Appendices 11 and 12, ibid. The significance of these conversations can be perhaps most clearly seen in Watkins and Shepherd, op. cit. It is significant that, early on in the project, we used grounded theory approaches in analysing the data, ably assisted by Deborah Bhatti, but these methods were later abandoned, in large part as they were not suited to a participative, conversational reading of the transcripts.

17 Graham, op. cit. 164. A criticism repeated by Boyd, op. cit. 42 and elaborated by Gary O'Neill, O'Neill and Shercliff, op. cit. 157–158.

18 See above chapter 2, pp. 21–22.

19 It is notable that for a number of the capacity building groups worked with subsequently, and later theological action research projects, this 'insider/outsider' language has been modified to reflect better the experienced realities of a greater correspondence between the co-researchers than this initial language might convey. So: practitioner/academic; local/university, for example. All have their problems.

20 For this see, most helpfully, Peter Reason and Hilary Bradbury eds. *The Sage Handbook of Action Research: Participative Inquiry and Practice* (2nd ed., Sage, 2013).

21 Chapter 2's account of the professional and personal journeys and priorities of the team illustrate where this is rooted.

22 Swinton and Mowat, op. cit. 2554–2555.

23 Ibid. 255.

24 Peter Reason and Hilary Bradbury, "Introduction." Peter Reason and Hilary Bradbury eds. *The Sage Handbook of Action Research: Participative Inquiry and Practice* (2nd ed., Sage, 2013): 7–8.

25 Ibid. 7.

26 Ibid. 7–8.

27 It is striking that Nick Healy's work, discussed in chapter 1 above, draws on much pre-modern ecclesiology to highlight the difficulties with modern ecclesiology – especially in so far as these difficulties are to do with the abstraction of knowledge about the church. The call to the post-modern and the retrieval of the pre-modern are closely allied, as proponents of 'Radical Orthodoxy' make clear: John Milbank et al., *Radical Orthodoxy: A New Theology* (Routledge, 1999). This appeal to the pre-modern is, in a different way, a feature of the current work as it unfolds.

28 Graham, op. cit.

29 Boyd, op. cit.

30 David Coghlan, *Attending to Experience: Reflections on Engaging in Action Research*, (2003). Available at: www.aral.com.au/whyar/Coghlan.pdf; "Seeking God in All Things." *The Way* 43, no.1 (2004): 1–14; "Ignatian Spirituality as Transformational Social Science." *Action Research* 3, no.1 (2005): 89–107; "Authenticity as First Person Practice." *Action Research* 6, no.3 (2008): 351–366; "Interiority as the Cutting Edge Between Theory and Practice: A First Person Perspective." *International Journal of Action Research* 6, no.2/3 (2010): 288–307.

31 Boyd, op. cit. 42–53.
32 It is no coincidence that one of the most fruitful and instinctive experiences of the ARCS research was with the London Jesuit Volunteers, whose commitment to Ignatian spirituality positively shaped their response to and participation in theological action research. See Account of Practice A 57ff below.
33 This is a well-recognised and persistently unavoided risk in the contemporary use of the pastoral cycle. This is discussed in more detail in chapter 4.
34 Swinton and Mowat, op. cit. 255.
35 Ibid.
36 Ibid. 256.
37 On one level, of course, this statement can be negated when we consider that there is always a 'problem' with Christian action in that it is marred by that sin and results of the Fall which inevitably make it fall short of its aim. It is eschatologically conditioned. This is, I suggest, a rather different context for 'problem-solving' than that recognised by action research more widely.
38 Swinton and Mowat, op. cit. 257.
39 Graham, op. cit. 160.
40 Cameron et. al., op. cit. 52. This account of the work of the Spirit in the 'progress of revelation' seems to have been missed by Gary O'Neill in his criticisms. See O'Neill and Shercliff, op. cit. 159.
41 See Thomas as Aquinas: "Holy teaching (*sacra doctrina)* while remaining single nevertheless embraces things belonging to the different philosophical sciences because of the one formal meaning which is its interest in all manner of things, namely the truth they bear in the light of God. Whereas some among the philosophical sciences are theoretical and some practical, **sacred doctrine takes over both functions, in this being like the single knowledge whereby God knows himself and the things he makes"**. *Summa Theologiae* I.1.4. My emphasis. This is discussed further in chapter 13, pp. 241–243 below.
42 Op. cit. 259.
43 Ibid. I note here the resonance with von Balthasar's theo-drama, that provided Nick Healy with the theological framework in which to speak about the co-operation of divine and human his ecclesiology. See: Nicolas Healy, *Church, World and the Christian Life: Practical Prophetic Ecclesiology* (CUP, 2000): 52–76.
44 Swinton and Mowat, op. cit. 5–6.

4 Theology in four voices

The four voices: origins and questions

As we have seen, theological action research has been described by its originators in terms of five characteristics. The first of these – being 'theological all the way through' – can be considered the prior basis of the approach, and has already been an important part of the discussions so far. The second characteristic – an understanding of 'theology in four voices' – grew out of this primary position. The theological action research 'understanding of theology in four voices' refers to the way in which we presented the various *loci* for theological authority in our ARCS reflections. These were described as: the operant voice, embodied in the practices themselves; the espoused voice, found in the practitioners' own theological articulation of their practices; the normative voice, expressed in the established Christian tradition, in its various understandings of scripture, church teaching, liturgy and so forth; and the formal voice, articulated in academic theology and wider thinking of the academy. Despite only occupying three pages of *Talking About God in Practice*,[1] this idea of the four voices of theology has gained significant currency among researchers and teachers and seems now an established way of speaking about and reflecting on theology and practice – somewhat to the surprise of its originators. At the same time, this up-take of what was only a small feature of the earlier book has inevitably led to the need to refine and clarify the four voices framework, and in training, teaching and conference papers, this has increasingly been done.[2] More, however, needs to be said about the origins, purposes and meaning of this approach in order to appreciate and develop its fruitful use and clarify the instincts of those of us who first articulated it. What follows not only draws together the developments of the last eight years, but also, and in doing so, reveals some of the significance and richness of this 'second characteristic' of theological action research[3] – significance and richness of which we were not fully aware when we wrote in 2010.

The place of the four voices in theological action research

The ARCS research set out with the understanding that the church practices with which we worked were bearers of their own theology – were, in their own ways, expressions of 'faith seeking understanding' – and that they therefore were proper sources for theology from the outset, having their own theological authority. This position demonstrates a commitment to the insight that, far from there being a gulf between theology and practice, as is so often supposed by what goes under the name of practical theology, faith-full practices are themselves embodied theology before the 'theologian' even brings her attention to bear on them. However, such a commitment becomes demanding when we consider how such embodied theologies are to be read and discerned; they are, after all, in common with all human practices, including speech and thinking, flawed and broken expressions of faith, intractably affected by sin, and in need of the constant illumination of that divine revelation which is the basis of all Christian theology. Our faith in human actions as *loci* of the Spirit, and the call to discern that activity of God within them, meant that it became a crucial question for the ARCS team as to how the theological authority of practice could be articulated and heard in ways in keeping with our fundamental sense of the wider theological and church traditions as, alongside contemporary practice, and in different ways, *loci* of revelation. Theology in four voices was an understanding which developed in response to this basic question of theology.[4]

In fact, looking back at our earlier, all-too-brief account, it seems clear to me now that the four voices always had a pivotal role in what we were doing. Not only did it answer the conundrum of our first conviction about the nature of theology as embodied in practice-and-traditions but it also gave rise to and gives explanatory weight to the other three characteristics – of conversational practice and the transformation of both practice and academic theology. The understanding of theology in four voices makes conversations across disciplines, traditions and perspectives, as well as across practices (including scholarly practice), essential. This is *essential* not only – or primarily – as a pragmatic consideration of method but as a quality intrinsic to the way in which theology as such is here envisioned in the interplay of the four voices. It is in this conversation of theologically authoritative 'voices' that truth – something of the word and action of God – might be discerned.[5]

There is one thing that was not clear in the book of 2010 whose importance has become evident in the ensuing years, especially as we have seen the ways in which the four voices framework has been used. This concerns the way in which the framework was arrived at and the implications of this. The identification of the operant, espoused, normative and formal voices of theology was, first and foremost, the fruit of an inductive learning process for the ARCS team; indeed, it can be seen as a result of the action research processes as they changed our own intellectual practices as theologians. I want to stress that this was not a 'model' that we devised and then brought to bear on our theology; it was much more a matter of discovering – as we went along, listening to research participants, attending to the data we were gathering, listening to our own conversations and 'intelligent hearts' – an emergent language which we were using more and more. Over time, we identified with more confidence four 'places' or sources where we felt we were 'hearing' important theological wisdom about what we were seeing and thinking. Our conversations, across our various personalities, traditions and experiences interweaved these theological sources – sometimes with some knotting and jarring – leading us to recognise that it was in this coming together of these 'voices' that fresh learning was gained and 'moments of disclosure' encountered.

Something more is said about these 'disclosure' moments below. Here I want to draw attention to the implications of this inductive learning of the four voices understanding. What this makes clear is that the four voices of theology should not be seen as something like a theological reflective method or adapted pastoral cycle; it is not a framework to be objectified and applied. The reader will not see the voices explicitly mentioned very often in the theology that arises from this work, as described in chapters 5–11; they are, rather, the hidden infrastructure of that 'disclosed' theology. Too often I have seen the four voices used as *headings* under which some kind of theological reflection is attempted. This may be more or less successful as a way of theological reflection, but it is not true to the nature of the four voices of theology as envisioned and practised by its originators – though this may hardly have been clear in our account of 2010. In particular, the four voices approach is not being presented as a method for holding together separate theological accounts. Rather, it arises from theologians' looking at practices in ways which are assumed to be integral with the wider theological and ecclesial traditions in which they work. Our assumption is that the voices already belonged to one another and are intrinsically inter-related; our task is to discern the complex interrelations of the various authorities within the conversation so as to discover renewed theology and practice. The four voices framework is a diagrammatic account of what we saw going on in our conversations, thinking and hearts. The unavoidable paradox is that once the diagram was conceived and published, it lent itself to being used as (yet another) deductive 'model' to be applied. Recalling how it was learnt by the ARCS team is important in challenging any too rigid codification of the four voices as a tool.

These considerations, and some evident misunderstanding of the four voices, has – as set out below – led to a re-visioning of the diagram in my current publication and teaching. The diagrammatic account presented in *Talking About God in Practice*,[6] whilst naming and describing the four voices themselves, did little to demonstrate their inter-relation, and tended to rather a static imaging of what was – and is – experienced as a dynamic of conversational and conceptual interplay. The text surrounding this diagram does, in fact, make the inter-relation of the voices and their proper complexity clear;[7] however, it seems that the brevity of these words, and the power of the image, has often distorted the understanding of the four voices.

As well as understanding the four voices through their inductively-learnt origins, it is also useful to make clear that they are rooted in a basic theological sense which is not primarily concerned with practical theology as a discipline. The four voices approach arises from the sense that what we set out to do was not 'practical theology' but, simply, *theology* – all be it a theology interested in and committed to practice and action. In part, this reflects the fact that two of the ARCS team – James Sweeney and myself – are Roman Catholic, and so work in a tradition where practical theology as such does not have the same currency as in other traditions.[8] We understood ourselves as doing ecclesiology within a systematic and ecclesially informed approach. Indeed, something of this is evident in the 2010 account of the four voices when we write of our "conviction that Christian practice is, itself, 'faith seeking understanding', a kind of theology, [which] leads to a properly complex view of theology as such".[9] This traditional understanding of theology is the motivation in our work, and it is the basis on which we attend to practices. We arrive at the value and the theological significance of practices not from a sociological or political conviction, but rather as a deeply held, obvious consequence of our theological faith about the kind of God that the Christian God is. The understanding of the four voices of theology was not, for us at least, primarily conceived in response to the agendas and questions of practical theological discourse but started in a rather different place, in which the integrated nature of theology-and-practice was assumed as the dynamic of divine revelation. This does, I suggest, make a difference.

The problematic context of 'practical theology'

In order to understand this difference a little better, I want briefly to acknowledge some of the problematic issues with practical theology and question their effects on how theology in four voices is understood. I would suggest that the problems that we've had with the understanding of the four voices are symptomatic of endemic problems within practical theology as a whole. In particular, the ways in which we habitually think about practice and about thinking/articulation in practical theology has made it difficult to understand fully what we were trying to say in the four voices of theology.

Here I have in mind that 'correlative paradigm', so formative of practical theology, about which I have written elsewhere.[10] The conceiving of practical theology – and especially theological reflection – as the bringing together of 'polarities', or a critical conversation between theory and practice,[11] suggests that at the start of much practical theology, there is an assumption of dis-integration. Practical theology can then see its particular task as the bringing (back) together of theology (understood often as 'theory') and practice, on the assumption that they are separate – all be it tragically so.

Against this, the ARCS project as an ecclesiological project concerned with practices (in keeping with many great ecclesiologists, such as Karl Rahner and Edward Schillebeeckx, I suggest),[12] and out of which the four voices of theology arose, assumed from the start a proper and alive integration of theology and practice. Indeed, the starting conviction that practices are theological expressions evidences this. For us, the 'problem' was not one of how to connect the separated realms of practice and (abstract) theology; rather, we were concerned to elucidate how the action and word of God might be discerned and responded to in a whole, ecclesial theology, in which the different *loci* of revelation were properly attended to as diverse but true and authoritative witnesses to that revelation. Far from being a tool or method for answering practical theology's dominant question of disintegration, theology in four voices is rather an expression of a theological conviction concerning the reality of an integrated 'whole-theology'. When you read the four voices with an assumption of disintegration, you get a different understanding of it.

The reception of the four voices – and questions arising

The next task in this chapter is to give an account of some of the clarification and nuancing of the four voices which has taken place since the publication of *Talking About God in Practice*. To do this, I want first to identify certain 'questions arising' in the reception of the four voices of theology, in response to which these clarifications and proper complexifications have taken place. In my experience of teaching and training in theological action research, I would identify three significant areas for questions concerning the four voices: the relation of the voices to one another; the problem of the operant as a 'voice'; and the asymmetry of authorities between the four voices, with particular attention to the question of the normative. Consideration of these three questions will shape the next section's renewed account of the four voices of theology. However, before exploring these questions, I want also to make some mention of the place of the pastoral cycle and related 'models' of theological reflection (or action-reflection more broadly) in theological action research, and their relation to the four voices of theology.

It is in chapter 4 of *Talking About God in Practice* that theological action research as such is presented, and the understanding of theology in four voices first articulated. The chapter begins with a diagram of a typical action reflection model which corresponds to many representations of the pastoral cycle.[13] The move from 'experience' through 'reflection' and 'learning' to 'action' lacks some of the explicitly theological resonances of the 'See-Judge-Act' of the pastoral cycle, but nonetheless will be widely recognisable to practical theologians. In the context of the chapter, the diagram serves not so much to describe theological action research, but rather to act as an introduction to the distinctiveness of theological action research by starting with an already recognised pattern of reflection and learning, after which what is different about theological action research is set out. In fact, I would argue, theological action research's understanding of theology in four voices challenges much of the dominant use and understanding of the pastoral cycle in contemporary practical theology.

The pastoral cycle has its proximate roots in the 'See-Judge-Act' ministry of the Belgian Catholic priest, Joseph Cardijn, and his work with the Young Christian Workers Movement, which he founded in the 1920s. This is a movement committed to the three 'truths' of faith, reality and method, where the See-Judge-Act method seeks to enable a greater congruence between these truths.[14] By 1961, this approach had found its way into the papal teaching of the Catholic church, being referred to in Pope St. John XXIII's encyclical on social issues, *Mater et Magistra*.[15] It later became the mainstay of much Latin American liberation theology, as is more widely recognised in the practical theological literature. The Roman Catholic provenance is of significance in understanding the ecclesiological context of the pastoral cycle as originally conceived; this is a 'method' born out of a tradition in which there is a distinctive understanding of divine revelation, its *loci*, its transmission and the role of the church in these dynamics. More pragmatically, See-Judge-Act was not designed as an aid to academics seeking to relate their theology to practices, but rather as a communal and prayerful process engaged in by small groups of Christians reflecting on their day-to-day life. The pastoral cycle can still serve the practical theologian and theological reflector in these ways, but this awareness of ecclesial context and history serves to ward against any reification of the pastoral cycle which sees it in terms of a quasi-academic method or research tool. In particular, the Young Christian Worker Movement and the base communities of liberation theology gather around this method in a context of shared prayer and faith-community with the express intention of seeking to understand better what God might be saying to them about their own lives as Christians. Any translation of this into the rather more individualistic, academic (and protestant dominated) world of practical theology needs to take some account of this in chastening too uncritical a promulgation of the pastoral cycle to students and practitioners.

One of the risks of separating the pastoral cycle from its ecclesial, faith-community roots is that it allows for a more modern, academic epistemology, more akin to social sciences and educational studies, to dominate. In this context the pastoral cycle is too easily operated as *stages* of reflection, in which experience/practice, analysis, theological reflection and action are held distinct. This gives rise to the idea that theology is one of the steps in the process, and undermines any fundamental sense of the reflector being involved in theology 'all the way through'. It is notable, of course, that the original See-Judge-Act method did not include 'theological reflection'; such an inclusion would be unnecessary in the context of practising this way of discernment in explicitly prayerful, faith groups for whom – I suggest – the theology was operative throughout the process.

The significance of these reflections on the pastoral cycle for understanding the four voices of theology and their place in theological action research lies precisely here: if the pastoral cycle is understood in terms of a procedure of stages, in which theology is one rather late stage, it remains inimical to theological action research precisely because of the way in which the four voices of theology speaks of an integrated, whole-theology – in which all aspects of the research and its attendant practices are understood as theological. For an approach adopting theology in four voices as a basis, it is indeed questionable as to whether there can ever be so procedural a sense of a model; rather, the four voices commit us to sitting with the cacophony and occasional harmony of the voices, attentively waiting for the insight (disclosure) to become clear.[16]

Renewing the approach: reflections and clarifications

It now remains for me to clarify some key aspects of the four voices of theology, and, in doing so, offer an enriched, 'thicker' account of the approach.

The interpenetration of the voices

I mentioned above that the diagram used in *Talking About God in Practice* to describe the four voices had some weaknesses which have become clear in the intervening years. In particular, the diagram does not make clear enough either the interrelatedness of the voices or their dynamic interpenetration, at the heart of which lies a renewal of theological knowledge for practice. We do say in the text that it must be "constantly borne in mind" that "these four voices are not discrete, separate from one another.... We can never hear one voice without there being echoes of the other three",[17] and subsequent iterations of the diagram in teaching and training have reflected this more clearly. So, in Figure 4.1, we see a revised image in which double headed arrows between the voices are introduced to express the dynamic interpenetration of the voices: not only is there an expectation of constant back-and-forth conversation between the voices, but also a recognition that each voice 'contains' and is dependent on the others. Normative voices are historically dependent on operant, espoused and formal. Formal voices, likewise are not discrete. Rather, they stand in normative traditions, more or less critically, and are shaped, even unwittingly, by the voices and experience of practice. The practice-based voices of the operant and espoused themselves will derive something of their embodied and articulated theologies from being shaped and informed, in different ways, by aspects of the normative and formal. The voices are truly *not* discrete entities. Indeed, there is a real sense in which they are not separate voices at all; rather, they refer in a short-hand way to the manner in which the one voice worth hearing – that of the Triune God – might be heard.

This brings us to a second modification to this revised diagram: the inclusion of an extra heading, "a conversation of *disclosure*". What this addition

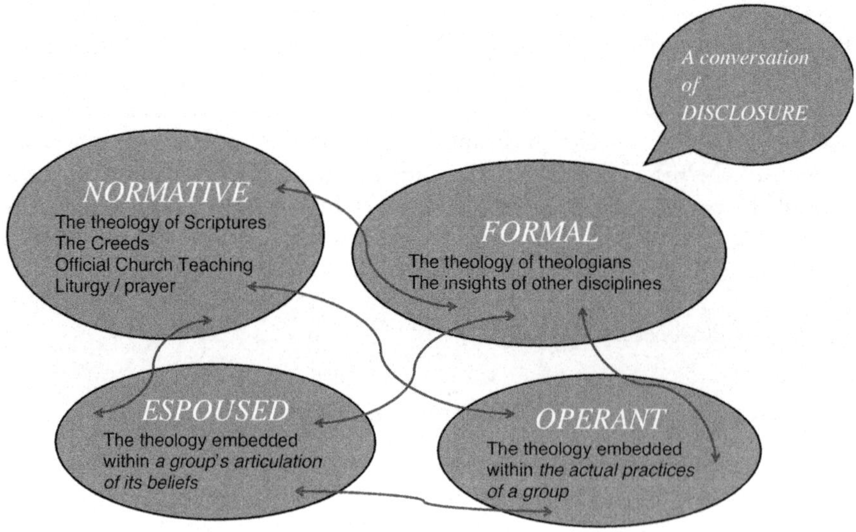

Figure 4.1 Theology in four voices

seeks to clarify is that theology does not (ever) exist in just one of the voices. As 'faith seeking understanding' theology only properly exists in the conversation *between* the voices – a conversation which can be more or less dissonant, or harmonious, but which is always multi-voiced. What concerns the theological action researcher is not so much the 'content' of the different voices but rather the insight that is gained through sitting with them all, in open, listening conversation. These insights are recognised in what we came to call moments of 'disclosure', or epiphany[18] – communally shared learning points, where we might just have caught a glimpse (all be it fragmentary and partial) of that divine word and action which we seek to discern. It is the identification of such disclosures that shapes the 'accounts of practice' that thread through this book, and which provide the practice basis for the 'disclosed' ecclesiology which results. In this way, the four voices' understanding is fundamental for the working out of the integrated, practically attentive ecclesiology that this volume surfaces and explores.

The problem of the operant as 'voice'

These observations lead to the second problematic area for the four voices: the understanding of practice as articulated in the 'voices' of the espoused and, most problematically, the operant. For, in including in this book 'accounts of practice' with their identified 'disclosures', I am nonetheless aware that these accounts are not, and cannot be, the practices themselves; indeed, they are not even detailed, thickly described case studies of those practices. They are simply accounts which name and evidence the 'disclosures' experienced in the reflective conversations on practice between the ARCS researchers and the practitioners themselves. As witnesses to the shared learning of practitioners and the ARCS team, they are also something of a window into the complex, polyvalent realities of the practices concerned, and care has been taken to include verbatim accounts from those involved. Nonetheless, the highly partial and selective nature of these accounts highlights the difficulty that persists in trying to be true to the operant 'voice'. For as soon as we have written about practice, as soon as we have discussed, interpreted and reflected on those actions, they have ceased to be practices as such, and the embodied nature of their theological authority is, at best, attenuated, and, at worst, lost all together.

There has been much written about 'thick description' in practical theology,[19] as well as about ethnography and how it might appropriately be used in ecclesiology. With regard to the latter, both ethnographic studies as such and the work of ecclesiological proponents of ethnography have voiced concerns as to the possibility of the core characteristics of ethnography being either sustainable within or even helpful to ecclesiology.[20] Social scientists and ethnographers themselves struggle to give proper, faithful accounts of the complexities of practice in what, ultimately, are representations of practice, and largely verbal ones at that. Nonetheless, there is a proper intuition for many practical theologians (including myself) that it is only in giving the most detailed, careful, 'thick' description of practices that we can be appropriately authentic to our commitment to these practices as theological authorities. What this book's Accounts of Practice witness to, however, is the decision to allow that authenticity to stay hidden from the page of words, so as to remain embodied in the real-life practices of conversation from which the Accounts and their learning points are articulated. For the ecclesiological purposes of this present argument, the aim is not primarily one of faithful practical description of complex realities, but rather attentiveness to these realities, communally discerned as carefully and complexly as possible, so as to read them as an authentic *locus* for discernment of the Spirit's work. So it is that a decision was made not to offer a detailed, action research narrative of the various research *loci* and their research experience – each of which deserved a book in itself; but, instead, to identify and give sufficient account of key points of learning for action that came about from the participative conversation and reflection on practice, so as to serve a demonstration of an integrated, practice-informed ecclesiology.

This leaves us with the question of what it means to translate practice into a 'voice' with all that is involved in such translation into words, ideas and their simplifications. Fundamentally, this paradox of the operant voice cannot be resolved; there is always a certain 'surdic'[21] quality to lived reality which cannot be fully accounted. Not being able to resolve this paradox does not mean, however, that it can be ignored in using the four voices of theology, not least for the ways in which it shapes the nature of the authority of the operant voice. For this authority is not only to be found in the verbal representation of practices nor the discerned learning from practice; rather, it is only truly embodied in the actions themselves. We cannot fully give an account of this verbally and so are consistently compelled back to the practices and their doing, where the authority is lived and experienced and presents new challenges for the whole-theology dynamic of theology in four voices. The operant voice, with its unresolvable paradox of articulating the 'mute' (*surdus*) voice of embodied theology, pulls theology in four voices consistently back to the lived realities of practice. It is here that the central Christian mystery of the Trinity who is always utterly other and utterly alongside can be glimpsed.

The asymmetry of authorities and the question of normativity

These reflections on the surdic nature of the operant voice bring us to a third important issue for the four voices of theology. One of the most frequently asked questions in teaching and training has concerned which voice has dominance—which has the final say. It is to this question of the (a)symmetry of authority between the voices that I now turn.

In principle, the commitment to the interpenetrating four voices as a diagrammatic account of a vision of a whole-theology does not admit of any of the voice being ultimately corrective in any straightforward way. Both as action researchers (of a type) and as theologians, our conversations could never be closed down by appeal to one voice or another as the final word. Where dissonances were felt between the voices – as we shall see – the commitment was to remaining with that tension, even indefinitely, in the conviction that somewhere, precisely *in* the tension, the voice of the Spirit would, at some point, be discernible.

That being said, it would be ruinously naïve not to recognise the in-built asymmetries of these voices as 'authorities'. The unresolvable difficulties surrounding the authority of the operant voice have already been highlighted, and these are further problematised when they are brought into conversation with the other voices. The formal voice(s) have the claim to a certain expertise as a basis for a well-established and recognised authority whilst the espoused has at least a working authority for the practitioner co-researchers. It is the normative which is perhaps the most problematic, representing as it does – at least potentially[22] – the whole weight of the long, historically discerned Christian tradition, with its claims around Scripture and (for some) church teaching as the privileged places of God's Word. For some, it would appear that the very naming of these traditions as 'normative' demonstrates an approach in which this church/scriptural authority has the last say.[23]

It is true to say that, like Swinton and Mowat,[24] the originators of the four voices approach would give a certain logical priority to theological knowing based on its commitment to the authentic discernment of divine revelation. However, what has already been said about the essentially theological nature of *all* the voices, and their mutual need of each other in making such discernment, should indicate that there can be no sense in which the normative can assume a simply corrective authority in the conversation of the four voices. Indeed, the normative as such never stands alone as a separate voice and so cannot be seen as exercising some kind of simply hierarchical authority over the other voices. Nor is 'the normative voice' single, in that its referring us to traditions, scriptures and worship inevitably draw us into diverse *normativities* which require, themselves, discernment and interpretation. Even as such, the normative voice holds in the conversation the *ecclesial* knowing of God, shaped into shareable and transmissible forms in texts, rituals, traditions and doctrine. This undeniably gives the normative voice a well-recognised and, for many, formidable authority, but in the four voices approach, this is not something to be exercised *over* the authorities of practice and the academy but rather as a *service* to a mutually attentive conversation seeking understanding in faith.

In practice, this account of the authorities of the four voices can be difficult to sustain in the research conversations. Many of us practitioners and ARCS team members would have our own preferences – even prejudices – in relation to the voices, which, if left unchallenged by others in the conversation, might lead to the dominance of one voice *over* the others, to the detriment of the *service* of the voices to one another. One helpful way of mitigating this is to think of the authority of the voices not so much in terms of their relation to one another – which has authority *over* which – but rather as different *kinds* of authority, each of which has a particular service to the discernment as a whole, and so to the other voices and their authorities. This notion of different kinds of authority is hardly strange. In human living and decision-making, we are aware not only of the intractable, visceral authority of experience that shapes us and radically informs our thinking and doing but also of those authorities of faith, and of reason, which hold our experience open to bigger stories and communally discerned realities and learning. Indeed, this nexus of authorities lies at the heart of the long tradition of Christian discernment which has significant resonances with theology in four voices.[25]

A practical fundamental theology?

I finish this chapter with a short section making a suggestion which will be taken up in Part IV of this book: that the understanding of theology in four voices can be understood as a diagrammatic representation of a *practical fundamental theology*. In making this suggestion, I am aligning myself more with Johann Metz[26] than Don Browning[27] – though the latter is likely to be better known by readers familiar with practical theology. For whilst Browning's classic work seeks to describe a *fundamental practical theology*, Metz's writing works from an established fundamental theology and demonstrates that this is intractably practical – a *practical fundamental theology*.

The notion of 'fundamental theology' will be more familiar to Catholic readers than non-Catholic, as it remains a key element in Catholic theological studies, particularly in seminaries. At its simplest, fundamental theology can be understood as offering a theological account of how we can do theology at all – how God speaks to us, and how we can hear that word. So, as one leading writer in the field describes it, fundamental theology is to be understood first as "that discipline which in the light of faith reflects critically on the foundations of theology and basic theological issues". Secondly, it is characterised as working "from the inside", "an exercise of faith seeking understanding, justice and prayer", and so should be clearly differentiated from the philosophy of religion. Whilst there are inevitable overlaps with systematic theology, fundamental theology is, thirdly, different from systematics, in that it offers a formal study of what *theologically*, makes doctrine and systematic theology possible. These characteristics lead to the content of fundamental theology being describable as: "1) the self-revelation of the tripersonal God in Jesus Christ, 2) the credibility of that revelation, and 3) its transmission and interpretation".[28]

From this brief description it is already possible to see how theology in four voices can be construed as a diagrammatic response to the central questions of fundamental theology. What is crucial is that, in answering the questions of how God speaks and how we hear and respond, the practices of faith are recognised as integral. In this way, the four voices resonates with Metz's instinct that fundamental theology is necessarily practical/political by the very nature of fundamental theology itself. Practice, the daily living of faith in ordinary, has an *essential* place in fundamental theology, whose questions cannot be authentically responded to without recourse to such lived realities. Here, Metz is reflecting that fundamental theological position to which we referred in *Talking About God in Practice*, when we quoted from Vatican II's Dogmatic Constitution on Divine Revelation – a text of Catholic normative theology concerned with fundamental theology. It is worth quoting again here:

> This tradition which comes from the Apostles develops in the Church (*in Ecclesia proficit*) with the help of the Holy Spirit. For there is a growth in the understanding of the realities and the words which have been handed down. This happens through the contemplation and study made by believers, who treasure these things in their hearts (see Luke, 2:19, 51) through a penetrating understanding of the spiritual realities which they experience, and through the preaching of those who have received through Episcopal succession the sure gift of truth. For as the centuries succeed one another, the Church constantly moves forward toward the fullness of divine truth until the words of God reach their complete fulfillment in her.[29]

The conviction is that divine revelation, embodied in the 'tradition' (written and unwritten), makes progress (*proficio* – to advance, go forward) in all the complexity of ecclesial life, and its various activities, offices and experiences. From such a perspective, fundamental theology is necessarily engaged with practice and ordinary living. It is something like this account of revelation and its progression in faith-full living to which the understanding of the four voices of theology witnesses. This is the practical fundamental theology which underpins the ecclesiological insights which are the central content of this book.

Notes

1 Cameron et. al., op. cit. 53–56.
2 I am frequently asked to give teaching based on the four voices to research groups, and the current chapter is indebted to the time spent with Durham DThM students in Autumn 2018 discussing the four voices.
3 It should be noted that the 'four voices' are not essential to theological action research as such, but they do describe some fundamental aspects of the ARCS theological action research which have been sustained and developed in later theological action research, especially as carried out by the present author. So see: Clare Watkins, "Practising Ecclesiology: From Product to Process." *Ecclesial Practices* 2 (2015): 23–29. The four voices have remained a helpful part of the subsequent theological action research projects named in chapter 2, and reported on the TARN website: www.theologyandactionresearch.net.
4 Gary O'Neill misunderstands the four voices when he describes them as encouraging "a conversation between those outside and inside a context" in comparing them to his own theological reflection model (Gary O'Neill and Liz Shercliff, *Straw for the Bricks: Theological Reflection in Practice* (SCM, 2018): 166.) The four voices are not so much a model for theological reflection nor a pragmatic method for facilitating groups, but rather an attempt to diagrammatically represent the fundamental theological approach of the originators of theological action research and thereby elucidate the ways in which we work with practices theologically.
5 As a Catholic, I find it striking that in my own tradition, there is an explicit commitment to the discerning of truth through (even misinformed?) conversation: "Truth, however, is to be sought after in a manner proper to the dignity of the human person and his social nature. The inquiry is to be free, carried on with the aid of teaching or instruction, communication and dialogue, in the course of which men explain to one another the truth they have discovered, or think they have discovered, in order thus to assist one another in the quest for truth." Second Vatican Council, Declaration on Religious Liberty, *Dignitatis Humanae*, 3. This is quoted to support our thinking in Helen Cameron, Deborah Bhatti, Catherine Duce, James Sweeney, and Clare Watkins, *Talking About God in Practice: Theological Action Research and Practical Theology* (SCM, 2010): 57.
6 Cameron et. al., op. cit. 54.
7 Ibid. 53–54.
8 See *Keeping Faith in Practice*, esp. Stephen Pattison's observations in the Foreword, ix–x.
9 *Talking About God*, 53.
10 Clare Watkins, "Practising Ecclesiology: From Product to Process. Developing Ecclesiology as a Non-Correlative Process and Practice Through the Theological

Action Research Framework of Theology in Four Voices." *Ecclesial Practices* 2 (2015): 23–39; and "An Argument for *Non-correlational* Approaches in a Catholic Practical Theology." *Cahiers Internationaux de Theologie Pratique. Actes no. 8*, (March 2016): 141–158. Available at: www.pastoralis.org/CITP-Actes-no-8-Groupe-Santiago.

11 So see Stephen Pattison, "Some Straw for the Bricks: A Basic Introduction to Theological Reflection." *Contact*, 99, no.1 (1989): 2–9; and; Elaine Graham et al., *Theological Reflection*, vol. I, 6: "At the heart of theological reflection are questions about the relationship of theory to practice, and how to connect theological discourse about the nature of God to the exercise of faith".

12 I mention these authors particularly to make clear that there is an established tradition of systematic theologians attending to ecclesiology in its practicality. What may be significant for how these, and others, achieved this without recourse to 'practical theology' as such, is their practising of theology within a clearly ecclesial context, as, above all, churchmen.

13 Cameron et. al., op. cit. 50. For other diagrams of the pastoral cycle and its variants, see: Judith Thompson, *SCM Study Guide to Theological Reflection* (SCM, 2008): 56, 58, 60.

14 See www.ycw.ie/about-us/ accessed August 2019.

15 John XXIII *Mater et Magistra* (1961) 236: "There are three stages which should normally be followed in the reduction of social principles into practice. First, one reviews the concrete situation; secondly, one forms a judgment on it in the light of these same principles; thirdly, one decides what in the circumstances can and should be done to implement these principles. These are the three stages that are usually expressed in the three terms: look, judge, act". Significantly the encyclical continues: "It is important for our young people to grasp this method and to practice it. Knowledge acquired in this way does not remain merely abstract, but is seen as something that must be translated into action" (ibid. 237). See: http://w2.vatican.va/content/john-xxiii/en/encyclicals/documents/hf_j-xxiii_enc_15051961_mater.html.

16 I suspect that different members of the ARCS team would have different accounts of the pastoral cycle and its relative merits. Helen Cameron, in particular, has explored the use of this model in a variety of settings, with a facilitatory skill that goes some way to mitigating the problems I would have with its contemporary use in practical theology. So see Helen Cameron, *Theological Reflection for Human Flourishing: Pastoral Practice and Public Theology* (SCM, 2013). Gary O'Neill's critique of theological action research is fundamentally flawed in identifying this work of Helen's with theological action research as such: see O'Neill and Shercliff, op. cit. 153ff.

17 Op. cit. 54.

18 This is especially spelt out in Clare Watkins and Helen Cameron, "Epiphanic Sacramentality: An Example of Practical Ecclesiology Revisioning Theological Understanding." Christian B. Scharen ed. *Explorations in Ecclesiology and Ethnography* (Eerdmans, 2012): 71–89.

19 A simple and helpful account of this term, its provenance and its place in practical theology is given in Judith Thompson, *SCM Study Guide to Theological Reflection* (SCM, 2008): 53.

20 So see Nicolas Healy, "Ecclesiology, Ethnography and God: An Interplay of Reality Descriptions." Pete Ward ed. *Perspectives on Ecclesiology and Ethnography* (Eerdmans, 2012): 182–199; Paul Avis, "Ecclesiology and Ethnography: An Unresolved Relationship." *Ecclesiology* 14 (2018): 322–337.

21 My experience of using this neologism in teaching suggests it needs explanation. It refers to the mathematical use of 'surd' referring to irrational numbers –

numbers that can be meaningfully referred to, but never numerically counted (e.g., the square root of 2). Etymologically the term is related to the Latin for deaf, mute (*surdus*), and translated the Greek word *alogos* (irrational, speechless) in Euclid. These meanings resonate well with what I am trying to say about the essential nature of practices as theological authorities.

22 In working with different practitioner groups, care was taken to describe the normative in ways consonant with their own tradition. So different weight would be given to scripture, liturgy, tradition, church teaching according to the kind of Anglican and Roman Catholic church traditions which provided the context.

23 These questions are well discussed by Tone Strangeland Kaufman, "From the Outside, Within, or In Between? Normativity at Work in Empirical Practical Theological Research." Joyce Ann Mercer and Bonnie Miller-McLemore eds. *Conundrums in Practical Theology* (Brill, 2016): 134–162; and "Normativity as Pitfall or Ally? Reflexivity as an Interpretive Resource in Ecclesiological and Ethnographic Research." *Ecclesial Practices*, 2, no.1 (2015): 91–107. See also Tone Strangeland Kaufman and Jonas Idestrom, "Why Matter Matters in Theological Action Research: Attending to the Voices of Tradition." *International Journal of Practical Theology*, 22, no.1 (2018): 84–102.

24 See especially Elaine Graham's criticism of Swinton and Mowat here: "Is Practical Theology a form of 'Action Research'?" 160.

25 This is discussed a little more in chapter 12 of the current work. See also See also Marc Henri Lavallee, "Practical Theology From the Perspective of Catholic Spirituality: A Hermeneutic of Discernment." *International Journal of Practical Theology* 20, no.2 (2016): 203–221.

26 Johann Baptist Metz, *Faith in History and Society: Toward a Practical Fundamental Theology* (Seabury, 1980).

27 Don Browning, *A Fundamental Practical Theology* (Augsburg Fortress, 1959).

28 Gerald O'Collins, *Retrieving Fundamental Theology* (Geoffrey Chapman, 1993): 40–41.

29 Second Vatican Council Dogmatic Constitution on Divine Revelation, *Dei Verbum*, 8. Available at: http://www.vatican.va/archive/hist_councils/ii_vatican_council/documents/vat-ii_const_19651118_dei-verbum_en.html

Part II

Contextual themes

Rationale for Part II

Having described the approach, context and purposes of the research work from which this book's argument arises, the move is now made toward a more detailed and substantive consideration of the findings and their ecclesiological implications. To this end, parts II and III intersperse 'Accounts of Practice' (A-G) with chapters of analysis and discussion. As described at the start of this book, this design was felt to be important in order to keep all four theological voices to the fore of the work and avoid the danger of appearing to set aside practices once the 'real work' of analysis begins. (See the 'A Word to the Reader' above.)

Part II is concerned with the contexts of our co-researchers' practices – both geographical (chapter 5) and organisational (chapter 6). These chapters reflect the basic *locating* of the ARCS work, recognising that when ecclesiology seeks to integrate ecclesial living, it must of necessity honour the particularity and contextual specificity of those practices. Practical ecclesiology is necessarily contextual and inter-disciplinary, and these chapters enable our theological action research methods and attentiveness to the four voices of theology to illuminate the practical-and-ecclesiological significance of context, in their shaping, challenging and enabling of faith-full action. Indeed, the four voices of theology are, themselves, contextually shaped: the operant and espoused voices are entering into a conversation about a particular set of practices that are embedded in a time and place; the normative voice, whilst drawing upon the historic tradition, relies for its effect upon the understanding of normativity held by the practitioners, and the practices of authority and influence undertaken by those who have power in the practice setting; the formal voice, despite its frequent modern pretensions to abstraction and generalised truth-telling, always arises in a particular context, and the role played by academic voices in the life of the church is affected by the relationship between church and academy that varies across denominations, geography and time.

In writing these chapters – and those of part III – I struggled particularly with structure: should the chapters each begin with learning from the

Accounts of Practice and move to theorization (risking the overly descriptive emphasis of much practical ecclesiology)? Or should a summary of the theme from the literature be given first and then the data learning discussed (risking the 'flattening' of the practice-data into a pre-established theoretical framework)? Whilst instinctively tending to the first position rather than the latter, in what follows, I have tried, as far as possible, to work 'from the middle of things' in a way not only inspired by the understanding of theology offered by Rowan Williams[1] but also true to what has been said about the theological position embodied by the commitment to theology 'in four voices'.[2]

Throughout chapters 5–11, references are made in the text to the Accounts of Practice and their disclosures through identifying these by letter, number and source (e.g., A2, Joseph = Account of Practice A, disclosure 2, quote from Joseph). In terms of methodology, what follows is not so much an account of action research as such, but rather reflections on the learning achieved and identified through the meta-reflection on the range of theological action research processes in which the ARCS team were engaged, as represented in Accounts of Practice.

Notes

1 See Rowan Williams, *On Christian Theology* (Blackwell, 2000). This position has recently been highlighted within practical theology by Pete Ward, *Introducing Practical Theology: Mission, Ministry, and the Life of the Church* (Baker Academic, 2017): 11–12.

2 See chapter 4 above.

Account of practice A

London Jesuit Volunteers

Project time frame: October 2009–September 2010

Introductory narrative

London Jesuit Volunteers (LJV) is a small volunteer-placing agency, which is an initiative of the British Province of Jesuits based at the Mount Street Jesuit Centre in Mayfair, London, closely associated with the central church of this Jesuit Province. LJV approached the ARCS team for help in reflecting on their practice as they were receiving approaches to replicate their work in other parts of the United Kingdom, and wanted to capture the essence of what they were practising so as to be better able to hand it on.

The particular structural make-up of LJV is significant: run by a lay-person Director, the group is supported by a team of Spiritual Reflectors who facilitate the small groups of volunteers and overseen by staff of the Jesuit Centre. As such, it is both a lay-led. 'entrepreneurial' agency, and an ecclesially integrated activity. Starting in London in 2007, the agency was built upon an American parish model that originally aimed to match the skills of semi-retired parishioners to volunteer placements within a local community. This model was adapted for a central London context and at the time of the research, LJV coordinated placements for more than 30 adult volunteers of all ages (from 25 to 75+) who wished to give part of their time to serving marginalised people in London. They are placed in a wide range of contexts, including homelessness agencies, prisons, and youth clubs. What is distinctive about the work of LJV is that these volunteers also join a small group which meets monthly and uses practices learnt from Ignatian spirituality, centred on prayer and scripture, to reflect upon what has been experienced in the volunteering. In this way, LJV presented us with the opportunity to work with people whose practices exemplify the Ignatian ideas of contemplation in action, community commitment, and spirituality for justice in the world. The LJV leaflet of the time illustrates this, quoting from a document of the General Congregation of the Society of Jesus (Jesuits), to sum up their vision and link it clearly to the Jesuit tradition:

> Ignatius and his followers began their preaching in poverty. They worked with the powerful and the powerless. Today, whatever our ministry, we ... enter into solidarity with the poor, the marginalized, and the voiceless, in order to enable their participation in the processes that shape the society in which we all live and work. They in turn teach us about our own poverty.[1]

During the one full cycle of action research with which we worked with LJV, the process was especially enriched by the previous research experience of two of the LJV team, and the culture of reflection that the agency nurtured. Here was a group of people for whom deep, communal reflection aimed at discerning the presence of God in the everyday experiences of their members was a core call. This both resonated with and illuminated our theological action research practices.[2]

The initial warm up meetings (summer 2009) led to the identification of two key research questions for the LJV team aimed at capturing the essence of their process so as to discern how – and if – it might be transferable to others:

1 What are the implicit and explicit values in the 'reflective talking' that take place in the *London Jesuit Volunteers* community?
2 By what processes do people engage in reflection at LJV?

The LJV's expertise and experience enabled a co-designing of the research which included a mixed-method approach to data gathering, especially appropriate to the participants. Firstly, nine volunteers submitted a piece of reflective writing about an aspect of their volunteer placement, providing layered, personal, reflective materials, out of which key themes were to be discerned.[3] The nine participants wrote honestly and openly about experiences of working in a prison, hospice, homeless shelter or with the disabled. The extent to which these written texts were able to integrate references to scripture and formal influences varied, but it was clear to the outsider team that here was a group of Christians who were at ease with the use of journaling as a tool for reflection.

In addition, following training given by a member of the ARCS team, four of the group Spiritual Reflectors carried out participant observation in a volunteer reflection session (a session different to their own) to tease out implicit and explicit values emerging in volunteer discussions. Inside rather than outside observers were used in this case study to minimise impact upon these confidential, close-knit groups, contributing further to that practitioner-led learning and renewal, which is a core aim of theological action research. As a final element of the research's data gathering, a volunteer focus group with six people was conducted to explore in more depth the reflective processes at work in the groups, with particular attention given to the (often varying) use of Ignatian spirituality.

A particular novelty of this research was that – reflecting their particular organisational structure – LJV decided to formulate two insider teams to reflect on the data and so created a three-way conversation with the outsider ARCS team. So, there was a Mount Street Jesuit Centre (MSJC) management group reflection team which was added to a group of Spiritual Reflectors (facilitators of the monthly reflection groups). These teams reacted differently to the experience, and to the possibilities and challenges raised by the use of the ARCS four voices in theology. In particular, some on the management team were less familiar with the use of empirical research in theology, such as the task of extracting theological reflections from participant observation data. What was striking here, however, was the learning evidenced by the management reflectors in this process: not only did they express happy surprise expressed at the quality and depth of LJV members' engagement with the volunteering and reflection processes, but they especially valued the theology in four voices approach. One management team member commented about the narratives: "I felt wrapped in it – it was an encouragement to me to engage with this sort of activity too".[4]

Six disclosures

1 Effecting church as a lay-led agency

As with the other agencies we worked with, the research was set up with relative ease, and access to participants was readily forthcoming. However, it was striking how LJV's peculiar organisational nature shaped its ability to carry out its mission. As a lay-led, non-diocesan agency, LJV had freedom of action; but at the same time, it benefitted from being embedded in the structures of Mount Street Jesuit Centre. This context of an established community of religious, living a charism of reflection and discernment, presented LJV as a type of agency unique in the ARCS research. An evaluation interview with the Director of LJV when the research had finished highlighted these points:

Q. What has been of value to LJV in the partnership with ARCS?

- Gaining greater awareness of the reflective process and its value in the work of LJVs
- Appreciating the fact that we have a clear sense of our espoused theology (through Spiritual Exercises and Catholic Social Teaching) against which we can measure what we do in reflection
- Enhancing the sense of the importance of what we do together which in turn has helped in team-building within reflection groups, between reflection facilitators and also within the MSJC management team

- Increasing confidence in the authenticity of what LJV does and how it works in practice, and being able to articulate this
- Involving the wider Mount Street Management in ownership of LJV so that it is now seen as integral to the life and work of Mount Street as a whole

Taking part in the research had increased LJV's confidence for what might be needed in setting up a similar group elsewhere, but at the same time led to their appreciating in a new way how their particular organisational situation enabled them uniquely, and how difficult this might be to replicate. For the wider research, we were able to see here a model of agency and ecclesial/community support, which was especially effective and which shone some light on the possibilities of effective agency in and for church.

2 *Living received traditions*

One of the over-arching interests that developed in the ARCS research was the question of how normative voices of scripture, church practices and the longer tradition found a place within the contemporary outreach practices we worked with. In the case of LJV, we found clear examples of such contemporary living of received, normative traditions.

LJV self-consciously locates its work within the Ignatian spiritual tradition. This gave coherence to its approach which other groups we worked with struggled to achieve. It also, however, drew upon practices, such as small group work, which were a feature of other groups: for example, St Mary's Alpha course. This raised, for the ARCS team, questions both about what constituted the Christian tradition in action and also what methods were effective in the transmission of that tradition in the context of the global city.

Knowledge of a tradition cannot be assumed, as one respondent made clear:

> I would like to say (that if LJV replicates their work) . . . don't take it for granted that people know about Ignatius and Ignatian spirituality because I didn't know much and I think a good few people felt the same and it was really helpful to be brought into it and to have it in action, to have it as part of the reflection group where we did something like we talked about discernment of spirits, for example, which is completely new to anybody who hasn't done this sort of thing before.
>
> (Sarah in Focus Group)

Yet growing fluency with a tradition allowed it to be integrated into daily life and not separated out as a practice different from daily living:

> The spirituality for me or the progression has been more in terms of everything. So at first, I thought of something like the actual placement

and the reflection, but now it's more the reflection and everything else. So it's not that it disconnects from the other thing but rather that it just links to everything else. When I think of Ignatian Spirituality, then it's not about going to Feltham on Sundays. It's about the coffee that I make in the morning and whatever I did before and what I'm doing after and brushing my teeth, where just all the time, this whole awareness that is not just for when I'm sitting down and thinking that I am aware. So it's been incredible and sharing that now, when it comes to the actual method of sharing, it's hard to just stick to the actual placement. Sometimes I want to talk about other things that I have gained from the Ignatian Spirituality.

(Joseph, p. 6)

I don't see it as something completely discrete anymore. It's not something I just do on a Monday with the SVP. It affects my life in other ways and I don't really like to see it as compartmentalising what I do in volunteering.... So I find that helping with the homeless people has sensitised me to homeless people when I meet them. So I never used to buy *The Big Issue* but now I always try to buy *The Big Issue*. So it's that, it's changed.

(Sarah, p. 6)

There was an awareness of Ignatian spirituality as a living tradition exemplified by the Jesuits that participants came into contact with; again, this highlights the particular locating of LJV as an agency. In successfully conveying the idea of tradition as something living and dynamic that both forms and is reformed by Christian living, LJV seems to have benefitted from being 'homed' within a contemporary community living the tradition.

As well as this ability to embed the Ignatian tradition, LJV seemed also to provide a new context for appreciation of the central practices of Catholic Christianity – in particular, reflection on Scripture and the centrality of Eucharist. The practices of reflective meeting integrated with social outreach shaped the prayer and sacramental celebration of the volunteers:

The 90 minutes of prayer and listening to each other in the reflection groups are 'very precious'. This isn't like an ordinary meeting when people argue and prove their point, but a place where you will be really listened to, and where it is safe to share difficulties. The same is true of the Mount Street LJV days, where as well as meeting and sharing with other volunteers, the liturgy and the way the Eucharist is celebrated using special symbols – journals, anointing, being sent out for mission – both affirms and deepens the sense of being held together within a spiritual framework.

(Joint Feedback Meeting, p. 2)

The regular meetings reflecting on scripture were opportunities for volunteers to link, in challenging as well as encouraging ways, the words of the Gospels with their own experiences. These accounts from one of the Participant Observations sessions is typical:

> *Barbara's story:* Barbara volunteers as a befriender to vulnerable people, and also has a busy career that at present is making heavy demands on her (12-hour working day, etc). Normally, she visits a man with schizophrenia living in very stark and squalid surroundings. She appreciates the flexibility of the visiting arrangements, but this month she hasn't managed to make contact at all: "I haven't been building these relationships". Her reflection was about the importance of doing things regularly – "if you don't put so much in, you don't get so much out" – and she commented on the gospel reflection (Matthew 25: 31–45) that the goats' real problem was with things omitted rather than committed. Implicitly, Barbara was identifying values around reliability, fidelity and commitment.
>
> (Participant Observation, Reflector Two)

> *Carla's story*: Carla came to the United Kingdom some years ago and described to us her a childhood in relative poverty, in the midst of which her mother always had something to give to the people poorer than themselves. As a child, she always refused to do the washing up – so now she sees her volunteering as a source of reconciliation. More than that, "I feel as if God has been telling me I am his volunteer in my own home too – when I wash up my own plates, now I feel I am serving God". Carla went on to tell us how she feels she has too many clothes (even though they are from charity shops) – although she finds Matthew 25 consoling, she is distressed by the story of the rich young man – how should she respond to this? This opened up a theme in the group's conversation "what is enough?"/ "is there such a thing as enough?"
>
> (Participant Observation, Reflector Two)

In all this, there are vivid glimpses of longer Christian traditions being taken up and effectively lived in a contemporary, urban and largely lay, secular context. And in these practices, a felt-need is being answered for the volunteers themselves, as an integration of faith, liturgy, social action and ordinary life is enabled. This excerpt from the final Joint Feedback document sums up what all reflectors discerned to be taking place:

> The LJV experience enriches their whole lives as they allow Ignatian values to become part of a life-changing journey. In some ways, the gently reflective, thoughtful way of processing the volunteering experience seems to be in sharp contrast to the rest of the volunteers' over-busy lives. But rather than being an escape from pressure and the impersonal nature of modern working life – as was suggested it

might be – it was felt that the LJV perspective and the regular use of the examen and prayer enabled participants to look more carefully at their own reality, softening and deepening the experience of the rest of their lives. Of particular importance for LJVs was being able to come to the reflection groups knowing that they will be really 'heard'. This sense of being well-listened-to contributed significantly to discovering how 'new reality breaks old assumptions' and to bringing changes across all areas of their lives.

(Joint Feedback Document, p. 1)

3 *City life, spirituality and expressions of community*

Living in a global city can be a strange mix of enjoying the fluidity of life whilst also seeking a sense of belonging to a community. Many of the LJV volunteers were living in central London because they were working or studying in London. They were seeking a way of connecting with the life of the city and the volunteer placements and LJV small groups gave them an opportunity to do that. Like so many activities in central London, some (but not all) of the small groups had a fluid membership. One participant reflected upon this as follows:

> I think community has had a different importance for me partly because of my placement. Sometimes if I see an inmate [in the prison where I volunteer], I might not see him again the next week or two, so I don't rely on that history with people or stability but rather on whatever I'm doing on the premises on the day, as if there was no tomorrow. And when the [LJV reflection] group was fading also, this happened to our group last year, it was also a bit like that. Even if the session is very successful and you get a lot out of it, I wasn't necessarily expecting that following one [to be the same]. It was just like, there doesn't have to be a tomorrow for there to be some community today. So I guess there is some sense of community, of sharing with others, of thinking with them, praying with them and just being them without there necessarily being stability.... I think it's always important to be relating to the person, to the neighbour, to the person I'm working with, the person I'm working for. Maybe in a different way, not with stability, over time, maybe in a different way. But it's always good to feel related, to feel bonded. Maybe it's not community anymore but I do think the bonding is necessary.
>
> (Joseph)

Here, we can see here a certain struggle to articulate 'a different way' of being community, one in which bonds are experienced 'as if there were no tomorrow' – and perhaps one more in keeping with the realities of urban life. The potential for learning about a more grounded, complex understating of that much used word 'community' presents itself.

It is also the nature of the London community that lies at the root of the diversity of the participants, and the variety of the respondents' responses to the LJV groups – an especially notable observation given that, at the time of the research, all the participants were Roman Catholics. The ARCS reflectors commented:

> ***Individual and Group Diversity***: In terms of the reflective process, the data was a lot more diverse than the team was expecting. We thought answers might be more straightforward in relation to how personal Ignatian spirituality feeds into the reflective group work process. However, what appeared to emerge was a much more complicated process marked by diversity – people are not just part of LJV reflection groups but also engaged in other types of reflection groups (e.g., CLC); people are coming with very different levels of formation – some very aware of Ignatian values, some training for the priesthood, others picking it up as they go along. There are also very different personality types engaging with the process as well which both enriches the groups but also reveals an ambiguity in some cases about what the exact function is of the group in terms of each individual's own reflective learning. A few thought the group was fantastic, others thought it sometimes worked for them, and a few individuals held a question mark over the group experience as a whole.
>
> (Outsider Feedback Document Two)

Part of the experience of living in a global city is being aware of the wide array of spiritualties being practised. For some this can make a choice of spirituality almost like a consumer choice – finding something that will work for me and that fits into my life. The outsider team reflected that one of the things that made LJV effective was that it both accommodated the culture of choice (of placement and of spirituality) that was so much part of participants' lives but also challenged that culture by requiring attendance at small groups and emphasising the importance of committing to community.

4 *Encountering injustice: guilt, conscientisation and advocacy*

Volunteering brought participants face to face with the marginalised inhabitants of the city. The guilt, anger and powerlessness this induced were reflected in the data. Volunteers found themselves embedded in 'structural sin'.[5] People felt frustrated at the smallness of what they could do and the sense of being caught up in secular culture and its de-personalisation. These extracts from reflective writing and participant observation notes illustrate this:

> A number of things struck me over my placement at Christian Kitchen in Walthamstow. First was how stratified UK society is. There is a whole group of people who are completely overlooked and seem to survive, hidden and interweaved in our daily lives without us knowing it.... So often I find myself being judgemental. The lines which separate our lives are so fine. It could have been me and yet, it is them and they are so good.... How fine the line is which divides people, destinies are. It is by the grace of God that we fall one side or the next. Yet there is no line, we are one really. I was really in a bad place in Nov 2008 and without the support of the ones who love me I could have been there. Seeing love working where you do not expect to find it is a blessing. This is where I find the Examen prayer so powerful: you see God present in your life every day.
>
> (Reflective Writing Two)

> *Bea's story*: Bea described a visit to someone who is mentally unstable, living in poverty and totally disorganised.... Bea described her frustration – there was so little she could do for him, other than simply visit him – and she felt that the social services he needed simply weren't available. So she questioned the value of her visiting him – but having voiced all this, she came back to thinking that in the end, she wasn't there to sort out practicalities – she was there just as a friend.
>
> (Participant Observation One)

> *Isabel's story*: Isabel feels bad.... She often feels frustrated about her inability to do more for the people she tries to support. She realises that she is very demanding with herself and needs to remind herself that finally it is God who does these things through her.... She realises also that one can get used to the misery you see when you try to help destitute people.
>
> (Participant Observation Three)

This issue was picked up as one of particular significance in the Joint Feedback Meeting between insider and outsider teams:

> The issue of feelings of guilt/frustration/anger at the tiny fraction of help volunteers are able to provide those on the margins of society compared with the amount of evident need, was a recurring theme. This led on to the question of whether and when volunteers should be wary of simply propping up a system that cares very inadequately for the weak and vulnerable and the 'losers' in society. Should we, instead, be moving towards an 'advocacy' style of support, so that, rather than just accepting the status quo and trying to alleviate in very small ways, the sufferings of those who are victims of today's go-getting society, we are challenging and seeking to change the circumstances which cause the

> problems in the first place. It was suggested that the contemplative/reflective approach of the group process might not lend itself very well to challenge and advocacy, but reference was made to the Ignatian principle of "contemplation in action" and to a document available online describing a process of 'Ignatian Advocacy' produced by the Jesuit European Office (www.ocope.info/index.php?id=194). This might indicate ways in which advocacy could be developed within the work of LJVs.
>
> (Minutes of Joint Feedback Meeting, p 2)[6]

Interestingly, one member of the MSJC team suggested that what counted as 'guilt' in the United Kingdom might be viewed as 'conscientization' in, for example, South America – and that this liberation perspective might possibly provide LJVs with an alternative way of approaching issues of social justice. Discernment of this issue of felt guilt and the action it called for was a major learning for the LJV leadership.

5 Encountering Christ at the margins

A number of participants identified their volunteering as an encounter with Christ, as these excerpts illustrate:

> I remember clearly one special moment one evening seeing a novice Jesuit talking to "Peter", a suffering young man with multiple sclerosis. The novice would wait more than one minute for Peter's replies each time with great love and patience. That special dialogue let me see Jesus Christ's love through the Jesuit novice loving and respecting Peter unconditionally. In that moment, I understood "Anna's" reflections – our former Reflection Group leader at London Jesuit Volunteers – about seeing Jesus Christ in others. I had been in Peter's house several weeks – one and a half hour once a week – before, but honestly, I had avoided speaking to him because it was really hard for me, even, to look at him and actually, I thought he was not able to speak. Now, sometimes I enjoy giving Peter his dinner – if he agrees – and we have short chats. This experience has helped me too – sometimes – to reflect and decide to see Jesus Christ in others when I am not in really great situations, especially in the bus.
>
> (Reflective Writing Five)

> Every week, I visit a person with mental health problems. The person seems, to a large extent, unable to look after himself or his home. He throws everything on the floor. The main purpose of our weekly visit is to sweep up all the cigarette butts, food and empty containers from the floor. Everything goes into black bags and then to the bin near the flat. One thing that struck me as significant was a thought that occurred to me during such a visit. I was remembering the line from the Gospel 'whatever you do to the least of my brothers, that

> you do unto me'. It occurred to me that if I took this line literally – and really saw the person as Jesus – would I leave him like that? Could we not do more to help him?
>
> (Reflective Writing Seven)

In reflecting on this, the ARCS team were noted how LJV achieved this coherence between espoused and operant theology for so many of its participants, enabling a deeply realised spirituality of seeing Christ in others:

> In particular, the data evidences the emergence of a striking theology of the person, and a very strong sense of finding Christ in others. The relationships described are often deeply Christological, but at the same time, there is a sense of sharing a common humanity. This dual perspective seems to bring about in some of the encounters a sense, almost, of sacramental embodiment. This, in turn, feels very much in tune with the espoused Ignatian values of solidarity with the poor and marginalized, sharing the common need of those we accompany, and affirming the dignity of each human person. It is noticeable that the regular personal use of the 'examen' and reflection time with other volunteers strengthened the sense of God's presence both in the ordinary, everyday, small events, and in particularly memorable moments:
>
> > "These reflections have enabled me to ... realise ... that I have been a God's volunteer at home for many years and when I am aware of that, it makes it even easier to wash the dishes, for example".
> >
> > "This is where I find the examen prayer so powerful. You see God present in your life every day".
> >
> > "If ... I really saw this person as Jesus – would I leave him like that?"
>
> (Outsider Feedback Document, p 1)

The management insider team also commented that God is "all through this data – like a stick of Blackpool rock!" As people steeped in the Ignatian tradition, it was significant that they noted an "ethos – which is of the Spiritual Exercises, especially the Second Week – focussed on growth in faith and a personal love of Christ".

6 *Faith formation in and for ecclesial* ad extra

When the outsider team read the reflective writing by volunteers, we were struck by the way in which this engagement outside the church was contributing to spiritual formation. Here we quote form the Outsider Team Feedback:

Examples of lay formation include:

- The discovery in practice of the reality of things they already 'knew' in theory:

- "I have learned to be less surprised when the immanent God of all creation turns up in my science teaching".
- "Understanding the rich interplay between justice and mercy (not from a book this time, but from the real world) has made me understand better the way Jesus sees me".

- The quality of deeply formative learning derived from their experience, demonstrating growth in self-knowledge and self-awareness:
  - "Seeing how long it takes for a life-changing experience to take place and act has made me aware of how patient God is with me, which will hopefully revert on my attitude towards others in this sense".
  - "My encounter with this man affected me quite deeply as it showed that the human conscience can lead you to show humanity under the most difficult circumstances".
  - "I try to engage more with people, individuals; to listen a little more. It's not just about feeding their bodies but nurturing their lives. It's not really nurturing, even, but just being there.... Jesus asked, in the song, 'Were you there?' not, 'What did you do?'"
- The marked crossover between placement experiences and the everyday life and work of the volunteers, leading to real change in their approach and understanding:
  - "I feel as if God has been telling me that I am his volunteer in my own home too – when I wash my own plates now I feel that I am serving God".
  - "As I result of volunteer experiences, I am growing in patience.... I see that money is not the important thing in life, but justice".

(Outsider Feedback Document, p. 1)

Both outsider and insider teams were able to affirm LJV as a vehicle for lay formation – enabling the laity to take on their distinctive part in the church, that of ministry to the world. The management team described this lay formation in the following way:

> The MSJC team felt that the presence of Jesuits in Formation (JiFs) among the volunteers and the reflection-facilitators could only be mutually beneficial, and that the more JiFs who could be encouraged to join the LJVs the better! They also noted that not only the JiFs but many of the volunteers often spoke in vocational terms of the ministry they offered through their volunteering – and that this was expressed by women at least as much as men. Hope was expressed that this significant and distinctive aspect of LJV reflection might be brought to the awareness of church authorities.
>
> (Joint Feedback Document Management/ARCS, p 2)

The following reflection from one of the volunteers beautifully articulates this sense of deep, integrated and personally transformative learning through practice and reflection:

> Urban Table is based at the Round Chapel in Hackney. On Sunday afternoons, soup and sandwiches are prepared by the volunteers and fruit, cake and hot drinks are also provided to the guests. Many of the guests are from the accession EU countries (e.g., Poland, Lithuania), but there are also a number who are local to Hackney. Some sleep rough, others live in squats. Others still are simply isolated and struggling to cope. At the end of the afternoon, the volunteers meet up to discuss how the day went, normally followed by a period of readings, reflection and prayer. There is an iconic Catholic Worker image which is set up in front of us, with two small candles, namely 'Christ of the Breadlines' by Fritz Eichenberg. It depicts down-and-out men and women in line, huddling in their ill-fitting clothes for warmth. In the centre, in silhouette, stands Christ, radiating light and warmth in the darkness. It is such a stark and powerful image and never fails to resonate with me personally. It expresses visually Christ's words 'I was hungry.... I was thirsty.... I was homeless.... I was naked.... I was a stranger.... I was a prisoner'. Occasionally, at the end of the check-in, a volunteer will apologise for spending too much time at the tables with the guests, and not helping out so much in the kitchen. This is a needless apology, as sharing a meal, sitting and chatting with the guests is at the heart of what the Catholic Worker offers. When I look back over my first year with Urban Table, I am aware that on the Martha and Mary spectrum, I have veered too much to the Martha end. Too often it's easy to retreat into your comfort zone, and find yourself simply serving the food, washing and drying up. Urban Table values the Mary approach equally; the act of sitting and listening to the guests, and it is something I aim to do more of in the future.
>
> (Reflective Writing Four)

Concluding reflections

In this research, the ARCS team and LJV discovered a common passion for effective formation developed through an inductive and participatory pedagogy, and together were able to identify some of the challenges involved in fresh ways. This made for a fruitful research relationship, enabling something of a voicing of this particular way of being church: lay apostolic living in the places of need and injustice in the late modern city, embodying the longer faith tradition authentically for today.

Notes

1 *Our Way of Proceeding*, Documents of the Thirty-Fourth General Congregation of the Society of Jesus, 1995.
2 There is a clear link here to the action research work of the Jesuit David Coghlan, referred to in chapter 3 above 32.
3 Such processes of reflective writing and 'reflecting-upon-text' have a long history – see Elaine Graham et al., *Theological Reflection: Methods* (SCM-Canterbury Press, 2005): 18–45 – and have grown to prominence ever since Anton Boisen coined the term 'living human document' in the 1920s. The strength of this method is that it is accessible and encourages individuals to express themselves inwardly and reflexively to learn and change from their practice.
4 Insider feedback document of the management committee, 1.
5 Sometimes referred to as 'social sin' this is a notion with its roots in the traditions of Catholic Social teaching, and important in liberation theology, referring to the ways in which the structures of human society and cultures can themselves be 'sinful', as distinct from a sole focus on the personal sin of the individual.
6 The link referenced in this quote no longer functions. More information about the Jesuit approach to advocacy can be found at *Ignatian Advocacy*. www.ignatianadvocacy.org. Accessed August 2019.

5 The geographical context

London, the global city

> There is a whole group of people who are completely overlooked and seem to survive, hidden and interweaved in our daily lives without us knowing it. … So often I find myself being judgemental. The lines which separate our lives are so fine. It could have been me and yet, it is them and they are so good. … Yet there is no line, we are one really.
>
> (LJV volunteer: A4, Reflective Writing Two)

The funding for the ARCS project required that the practices worked with would reflect Christian outreach work in the London area.[1] This locates our practices – in the main – within a global, diverse city, which is itself the subject of much sociological and religious research.[2] Furthermore, in studying specifically outreach, or *ad extra* Christian work, we were committed to co-researching with participants whose practice was intended to respond to and even change the context in which it took place. This makes the social context an important matter both for appropriate understanding of the shaping of the practices and for proper discernment of graced responses and engagement.

There are a number of key features of this geographical context that are especially significant for understanding the ARCS practices and their contribution to ecclesiology. London is recognised as manifesting unusually high levels and diversity of religious affiliation and practice compared to the rest of the United Kingdom.[3] This is partly explicable by the high levels of ethnic diversity,[4] but also, it might be suggested, reflects other features of urban life, around belonging and the demographics which demonstrate larger numbers of younger, single people. There is a culture of choice and freedom that characterises such 'postsecular' cities, which inevitably shapes religious, and so ecclesial, life.[5] In responding to the disparities of wealth and urban deprivation, the activities of churches and faith-based organisations (FBOs) alongside and in cooperation with civil, secular agencies are well recognised.[6] At the same time, the high levels of single living and the widespread experience – among young Londoners and the large immigrant population particularly – of having moved away from organically developed support networks of family and neighbours, leads to often painful experiences of isolation and a struggle to find new ways of belonging.

Of particular significance is the recent identification by a number of scholars of such global, late modern cities as 'postsecular'. This is a description of the London context which fits well with the ARCS data, and is adopted as a fundamental descriptor in the details that follow. It refers not simply to the ways in which the religious vibrancy of London challenges the established trajectory of religious decline, especially in urban areas, but more fundamentally, it recognises the ways in which the flourishing religious diversity *and* persisting secularism of London society reshape questions of the secular and sacred within this space. So, Justin Beaumont helpfully describes 'postsecular' as a term that refers to "the limits of the secularization thesis and the ever-growing realization of radically plural societies, in terms of religion, faith and belief within and between diverse urban societies".[7] What becomes crucial here are the relations between these diverse groups within the public frame of liberal secularism. The voices of faith are, in fact, still present in secular societies, but they exist in late modernity as voices among a plurality of voices in which none can claim absolute authority over the others. For Beaumont and Baker, this notion of postsecular can enable an account of the contemporary city which is neither simply a fragmented, postmodern plurality nor a context whose relativism leaves us no way forward. Rather it "presents a new, important and exciting conceptual apparatus in order to understand cities in ways that transcend the excesses of postmodern heterogeneity and nihilistic relativism with something fresh and new".[8] This radically shapes the 'church-world' relationship as one not of polarities, but rather one in which the church is enmeshed in the world's plural conversations as one of its authentic, but non-privileged, contributors.[9] As James Sweeney puts it: "The proposal that religion be treated as a purely private matter is just that – a proposal, and a cultural bias – the *political fact* is that religion is much more".[10]

All these dominant features of London as a global city can be recognised in the Accounts of Practice – accounts which describe the ways in which voices and activities of faith are still vibrant contributors to the late modern multi-voiced expressions of post-secular city life. The awareness of religious plurality and the important part that secular tolerance has to play lies behind the Housing Justice volunteers' reluctance to use explicitly faith language (E3), and contributes to the Messy Church leadership's anxieties around inquiring too directly of their friends in matters of faith (D Introductory Narrative). Such diversity is also held fruitfully by the common cause to alleviate poverty in CAFOD's work. At the same time, the experience of the isolation inherent in London life is reflected in the often hidden loneliness of middle-class mothers (D4), and busy city-dwellers (C), as well as more starkly through the almost overwhelming encounters with poverty and exclusion responded to by Housing Justice and the London Jesuit Volunteers (A4; E) Running through all our London-based participant practices is that desire to re-envisage community and care in the demanding context of the global city. As Philip Sheldrake describes it:

> In urban environments, effective community is fundamentally brought into existence by the everyday encounters of people on the streets and the narratives that they share rather than by top-down planning or politically-driven policy. In Michel de Certeau's powerful and evocative expression, it is human gestures that remake the city day by day. A critical question, therefore, is how we are to enable our streets and our neighbourhoods to be effective places of mutual engagement, often of a casual nature, rather than places of exclusion for some people and of threat for others.[11]

It is such 'human gestures', lived out in faith, that characterise the practices with which we have worked. In particular, we need to move to learning from the faith-full practices that negotiate this particular urban, late modern and postsecular context. To enable such learning, the following sections focus on three themes emerging from across the data: hospitality; civility and inclusivity; and inequality and injustice.

Hospitality: gifts and limitations

The theme of hospitality was prominent across all those practices we worked alongside which were engaged in immediate and hands-on outreach. Most often, this faith-full response to life in the city took the simple human form of sharing meals – with the homeless (Housing Justice, E), with families (Messy Church, D) and with anyone in interested in friendship and conversation about belief (St. Mary's, C). It is now well recognised that at least a part of the extraordinary success of the evangelism programme *Alpha* is related to the way in which open and non-judgemental conversation is facilitated by the sharing of a meal, and this is well-attested by those attending the St. Mary's *Alpha*. It was typical to see the 'social' aspect as of particular importance (C1, Interview 6) and the building of friendships through the kinds of conversation not usually enabled by the liturgical life of the parish (C2, Interviews 3 & 7). Sharing a meal, something "most people enjoy doing", and talking informally but intentionally (C1, Interview 6) embodies something of that deep sense of Christian hospitality described by Luke Bretherton[12] and Elizabeth Newman.[13] We are not 'entertaining friends', nor are we involved in some corporate hospitality. Rather, food, time and conversation are shared so as to provide a space for the welcome and discernment of God in one another.[14]

The theme of hospitality has attracted its own theological literature.[15] Most compellingly, it has been offered as a way of construing Christian relationships with the non-Christian and plural 'other', who are our neighbours, in ways which go deeper than mere tolerance.[16] For Bretherton, hospitality has a specifically theological meaning as that metaphor which best describes the proper eschatological locating of Christian life and its relations of both continuity and discontinuity with wider society. He sums it up thus:

> the motif of hospitality maintains the key eschatological tensions of Christian specificity. It does not force a harmony either through abstraction: that is, the term does not dissolve the eschatological tension by appealing to some universal principle (love, justice and so on); neither does it demand that Christians enter into relations with their neighbours on the basis of a rivalry between competing traditions. Rather, the motif . . . allows for Christians to retain their specific criteria for evaluating the veracity of moral claims, while at the level of moral practice experiencing both continuity and discontinuity with their neighbours.[17]

Bretherton's account speaks powerfully as a formal theological voice into the particular moral plurality of late modernity which is his concern, and resonates with that image of faith and non-faith conversation which is at the heart of the postsecular city. His theological account of hospitality as a specifically Christian theme and practice is helpful in articulating a basis for practices of hospitality and has some clear and fruitful links with work on the ground.

The fact that this formal theology of hospitality, with its solid biblical roots,[18] is so clearly recognisable in our practices is notable; but it leads also to the surfacing of some of the problems experienced with the practical work, which the formal and normative accounts of hospitality seem to underplay. In many ways, St. Mary's (C) speaks most vividly of this, in their recognition that the core congregation's practice of hospitality might actually be keeping others in a permanent role of 'guest'. Their own anxieties around the experienced tension between the focus on inclusivity and the desire to build a thriving, committed community were 'liberated' by the introduction of the 'guest to host' language which the action research process identified (C1, Follow-Up meeting). The shadow side of 'successful' hospitality practice – the permanent guest – could be named and attended to. In a way similar to this, the leadership of Messy Church were both heartened by the success of their work in building relationships, but also had to take account of the testimonies which valued the social but with no desire to 'go deeper' (D2, Interview 7), with even the suggestion that 'the ideal' would be to have such a gathering as Messy Church but without any religious associations (D2, Interview 6). If it is the case, as Bretherton argues, that hospitality is key for constructive living in contexts of plural religious and moral convictions, it is not yet clear that hospitality is a straightforward practice for evangelism or church community building in the ways hoped for by these practice groups.[19]

Of course, not all Christian practices of hospitality are evangelistically orientated; indeed, many – such as Housing Justice – are at great pains to make clear that the offer of free and inclusive welcome and sharing is, of necessity, 'anonymous' as regards its faith identity. The very naming of faith could, itself, be seen as excluding and so inhospitable, in an urban plural context that prizes tolerance and the private practice and holding of faith (E1, Jenny, and Sarah). Rather, what is important for Housing Justice is the way in which the practices of sharing food and shelter build relationships and break down divisions, even to the point where the volunteer and the homeless guest are indistinguishable (E3, Chris). Yet here, too, we see something of the way in which a certain approach to hospitality also brings with it a verbal silence, a reticence, for all its intentions toward facilitating conversation. For St. Mary's, this 'reticent hospitality' made it hard to make any demands on new members of the community (C1, Feedback Document, C3); for Messy Church, it led to a fear that all they were doing was building a 'Jesus-less community' (D2), and for Housing Justice, it became clear that the faith language (and, perhaps, faith needs?) of the guests to the shelter could not be met by the volunteers with a similar vocabulary (E1).

What is emerging here is both the significance of the practice of hospitality as a way of responding to the isolation and fragmentation of urban life and, at the same time, a certain ambivalence about how such practices – precisely in striving to be 'hospitable' (and so 'polite') – may also silence the articulation of faith. This may not, of course be a bad thing; arguably the power of such wordless faith-practice is precisely what enables the kind of journey toward faith that seems necessary in today's missionary context (see the shifts of thinking in the Messy Church mothers: D1), as well as effectively reconciling estranged strata of society (E3).[20] It is an observation which does, nonetheless, raise significant questions for theologies which may seek to valorise such practices as evangelising, and urge practitioners to a greater realism as to what can truly be done in such practices.[21]

Civility and inclusivity: resonance and dissonance between faith and context

I have used the term 'reticent hospitality' to describe what seems to be a widespread muting of any verbally explicit talk of faith precisely in the name of hospitality. The ways in which the language of hospitality is used in formal theology – as an enabling of honest, difficult conversation across diverse convictions[22] – runs the risk of giving grounds for the idealisation of hospitable practice, whilst failing to enable the move into deeper hospitable practice of faith and non-faith sharing. Given the demands and potential of the postsecular city as described by Justin Beaumont and others, it is precisely in this deeper practice of hospitality that real transformation and fresh learning might be possible. The reticence of many of our practitioners concerning faith-talk would seem, however, to be part of wider cultural expectations, which are especially amplified in the plural and potentially conflictual global city. These expectations concern the qualities of civility and inclusion as essential to London life.

These societal behaviours of mutual tolerance are recognisably a part of the instincts of Christian practices in this context, as one would expect. The tentative use of the rather conservative evangelical *Alpha* resources, and their adaptation by St. Mary's Rector is done in sensitivity to the more inclusive, liberal ethos of that parish (C2). As referred to in the previous section, Messy Church leaders felt that discussion of faith matters with other mothers might harm their friendships, and Housing Justice volunteers seemed to feel that speaking of their work as faith motivated somehow undermined its value as a practice of care (E1). In all these cases, we see examples of Christian practices embodying not only faith-instincts around community, kindness and inclusion, but also cultural values. Whether late modern social accounts of inclusion and civility are identical with Christian understandings of inclusive community is a matter for hard discernment.

For example, St. Mary's prided itself on being an inclusive church (C1); the hospitality it offered was without condition or demand – and it was precisely this that made it such an attractive place for many – "It's so non-expectation it's magnetic!" (C4, Interview 2). Values of open-mindedness and unquestioning welcome were paramount (C4, Interview 3); indeed, this principled inclusivity, rather more than traditional, normative Church of England understandings of parish as 'located', seemed to be the driving force for many of those attending (C5). At the same time, this commitment was revealed to have certain tensions with the normative scriptural theology for this group. So, Jesus' ministry was recognised as 'inclusive and welcoming' in that he 'ate with sinners', often calling them to repentance (C4); but this biblical language of sin and repentance did not marry well with the liberal assumptions about inclusivity being espoused and practised. In the end, the gospel challenge is to whether there are any proper demands that can and should be made on Christians, whether in terms of discipline, behaviour or belief? It is, perhaps, no coincidence that the naming and visibility of the historical Jesus and his teaching (as distinct from liturgical celebration and presence) was recognised as a difficulty for this community (C3).

None of this is to negate the clear effectiveness of practices of welcome and inclusivity that is visible in the St. Mary's data; people were clearly finding much needed community, and a sense of belonging and being drawn more deeply into Christian practice (C4). Rather, this account stands as an example of the ambivalence and proper complexity of these Christian and culturally shaped instincts toward inclusivity. It identifies as an area for Christian discernment the relationships between inclusion/welcome and demand/discipline in the Christian life.

Inequality and injustice: helping, helplessness and hope

Two of the practitioner groups we worked with – London Jesuit Volunteers and Housing Justice – were directly engaged with outreach to the most marginal in the global city. As such, what was learnt from them particularly guides our attention to those darker features of the late modern city: the disparities of wealth and the realities of many who are isolated, suffering and surviving on the margins. Here, the challenges of context shift from those of hospitality and civility and render a more raw account of the problems of exclusion and the inability to belong. Formally and normatively Christian practice is fundamentally shaped by a care for the poor and marginalised, and, in recent times, the particular call to such care within urban contexts has been clearly voiced by both the Church of England[23] and the Catholic Church in England and Wales.[24] In fact, the two practitioner groups working in these areas demonstrated rather different responses to their experiences, with a greater depth of reflection being evidenced in LJV due to the particular spiritual disciplines which accompanied their volunteering work.

A key learning point from the volunteers working with LJV concerns how their experiences of coming alongside the most marginalised not only compelled a re-visioning of the city itself (A4, Reflective Writing 2) but also evoked feelings of helplessness and guilt. This may have been a sharper experience for these than for the Housing Justice volunteers, owing to the LJVs volunteering away from their own place of familiarity and relative comfort and moving into spaces – homes, prisons, hospitals etc. – in which they were the stranger rather than the host. Both Bea and Isabel suffered because of their volunteering, as they were exposed to complex and extremely difficult lives, before which they felt totally inadequate. The realisation that this instability, poverty and exclusion are going on and cannot simply be fixed by any one of us led to a sense of frustration, helplessness and thoughts of giving up, as visiting and caring clearly wasn't moving people out of these situations (A4). In the late modern city, such problems are endemic and part of the very fabric of the city's life and dynamic; in the face of such structural and societal shortcomings, the individual can be reduced to passivity and hopelessness.

Commonly expressed among the LJV volunteers was a sense of 'guilt'; they were meeting with those in dire need, doing a little, but then heading back to relatively comfortable and secure lives. The language of guilt evokes, for many Christians, the language of sin, and raises questions in this context concerning structural sin and the ways in which the individual may be implicated in it. Reflection on this led to the alternative naming of what was experienced as guilt – despite no personal wrongdoing in relation to the suffering encountered – as 'conscientization' (A4). This journey from helplessness through guilt to conscientization enabled a move to complement volunteering with advocacy – a step which might be understood as one from charitable action to (additional) political action (A4).

However, we should also recognise how negotiating the world of the poverty and injustice of the city also drew on specifically Christian, spiritual practices for the LJVs. For what kept them visiting and attending to places of suffering, even in the face of their own helplessness and feelings of guilt, was a sense that here, it was really Christ that was encountered (A5). The experience of volunteers was often very difficult, and they could admit to finding it hard even to speak to or look at those they visited on occasions (A5, Reflective Writing 5). Persisting with the Ignatian commitment to see 'God in all things', supported by their reflection groups, enabled a movement through these very real challenges to a place where the smallest of tasks and hardest of relationships were recognised and celebrated as encounters with Christ (A5, ibid, and Reflective Writing 7). Ultimately this theological insight concerning God and humanity shaped this LJV engagement with the poverty and injustice of the city. This resonates strongly with Philip Sheldrake's thinking on what is required for the building of bridges and relationship in the fragmented populations of the city. Central to such activities of reconciliation and hospitality is, he argues, a Trinitarian anthropology which stresses "that God's presence in every person … is the source of and goal of the inner dynamics of human identity".[25] Such a theological anthropology demands a response of solidarity from Christians who are called to live "within the 'whole story' of Jesus Christ [which] implies coming to grips with a narrative of human ambiguity, incompleteness and failure".[26]

Conclusion: building community in the postsecular city

Within Christian theological tradition, the city has featured as both eschatological goal – the New Jerusalem – and as the place of iniquity – Babylon. It has had a central part to play in the understanding of the public contribution of Christian faith, from antiquity, and into the modern period.[27] In Augustine's great and enduring work, the "city of God" is both distinguished from and (partially) recognised in the earthly city,[28] and some 1600 years later, something of this mysterious dynamic can be discerned in the practices and their theological contributions outlined in this chapter.

At the same time, theological learning from practice demonstrates the proper complexity of notions such as 'hospitality' and 'inclusion', whilst vividly witnessing to the painful realities of attempts at solidarity with the suffering in contexts of structural sin in which we are all implicated. The gift of these practitioners' struggling with and reflecting on these realities is not only that a more authentic account may be given of them but also that fresh approaches to proper Christian responses to these realities are surfaced for sharing more widely. So it may almost seem too simple to mention, but the dominance of the egalitarian meal as a free act of hospitality is clearly a mainstay of the operant theologies we encountered, echoing the biblical table-fellowship of Jesus, as well as the Eucharistic practice of liturgical churches. However, as these practice accounts show, even so simple a thing as eating together raises more complex questions of guest and host, and the substantial ecclesiological question, of what the faith-full community are welcoming others into. A practice-based ecclesiology for today must not only witness to the importance of hospitality and practices of inclusivity in the urban environment but also acknowledge the theological and sociological complexity of such practices, building in opportunities for reflection and careful consideration to accompany them. It is no coincidence that central to Philip Sheldrake's 'urban virtues' is the practice of *discernment*.[29]

In the introduction to this chapter, we referred to Sheldrake's concluding observation that "in urban environments, effective community is fundamentally brought into existence by the everyday encounters of people on the streets".[30] The image of urban community here, inspired in part by de Certeau, is less of a gathered or regularly gathering community and more of a street-embodied, everyday way of living relationship. In contrast, our ecclesial practices of hospitality and inclusion tend to focus around a strong sense of a gathered community into which the 'other' is welcomed. Fresh Expressions, such as Messy Church (D), go some way to adapting this to the postsecular city by shaping their activities around the existing patterns of modern life in their contexts, which often exclude traditional gathering on a Sunday. However, there are more subtle shifts in understanding apparent. LJV breaks the mould with their model of volunteering outside of the faith community and returning to share prayer and reflection. In particular, the experience of LJV highlights a rather more (apparently) attenuated sense of community evolving from the ever-mobile global city and Christian outreach within it (A3). Joseph speaks of there "not hav[ing] to be a tomorrow for there to be some community today", both in relation to his volunteering and to the LJV group itself. 'Community' becomes a quality of encounter rather than a stable set of connections over time. The highly mobile, transitional quality of the majority of parishioners at St. Mary's (C5) suggests that this kind of reflective re-imagining of 'community' may be one important aspect of the ecclesial task in the global city, and one especially valued by its citizens, who find themselves greeting others on the street as a result of church outreach being "opened up to a new world" (D4, Interview1). Here inclusion might be more by way of shared practice and encounter than by way of the establishment of long-lasting, regular relationship.

It is clear, too, that this stretching of 'Christian community' into the places of isolation and need in the city brings its own transformation to Christians and their communities, as encounter with God is discovered as *not* the monopoly of the churchy and the liturgical (A6; E3, Richard). The city itself can be recognised as a *locus* of revelation, a place where the Spirit is at work ahead of us. However, whilst the ecclesiastical may not be the only place for divine encounter, it is equally the case that it provides – for good and ill – the structural contexts of the practices with which we worked. It is to these realities and their organisational significance that we turn in chapter 6. First, however, the reader is introduced to our second Account of Practice: that deriving from research with the Westminster Agency for Evangelisation.

Notes

1 In this sense, work with the Portsmouth diocese is untypical and was carried out building on the work done with the diocese in the pilot stages of the project.

2 The literature research that informs this chapter's reading of practice does not claim to be exhaustive, and the priority given to reflection on the practices themselves limits the space that can be given to these accounts of sociological research. Of particular help have been: Justin Beaumont and Christopher Baker eds., *Postsecular Cities: Space, Theory and Practice* (Continuum, 2011); David Goodhew, *Church Growth in Britain: 1980 to the Present* (Ashgate, 2012); David Goodhew and Anthony-Paul Cooper eds., *The Desecularisation of the City: London's Churches, 1980 to the Present* (Routledge, 2018); Elaine Graham and Stephen Lowe, *What Makes a Good City? Public Theology and the Urban Church* (Darton Longman & Todd, 2009); Timothy Gorringe, *A Theology of the Built Environment: Justice, Empowerment, Redemption* (CUP, 2002); Philip Sheldrake, *The Spiritual City: Theology, Spirituality and the Urban* (Wiley Blackwell, 2014).

3 Statistics relating to the time of the ARCS project suggest that "London accounts for 15% of England's population but 20% of its church-goers ... 60% of churchgoers in their 20s go to church in inner London." James Sweeney, "Catholicism in Britain: A Church in Search of Its Way." Staf Hellemans and Jozef Wissink eds. *Towards a New Catholic Church in Advanced Modernity: Transformation, Visions and Tensions*.(LIT Verlag, 2012): 172–173. Sweeney is here citing statistics made available through the Tearfund research: Jacinta Ashworth and Ian Farthing, *Churchgoing in the UK: A Research Report Form Tearfund on Church Attendance in the UK* (Tearfund, 2007). More recent data (up to 2012) confirms this pattern: Peter Brierley, *London's Churches Are Growing! What the London Church Census Reveals* (ADBC Publishers, 2013). In particular, the Anglican Diocese of London (covering Greater London north of the Thames, excluding east London / Essex) was unique in the Church of England for sustaining growth through the period 1990–2010. See John Wolffe and Bob Jackson, "Anglican Resurgence: The Church of England in London." David Goodhew ed., op. cit. 23.

4 "Growth was especially to be found among black majority and immigrant churches, which together accounted for 27% of all Christian places of worship in London in 2012 and 24% of churchgoers. Black people were far more likely to attend services than whites (19% against 8%), and in Inner London 48% of worshippers were black." *British Religion in Numbers*. www.brin.ac.uk/2013/london-churchgoing-and-other-news/, accessed August 2019.

5 For example, see Beaumont and Baker esp. chapters 2, 3 & 1.

6 Elaine Graham and Stephen Lowe, in Goodhew, op. cit, and their own book, op. cit.

7 Beaumont, "Transcending the Particular in Postsecular Cities." Arie Molendijk et al. eds. *Exploring the Postsecular: The Religious, the Political and the Urban* (Brill, 2010): 3–17. Cited Justin Beaumont and Chris Baker eds. *Postsecular Cities: Space, Theory and Practice* (Continuum, 2011): 3.

8 Ibid. 4.
9 This account of the ecclesial context of late modernity is set out by Lieven Boeve, *God Interrupts History* (Continuum, 2007): 13–29.
10 Sweeney, op. cit. 172.
11 Sheldrake, op. cit. 202.
12 Luke Bretherton, *Hospitality as Holiness: Christian Witness and Moral Diversity* (Ashgate, 2010).
13 Elizabeth Newman, *Untamed Hospitality: Welcoming God and Other Strangers* (Brazos Press, 2007).
14 Here, Sheldrake draws especially on the Benedictine tradition of hospitality: op. cit. 49, 168–170.
15 As well as Bretherton and Newman cited above, see: George Newlands and Allen Smith, *Hospitable God: The Transformative Dream* (Ashgate, 2010); Christine Pohl, *Making Room: Recovering Hospitality as a Christian Tradition* (Eerdmans Publishing, 1999); Lucien Richard, *Living the Hospitality of God* (Paulist Press, 2000); Arthur Sutherland, *I Was a Stranger: A Christian Theology of Hospitality* (Abingdon Press, 2006).
16 Bretherton, op. cit. 121–126; 147–150.
17 Ibid. 128.
18 For this see, for example, Bretherton, op. cit. 128–135.
19 I say this aware of the more positive account of hospitality for mission given by Cathy Ross, "Hospitality: The Church as a 'Mother with and Open Heart'." Cathy Ross and Stephen Bevans, eds. *Mission on the Way to Emmaus: Constants, Contexts, and Prophetic Dialogue* (Orbis Books, 2013): 67–83.
20 It is striking that Philip Sheldrake not only sees hospitality as an important Christian response to life in the late modern city, but builds this notion on strong theological instincts around reconciliation. Op. cit. 157–168.
21 A more clearly missiological light will be shed on this theme in chapter 7.
22 As in Luke Bretherton's work most notably, as cited above.
23 For example, Archbishop of Canterbury's Commission on Urban Priority Research Group *Faith in the City: A Call for Action by Church and Nation* (Church House Publishing, 1985).
24 For example, the Catholic Bishops' Conference of England and Wales Catholic Bishops' Conference of England and Wales *Choosing the Common Good* (Alive Publishing, 2010); and *Cherishing Life* (Catholic Truth Society, 2004).
25 Op. cit. 165.
26 Ibid.
27 For helpful accounts of 'the city' in Christian thought see Sheldrake, op. cit. chaps. 1–5; and Part I; and Gorringe, op. cit. chaps. 5–6.
28 Augustine, *City of God.* Gillian R. Evans ed. and H. Bettenson trans. (Penguin, 2003).
29 Sheldrake, op. cit. 179–199.
30 See note 11 above.

Account of practice B
Westminster Agency for Evangelisation

Project time frame: February 2006–May 2010

Introductory narrative

Westminster Agency for Evangelisation was, at the time of the research, an agency of the Roman Catholic Diocese of Westminster accountable to the archbishop for supporting catechesis, adult education, small groups and work with young people. This agency was established at the turn of the millennium as part of a process of pastoral renewal outlined in a Diocesan White Paper, *Communion and Mission*,[1] in which formation, education and catechesis were brought under the one umbrella agency with the overarching aim of evangelisation. This ambitious amalgamation of diocesan departments was designed to provide a more effective resource for parishes to nurture faith formation of adults, build understanding of Church teaching, and so equip adults with a vocabulary to reach out to others.

The Westminster Agency for Evangelisation was one of the earliest projects engaging with ARCS and it would be fair to say that the theological action research process was not yet fully established, and this shapes both the narrative of the research and the types of materials gathered and discerned. In particular, the insider team participation was less consolidated than in later projects and this at times disrupted the capacity of the agency to take ownership and a lead, especially around practices of data reflections and their potential impact. The reliance upon outsider team reflections, some points of which (as you will read below) were challenged by agency team members, highlighted to ARCS both the very real risk of outsider teams unconsciously passing on their own agendas and concerns to insider groups, and to the hugely significant emphasis in action research of committing to practitioner-led enquiry.

At the early stages of the ARCS project, James Sweeney approached the Director of the new Agency for Evangelisation to see if they would be interested in working in partnership with Heythrop College to take part in facilitated theological reflection upon their work. The agency staff member responsible for adult education work, who had recently completed a doctorate, heard about this invitation and was keen to work in partnership to deepen her reflection on the impact of faith formation programmes in the diocese.

After several warm-up meetings, the overall aim of the cycle one research was agreed: "to explore the role of faith formation programmes in evangelisation and renewal in specified deaneries in the Diocese of Westminster". In 2007–2008, the diocese of Westminster piloted a Deanery Talks project in 23 deaneries. It produced a directory of more than 60 speakers, each offering 2–3 talks on a theme, which were delivered at a central location in a deanery and advertised in local parishes. Talks on scripture were the most popular. Most speakers were Catholic priests, along with some lay women and men. In cycle one, the agency sought to discover more about the profile of people attending these talks and to discover more about attendees' beliefs and responses to the style and delivery of talks.

A mixed-method research programme was devised with the agency staff member responsible for adult education continuing her programme of evaluative questionnaires. At the same time, the ARCS fieldworker carried out in-depth interviews with three attendees and two speakers from a sample of deanery talks in the diocese. The speakers interviewed were Catholic priests working at a Catholic Seminary. Two female and one male attendee were selected for interview after responding positively to an agency e-mail invitation requesting participation in the research. Finally, the ARCS fieldworker attended a faith formation talk in north London to take field notes.

Reflections upon the data on this first cycle of research raised a number of issues addressed in this chapter. From the 60 initial questionnaire responses, more than 80% of attendees were brought up Catholics, more than 80% were female and more than 90% attended church services weekly.[2] Statistics such as these were a strong indication that faith formation talks were attracting already active and committed Catholics and were perhaps more properly seen as catechetical or educational than evangelising. Alternatively, the talks could be seen as events to re-evangelise the Roman Catholic community and equip Catholics to reach out to their local communities, rather than reaching out primarily to un-churched people.

Outsider team reflections highlighted the following points for feedback and further discussion:

- Ecclesial structural questions relating to the agency's location between diocese and parish
- The complexity of relationship between 'formation', 'education' and 'evangelisation'
- The existence in the data of what could be interpreted as a rather weak/fragmented 'theology of the world'
- A tendency for the agency's espoused theology to collapse in on itself and become normative due to a rather rigid (and disabling?) adherence to the 'bishop's mandate'

Some of this feedback, particularly relating to pedagogy, was questioned by the Director at the first feedback meeting. He felt some of the outsider team comments were "value laden". Having said that, it was the last point about the agency's espoused theology that triggered the most discussion and it led to the Director himself suggesting that a second cycle of research be carried out focusing explicitly upon the mission of the agency staff team as a whole.

In the second cycle of research, ten agency staff team members took part in two team exercises to draw out how they understood the mission and 'espoused' theology of the agency in the diocese. This took place in two sessions of one hour each, which were transcribed by the Agency. The research questions were:

- Session one: 1. What do you understand as the Agency's role or mission? What would a mission statement look like? 2. How do you see your area of work/responsibility as serving the Agency's mission?
- Session two: 1. Mindful of the Agency's aims and reflecting on how you go about your work, to what extent is the way you operate reflective of the Agency's aims/ mission? Are there any areas of contradiction?

It was clear in these sessions that dedicated time for staff team reflection was rare and it was a new (and not always comfortable) task for the staff to be invited to reflect alongside colleagues about the purpose of the agency and each person's role within it. It was especially sensitive when questions touched upon peoples' own personal faith commitments, which did not always align with the work of the agency and the Roman Catholic Church more generally. That said, what was striking in the second cycle joint feedback sessions was the appreciation expressed by agency staff for the space and liberty for reflection and conversation. In this second cycle, the team undertook their own reflections on the data, as did the ARCS team; this created a much healthier dynamic. Two (non-Catholic) members of the ARCS team met with the whole team for a session of joint reflection. The themes from this were taken up by the Westminster Agency team in a subsequent away day.

The learning emerging from cycle two reinforced many of the findings from cycle one and are outlined in full below. They raise particular questions about how 'official' church agencies might be effective in outreach (evangelisation) work, and challenge the ecclesiologist to consider questions of structures, the patterns of power distribution and their effects on ecclesial mission and pedagogy.

Five disclosures

1 The ad intra[3] *agency: between the Bishop and the parish priest?*

In this context, the word 'agency' signals an organisation authorised to act on behalf of a principal actor – that is, the bishop. The priorities, resources and approach of the Agency were shaped by the bishop's understanding of evangelisation. However, this episcopal authorisation did not seem to mean automatic right of entry to parishes for the Agency – parish priests felt able to act as gatekeepers selecting what support they wished to receive from the agency.

DIRECTOR: The tension for us is that ... we, given we are who we are in the life of the diocese and who we represent, as it were, is that we don't.... we've got to bear all that in mind all of the time. We don't have that liberty, to be an individual in the centre because our work is seen as part of this department and the tension for us is that you don't have the freedom of mavericks (Cycle Two, Focus Group 1).

AGENCY TEAM 1: I think one of the frustrations which might be considered to be a contradiction is when we have a certain espoused theology and we go into a parish and we can only do what we can do because you meet with a very different ecclesiology or a very different approach – in our case, to catechetics.

DIRECTOR: Do you mean ... is that from the catechists or from the priest or from the catechetical coordinator?

AGENCY TEAM 1: I think from a combination of them and from the people who are being catechised. For example, one of the challenges is often with Confirmation parents who believe that the Confirmation preparation is really a crash course in Catholicism and it takes their children up to their graduation service where they are 'done' and then the parents' responsibility is finished with the kids and so they have certain concepts of what should be included in the programme. And nobody has really ever taken the time and trouble to talk to them about the theology of the sacrament. So they don't ... and so many times they don't really understand the difference between religious education and catechesis or sacramental preparation. So I don't know if you would call that a frustration or a contradiction, but it feels sometimes like a contradiction (Cycle 2, Focus Group 2).

The ARCS team named this as a 'tension' in the feedback process – a term that didn't resonate with the Agency team:

> *Theme 4: Bridging communication between the diocesan Agency and local parish*
>
> One of the most striking themes emerging from the data relates to what seems to be a sense that there are real obstacles to communications between the central agency and a proportion of the local deaneries and parishes. Matching up local parish expectations with the capacity for delivery by the central Agency for Evangelisation is clearly a huge challenge (Cycle One, Feedback Document).
>
> The ARCS team felt that there was a constant tension emerging in the data, which again is a common difficulty found in many

> middle management organisations, whereby the Agency to some extent appears 'stuck in the middle' between fulfilling a Bishop's mandate on behalf of the diocese and communicating this to parishes and parish priests in such a way that it might be heard and responded to (Cycle Two, Feedback Document).

AGENCY TEAM 2: Felt that we are not "caught" in a tension. This is where we are at, at the moment. There will always be an ideal church and a real church.

AGENCY TEAM 3: Felt that their core belief in the Christian faith kept them persevering, without this and if, for example, they were a corporate business, it would be nonsense to continue working in this complex way as an organisation (Cycle Two, Joint Feedback Document, notes of discussion).

The ARCS team as outsiders were seeking some way of making the position of the agency 'in the middle' less messy. The staff of the agency, drawing on the motivation of their personal faith, saw their role as grappling with the reality of the church. This was an example of where outsiders and insiders did not reach a shared understanding of the situation – however, this does not diminish the exploration of the work of the Agency, which both teams found valuable, all be it in relation to different learning.

2 *The ad intra agency: whose espoused theology?*

The second cycle of research led to extended reflections from both insiders and outsiders on the purpose and identity of the team. Again, there were interesting differences with the way in which the two teams viewed the situation. The following extract from the Insider Team Reflections in Cycle 2 gives a sense of their perspective.

AGENCY TEAM 3: I did some summer work for M&S between university terms. They asked me to undergo a whole week's training and basically my job consisted of stacking shelves . . . but the first four of those training days was the instilling of the organisation's values. M&S ethos, how we should all be pulling to the same direction, work together to rescue the company. The last half of the last day was some training on how to work at the till. All that training was about pulling towards the same direction. . . . We all come to this work not necessarily to find that ethos or those values, but we come with them already instilled. This is probably the reason we came here at the first place. So that groundedness in faith comes from infancy; we have these values so deeply ingrained, so it would be surprising if we had more tension. We are roughly pulling to the same direction. And one of the things I remember Fr. D saying was that this is not just about us, this is about Holy Spirit. And [Agency Team 4] picked it up talking in realistic terms: 'if I could make a bit of difference today to get through this, this is my job, this is not what I do, this is not my project, this is part of something much bigger'. I think there can be a struggle to realize that this is something bigger than us, but if you do realise that and resist the temptation to think solely about yourself, or about the small team, or even about diocese of Westminster or even our parishes, there is something bigger … and then to feel part of that it is overwhelming and enriching. I think that's got to be what underpins our working.

DIRECTOR: The other thing that comes to me, to pick up what [Agency Team 3] was saying, is how we see ourselves as a team. I think we have a very clear idea of our being rooted in the bishop's work no matter what we might think individually at times. We say at the end of the day, "Okay, this is not my work; this is not my project or even the department's project. This is a department to facilitate the work of the bishop of the diocese". It might not seem startling or strange, but from my experience of going around to different parts of the diocese, I think it is something to be commented on. Certainly we clearly relate to what the bishop says even when the bishop might be coming from a slightly different perspective. We realise we have to engage with it, we cannot just circumvent it.

The ARCS team perspective can be seen in this extract from our Cycle Two Feedback Document.

> Could it be that the 'espoused theology' of the Agency, instead of being owned by the Agency itself, is rather taking the form of a kind of normative theology – the vision of the bishop – which short-circuits the possibilities for articulating powerfully a properly espoused theology; and so also limiting the freedom to explore new operant theologies? This point links to the 'in the middle' position the Agency holds. Does the Agency feel it has permission to espouse its own understanding of mission or does it need to repeat and reinforce statements from the bishop? Indeed, how can the Agency continue to renew and strengthen its own espoused theology?

The moment of disclosure for the team was realising that unlike M&S, they didn't spend time discussing what they were trying to achieve; it was all implicit or emerging from the bishop's wishes.

3 Clericalisation: power, the parish priest and the work of the agency

In the second cycle, the issue of the gatekeeping role of parish priests emerged. The point of disclosure for the Agency team was realising how much of their energy was spent negotiating with gatekeepers and how much work could be undone in the change-over between one parish priest and another.

AGENCY TEAM 4: Yes, I think sometimes I work with a group of catechists where I know that my model of church is in direct conflict with the model of church of the parish priest. So I wonder how what I do with the catechists is then manifested in. I do wonder about that sometimes. Well, I know that there are guys that have got you in because they know that they ought to get you in, but in fact they don't think of church like you think of church and churning it out to their people. I wonder sometimes. But that wouldn't stop me! (Cycle Two, Focus Group 1)

DIRECTOR: Has a canonical understanding of priesthood, where, particularly in relation to pastoral work, the work of the priest is the work of the bishop. He felt frustrated by those priests who resisted receiving help and resources offered by the agency.

DIRECTOR: Described how sometimes catechetical coordinators and small group leaders would ring them up requesting resources. Then when the agency contacts the parish priest to receive the order the priest refuses to pay and authorise the work to take place. This could be extremely frustrating for the Agency.

ARCS TEAM 1: When changeovers come – what opportunities are there to work more closely as a team to pre-empt the problems that might occur?

AGENCY TEAM 4: Said that, frustratingly, there is an issue about resources. She'd like to "put our money where our mouth is" and support those parishes struggling in situations whereby a flourishing formation programmes is left to flounder due to a changeover of priest. This is a constant challenge (Cycle Two, Joint Feedback Document, note of discussion).

Again, the difference between the two teams emerged, with the Agency team being more ready to accept that this was how things were than the ARCS team.

4 *Articulating purpose and practice: evangelisation or catechesis?*

The Westminster Agency for Evangelisation team expressed anxieties about whether they were really doing evangelisation or whether they were largely doing catechetical work to maintain parish life. They all expressed a personal conviction that evangelisation was important. This developed into a discussion about the lack of a clear-cut relationship between 'evangelisation' and 'renewal'. If you were renewing an adult believer in their faith, that might equip them to do evangelisation. If you were evangelising new people into the faith, that would renew the life of the parish. There was even a sense that all their different activities could be seen as having potential for both evangelisation and renewal, but that this was insufficiently explicit.

AGENCY TEAM 2: I have bought into the idea of our role really being facilitators of evangelisation at a local level, giving people the voice or the ability to realise that they have a voice or helping people where they don't know the words to express what it is they actually believe fundamentally. That's where I see our role, our duty and I think, I believe what we actually do represents that (Cycle Two Focus Group).

A significant disclosure moment for the Agency Team came with a discussion of the Emmaus Road story that took place in the final feedback meeting. Where did they position themselves on that journey? Was the journey back to Jerusalem a journey into the world to evangelise or a return to the church? There was a concern that *ad extra* activity was so often pulled back into having an *ad intra* focus.[4]

AGENCY TEAM 4: I think it is a challenge what we are trying to support in the parishes. It is difficult to them, I think, to see the value of the evangelisation. I think, theoretically, they understand the value of the evangelisation, but putting into practice, sometimes it might be quite difficult outside your usual context where people present themselves for sacraments. And I think sometimes we can bear the brunt of that difficulty when we present the things to parishes and ask them to come along to this. But I think we act as a constant reminder to them that you don't give up on this.

DIRECTOR: And the other thing I would say is that the data affirms our beliefs and values. A key document for us, and an operational principle, is found in the Road to Emmaus. We are attentive to where people are. We seek to bring the Scripture and the teaching of the Church to situations, to inform, and we do all this in a pastoral way. It seems to me that this is not just a value system of the Agency but is what we are called to do as a Church – to walk with people, to understand their challenges, to bring to those challenges the light of faith, Scripture, Church teaching, prayer and so on. This is how I would understand the documents on catechesis and certainly what I understand as good pastoral practice (Cycle Two, Insider Team Reflections).

The metaphor of the journey to and from Emmaus felt like a unifying narrative for the work of the team. Feedback after the research was over suggested that a greater sense of shared purpose had been one of the benefits of the research collaboration.

5 Faith formation, pedagogy and handing on

Data from the research raised sharp questions about adult faith formation and its relation to church mission and evangelisation. There were several examples of reflection of pedagogy in the Westminster Agency material in terms of styles, methods, process and content. Pedagogy was reflected upon in the interviews around the Deanery Talks and in the ARCS fieldworker's notes following a visit to a deanery talk:

> On the Diocesan website, the address of the talk was said to be the presbytery (not the Church Hall), so I surprised the priest arriving on his doorstep in the pouring rain! He walked me over to the hall. There were 45 people in attendance. The priest said 70 people had been there the week before, which was far more than expected and extra chairs had been brought in. There was a mixture of people from the parish – predominantly older, with one or two younger adults. Inevitably it was to be a challenge to tailor a faith formation talk to meet the needs of such a diverse range of people, all at different stages of faith formation. The talk delivered [deleted name] was quite scholarly with no interaction with participants or invitation for questions. There was no opening or closing prayer or any scriptural readings throughout the talk – just references made to them. However, the talk was very clearly structured with Powerpoint slides looking in depth at the differences between Matthew and John in the Passion Narratives for Palm Sunday with a background context to each gospel.
>
> (Fieldworker's Field Notes)

Something of this pedagogy is also reflected in interviews with speakers and attendees:

> Oh, it's a fairly straightforward biblical methodology really: my question first of all, is what is the author trying to say in this text, what is Jesus trying to say, what issue was he addressing, what was going on socially an psychologically in the background and then how does this maybe relate to us. Yes, I would always try and apply it somehow to our world today – nearly always certainly.
>
> (Speaker Interview – describing the format of his talks)

> Some of the talks I found helpful. It very much depended on the speakers.... Basically the format was the speaker would speak for half an hour or so. Sometimes they had questions for us and we got into groups to discuss things. Then there was feedback and people asked questions openly in one big group together.
>
> (Attendee One)

> The talk I attended, I had quite strong views about ... some of the things people had to listen to were not so good.... It was a young couple, still in their honeymoon period; basically they were just talking about the Catholic template for marriage. It included all the scriptural stuff about why you shouldn't marry outside the faith, and how that won't

work for you. You shouldn't marry anyone who isn't a Catholic, even marrying Anglicans, that would be difficult and in years to come; you will have a rift with God or your partner. And I just thought well, a) that's rubbish because I'm married to an agnostic and have been so happily for 11 years and I do not have a rift with God or my partner, b) it was an incredibly blinkered attitude from people who hadn't been married for very long. . . . The line was so fine. They actually came and apologised to me afterwards because I stood up and challenged them with my situation and experience.

(Attendee Three)

The outsider team made robust comments in both feedback documents about the importance of pedagogy in the work of the Agency:

Theme 2: Relationship between pedagogy, formation & evangelisation

There are some recurrent questions arising about the relationship between pedagogy, formation and evangelisation, which could merit deeper reflection and 'connecting up'. Where is the clarity of focus in the methods being used by the adult faith formation team? What are the limitations of a using a directive 'talk' for the purposes of adult faith formation? And where does the adult faith formation team identify *transformation* taking place in its current work in the diocese? The ARCS team is well aware of the pressure faced by the Agency in terms of managing limited resources. Nevertheless, ARCS too can speak from experience of the value of setting aside time as a team to carry out reflection on the on-going purpose of formation! (Cycle One, Feedback Document).

The Agency team is bound together by the pedagogical process

Recognising the complexity of this multi-stranded organisation, the ARCS team wondered whether the Agency might helpfully focus first and foremost on the pedagogical process which binds the Agency together. Could, for example, the Agency be more explicit about where people are fitting into this pedagogy, whether that be catechises, adult education and so on? How are all of these strands of work evangelising? How can the Agency make sure that all this pedagogy has a missional impact? (Cycle Two, Insider Team Feedback Document).

This was a theme warmly discussed at the final feedback meeting, at which a member of the ARCS Team was able to emphasise its importance and potential:

DIRECTOR: Felt that the unifying thread running between team members was a commitment to formation.

ARCS TEAM 1: Identified the Kolb learning cycle as perhaps a helpful tool to strengthen the team's interconnectedness. For example, at the experiential stage on the cycle would be the small groups and youth ministry, and at the stage of tradition would be catechesis. All groups are on a journey and understanding more explicitly where each strand of work is located on this journey might strengthen the agency's structure and mission. Individual agency team members are also journeying and learning from this cycle too.

DIRECTOR: People in parishes, the parishes themselves and even deaneries are all at very different stages of formation and growth on that journey. This can be very challenging to work with. For example, parishes can be very accepting of catechesis, but you can find yourself begging them to take up adult faith formation (Cycle Two, Joint Feedback Meeting, notes of discussion).

The moment of disclosure here came for the outsider team when they acknowledged the strength of their reactions to the lack of discussion of pedagogy in the Agency. This reflected in part our beliefs as practical theologians of the importance of adult education approaches in empowering the laity. It also reflected our growing realisation of the formational power of a multi-voiced approach to theology, which had sharpened our sense that, for us, the Agency was dominated by the voice of the bishop which was experienced as normative. It is important to reiterate that that was not the perception of the Agency team, who remained largely committed to 'directive, traditional styles of talks' as deemed appropriate for their older attendees (Director, Cycle One, Feedback Meeting notes).

Concluding reflections

The overall experience of working with the Agency raised a sharp question about what impedes and enables mature theological reflection within a team. A delicate set of questions around leadership, trust and group dynamics emerged in the research. It is significant to note the Director's comment in the Cycle Two Joint Feedback meeting, that "he had never had a sense of the team working so well together". This exemplifies the way in which the ARCS process enables structured conversations to take place that make a difference just by having happened, even when there is – as in this case – a sense of insider and outsider teams not having worked so well together in developing a shared and coherent vision.

A final, and perhaps important, reflection might be one of challenge to the ARCS team: Did we miss a 'negative epiphany' – a revelation of the non-disclosed – in the constraints the diocesan Agency accepted, but which we wished to challenge? In the post-research Evaluation Interview, the Agency Director was clear that he had felt that the ARCS Team never really understood the realities of his team and their work, especially as a diocesan group, mandated by the bishop. We might respond, of course, that we could see other realities in their work and practice, which they, too, were unable to receive. The importance of the hard work of receptive conversation is highlighted here. Beyond that, however, there is the possibility of a negative epiphany which casts light on the ways in which agencies located in the *ecclesia ad intra* are, in particular ways, necessarily bound to certain ecclesial understandings. Theological action research in these settings might need to take different forms from those carried out with more 'edgy' places of church.

Notes

1 This document no longer appears available.

2 Feedback from the Westminster Agency for Evangelisation faith formation questionnaire.

3 The language of *ad intra* church (and its partner term *ad extra*) is used extensively in this book. It is drawn from the debates surrounding the Second Vatican Council in which Cardinal Suenens differentiated the two Constitutions on the Church as pertaining to the *eccleisa ad intra* (the Dogmatic Constitution on the Church, *Lumen Gentium*) and the *ecclesia ad extra* (the Pastoral Constitution on the Church in the Modern World, *Gaudium et Spes.*). These ecclesiological perspectives are not in competition with one another as they simply refer to the same reality of church understood under different aspects of its life – pertaining to the 'internal' life and work of the structured community (*ad intra*) and the life and work of the church in and for the world (*ad extra*).

4 See note 3 above.

6 The organisational contexts

Dioceses, parishes and faith-based agencies

> given who we are in the life of the diocese and who we represent. . . . we don't have that liberty to be an individual in the centre because our work is seen as part of this department.
>
> (Westminster Agency for Evangelisation, B1, Director)

> I don't see it as something completely discrete anymore. It's not something I just do on a Monday with the SVP. It affects my life in other ways.
>
> (LJV, A2, Sarah)

Just as the parameters of the ARCS project defined the geographical context as focused on London, so too it shaped the ecclesial contexts by committing us to working with Roman Catholic and Church of England practices. What these ecclesial contexts share is, of course, an episcopal polity, shaped by the organisation of ordained ministry in the historic three-fold pattern of presbyteral, diaconal and episcopal 'orders',[1] and a concomitant culture of a certain differentiation, with varying degrees of separation, between lay[2] and ordained. In addition, both ecclesial traditions are recognisable as complex, routinised, 'bureaucratic' organisations,[3] whose long-established presence in British society and long historical legacies allow them also to be seen as public 'institutions'.[4] At the same time, there are notable differences between the social make-up of the Church of England with its establishment connections and identity and the Catholic Church in England, with its longer history of disenfranchisement and persecution in Britain and its historic and contemporary dependence on immigration.

These sociological, organisational realities already suggest certain characteristics for the organisational culture in which the co-researcher practices (and most of the ARCS team members) operated: such long-lived, complex organisations typically struggle with change and flexibility and have numerous points of information transmission and absorption, making communications complex.[5] This organisational complexity is added to by the largely voluntary nature of church membership in which people are members for reasons of belief and belonging,[6] rather than 'harder', and so more manageable, material benefits. In a post-associational culture,[7] and a global postsecular city characterised by freedom and choice, these sociological characteristics of church life are only made more problematic.

Such complexity is added to when we consider that these structures are, in varying ways and to varying extents, imbued with specific theological authority and weight, both explicitly in the form of ecclesial doctrine and culturally in the operant theology of ecclesial practices. Normative Catholic Church self-understanding not only names its ordered ministry as 'sacrament',[8] thereby giving these practices of hierarchy assured status in the economy of grace, but also sees the church as *essentially* 'hierarchical', even in its commitment to a communion of equality in Christ.[9] For Anglicans, too, ordination has been accompanied by a strong liturgically manifest sense of sacrament and permanence, although this is variably interpreted.[10] For both arguably, the 'clerical paradigm'[11] persists across many areas of church life and theology.

The specifically theological learning concerning ordained ministry (orders) will be discussed in chapter 10. Here, our concern is more with demonstrating the ways in which the practices were shaped by and responded to the organisational realities of their church location. There is a growing, if rather fragmented, academic literature concerned with the interplay of ecclesiology and church organisation to which the present author has made some contribution.[12] The insights of this discourse, particularly with its interdisciplinary wisdom on issues of power/authority,[13] inform this chapter, although detailed consideration of it is excluded for reasons of space. It remains the background to consideration of diocese and parish, as traditionally inherited structures of the ecclesial realities with which we worked. This organisational frame has also shaped the positioning and possibilities for the Faith-Based Agencies[14] (FBAs) in the ARCS project who demonstrated a more entrepreneurial, often lay-led form of practice, which was none the less affected by the wider ecclesial polity in various ways.

This chapter is also indebted to the literature on recent church growth and decline and the related shifts in structural practice and approach.[15] What this literature makes clear is that, as the historic structures of particularly mainstream churches have struggled to respond to rapid shifts in demography and social practice, older forms[16] of organisation have been forced to renew themselves to meet the new circumstances. This is the age of the diocesan pastoral plan and renewal programme.[17] At the same time, in both Catholic and Church of England communities, there have been flowerings of more grass-roots expressions of organised faith – through the Fresh Expressions which are now integrated into the 'mixed economy' of the Church of England,[18] and through the various 'movements' which characterised much lay renewal in the Catholic Church prior to the third millennium.[19] The discussions that such re-patterning of church life have engendered are an important part of the background to our own learning from the practices with which ARCS worked – in particular, for the ways in which they call into question the nature of the long-established practices of parish structures.[20]

By way of an outline typology, we can categorise our practices under three headings: diocesan practitioners (the Westminster Agency for Evangelisation and Portsmouth Diocese); parish practitioners (St. Mary's, Battersea; Messy Church); and FBAs (LJV; Housing Justice; and CAFOD). Even in this list, it is clear that such categorisation is open to challenge, and there are degrees of overlap. As a Fresh Expression, it could be argued that Messy Church was less of a parish practice and more that of an FBA; and CAFOD has the rather unusual status of being a mandated agency of the Catholic Bishops of England and Wales, a charity, and a lay-led Catholic organisation. In a different way, LJV, too, straddles identities, as a lay-led FBA which is homed, very significantly and intentionally, in the Jesuit parish and community at Mount Street. However, for all this complexity and inter-relatedness of structures, this three-fold typology can be useful in exploring the organisational contexts within which these practices worked.

The terms used to describe this typology may benefit from some clarification. In referring to *diocese/diocesan,* we described those practices associated with the diocese as the geographical territory under the authority and oversight of a bishop. This is the primary unity of an episcopal church, and is technically the 'local' church, within which the bishop's teaching and leadership has (at least in principle) a normative authority.[21] At the same time, the complexity and size of diocesan activities also sees dioceses shaped by the appropriate delegation by the bishop of key tasks and responsibilities. This bureaucratic organisational form can be well recognised in the Westminster Agency (B) and Portsmouth Diocese (F) data. The *parish* is the most geographically local unit of the diocese, whose ministers are generally appointed by the bishop, and whose activities come under his or her oversight. There is also a financial relationship between the parish and the diocese, which involves both set contributions from parishes to the diocese and the availability of resources to parishes from diocesan agencies. Like dioceses, *parish* boundaries are geographically understood in both the church traditions we worked with – although this locating of parish could clearly be seen as non-binding in a London context (for example, C5). When we look at the authority practices of parishes, it is notable that parish priests[22] in a Catholic parish have considerable leeway as to how much decision-making and work they share with the parish lay people, with parish councils being optional and only advisory.[23] Within the Church of England the parish priest or vicar works with a parish council (parochial church council – PCC) which has a clearer, institutionally established role, and authority is more communally held.[24]

The complexity of power relations – between diocese and parish, and within diocesan structures and parish life – is already becoming visible. The sociological realities of FBAs in these contexts are shaped by such relations, but also can be read as a move away from them, even a challenge to them, in their more 'entrepreneurial' practices. That is not to say that the FBAs with which ARCS worked were not dependent in some way on the more structured powers and community of church life; as we shall see, these relationships were often extremely fruitful to both parish/diocese and FBA. However, the origins of FBA initiatives and the consequences of such origins on day-to-day leadership and governance not only allowed them to remain disentangled from more bureaucratic structures, but also enabled a significantly different organisational culture from those experienced in much parish and diocesan life.

Our learning about the effects, blessings and limitations of these different organisational cultures in what follows will focus on three themes identified from across the Accounts of Practice: the FBA and the espousal of theology; the role of the parish priest as 'gatekeeper'; and the recognition of structure as a form of embodied normativity.

The FBA: deepening espousal

In the four voices of theology the 'espoused voice' represents the theology articulated by practitioners as a faith account of what they were doing and why. When asked about this, most practitioner groups would have recourse to their mission statement or established goals – making disciples (D), enabling evangelisation (B) and so forth – goals which would often feature in their own research questions. For larger organisations, such as CAFOD and Portsmouth Diocese, the scope of their overall purposes required a focusing down on one or two aspects of the espoused theology in order to make reflection manageable. However, in all cases – although to differing degrees – the question arises as to how far the 'officially' espoused theology of a group is, in fact, thoroughly espoused or appropriated by individual members or smaller teams.

This question as to how the espoused theology functions is brought into sharp relief when considering the differing organisational cultures of our practices. Indeed, the move from the publicly espoused to the fully appropriated might be seen as a major feature of concern for at least two of the practices worked with. For Portsmouth Diocese (F) the exploration of stewardship processes as a way of more deeply appropriating the bishop's pastoral plan can be read as a search for deeper espousal (F1), whilst the CAFOD project's desire to explore ways of better embedding its core publicly espoused theology of Catholic Social Teaching among its workers brought to the fore the complexity of large organisational espoused theologies and more personal or small group espousal (G, Introductory Narrative).

Our diocesan practitioners seemed to struggle particularly with the extent to which the public espoused theology acted as a local normativity, often limiting the extent to which effective personal espousal, and the creativity and possible diversity that attends it, could be put into practice. This is especially clear in the Westminster Agency for Evangelisation, where the naming of an espoused theology seemed caught between the bishop's mandate (B1) and the often unspoken and so rather unclear ethos of a shared faith and passion for transmitting it (B2, Agency Team 3; B4 Cycle 2, Insider Team Reflection). It was striking that for this group, one of the positive learning points of the theological action research process was the need to develop a stronger sense of shared purpose through giving time to team reflection (B4). In a similar way, Portsmouth Diocesan workers recognised as a particularly important part of their task the enabling of the effective espousal of the stewardship idea and process to both laity and clergy. The reflective skills of this diocese's team at the time enabled them to offer stewardship as a wider spirituality rather than as a narrow programme for structural change, bringing about 'dramatic change' for a number of laity who were able to espouse the ideas more deeply, seeing that "stewardship is recognising that everything comes from God and everything is a gift" (F3, Questionnaire). Clergy too had to embark on a sometimes difficult journey of personal espousal (F2 Cycle 1 Notes) before being able to appropriate stewardship as "the opportunity to celebrate who they are/rediscover gifts/talents" (F2, Parish Priest Interview).

When we come to look at the more 'entrepreneurial' and generally lay-led FBAs with which we worked, these tensions around public and personal espousal shift. The organisational context of the FBA seems to lend itself to providing a greater space for discussion, learning and creativity, enabling members to work with the espoused theology of the group in ways which enable both a deeper personal espousal and an enriched reading and even renewed articulation of the group's espoused position. Notable here were the LJVs whose built-in reflective practices saw volunteers growing in their ability to understand the espoused Ignatian theology in intimate ways (A2, Joseph and Sarah; A5, Reflective Writing 5 and 7). The intentionally contemplative culture that was nurtured in LJV gave space for the range of emotions and experiences to be reflected upon in the light of scripture and the community, giving the espoused theology living roots in the words and practices of the volunteers. It is relevant, too, that this FBA, whilst a properly lay-led venture, was nonetheless homed not only in a parish but in a parish run by a resident religious community of Jesuits. In this way, the espoused Ignatian way was not simply a matter of words or a mission statement but was a tradition being lived and embodied in an accompanying community – a relationship which the research surfaced as important both to LJV and the parish Management Team (A1).[25]

It seems likely that FBA-type structures are better equipped for deepening the espousal of publicly espoused theologies among practitioners. Here, the practices of CAFOD presented in the ARCS project have a particular light to shed in that they were deliberately setting out to embed more effectively aspects of their organisationally espoused theology (Catholic Social

Teaching) within their workers. The time and resources required for this reflective learning of action research were hard to negotiate in a busy, over-stretched workforce (G, Introductory Narrative), but were facilitated by the structural inclusion of the Spirituality Team within the organisation and the organisational commitment to theological formation in its work (ibid.). It was the experience of the fruitfulness of this use of time that allowed the continuation of theological action research processes for a number of years within the organisation. What the Account of Practice here demonstrates is the move from the 'fig-leave' of the 'Pope-quote' – a superficial adherence to a publicly espoused theology – to the more deeply formative understanding of this theology, seen now as the 'bay leaf' flavouring the whole (G1). The participants themselves clearly experienced some frustrated sense of a lack of real agency in their day-to-day work (G3, Advocacy Group, Quote 1), which contrasted with the creativity and sense of active ownership that the processes of theological action research and the related reflective spaces enabled (Ibid. Quote 2). The ability to share imaginative metaphors – such as the catwalk and the high street fashion store as an example of 'translation' – enlivened both the experience of the work and the espoused theology and was highly valuable (ibid.).

The parish priest: the power of the gatekeeper

If it is the case that the freer structures of FBAs are better at enabling a deeper espoused theology than more ecclesiastical structures, then a key point in those more bureaucratic structures of parish and diocese is that occupied by the parish priest. His or her ministry shapes the parish in subtle as well as more obvious ways, through preaching and liturgical 'style' (C5, Interview 3) as well as though more direct decision-making (C2, Warm-up Meeting Notes). We have seen above how the particular parish clergy of the Mount Street Jesuit Church enabled and supported the work of LJV, and similar patterns of support can be seen in the curate's and parish priest's involvement with Messy Church (D, Introductory Narrative), and the cooperation of parish clergy in the Housing Justice project – though in this latter case, the lack of hands-on involvement by such clergy may not have helped with a deeper understanding of the work (E1, Clergy Interview). FBAs may demonstrate a certain freedom and flexibility, but parish and diocese remain important to them as structures of wider ecclesial identity, commitment and support.

The enabling power of parish clergy in supporting these faith-full practices has its own shadow side: the ability to enable carries with it the potential for failing to nurture or even obstructing. Not that this was, in general, something experienced as a deliberate exercise of clerical power 'against' something; rather, the 'soft' power of the parish priest as the gatekeeper to parish communications and resources, and as often the first point of authoritative contact in approaching 'the parish', may often have been exercised unwittingly with a variety of unintended effects. For example, we mentioned in the previous section how the Portsmouth diocese project recognised the importance of working with clergy in aiding the espousal of stewardship as a living and effective theology. Anxieties around 'collaborative ministry' and pastoral areas diminishing the role (and status?) of clergy were apparent (F2, Clergy Advisor, final quote; and Introductory Narrative), and the need was felt to appoint a special Clergy Advisor on Stewardship to work with the diocesan priests (F2, Cycle 1, Feedback Notes). It was clear that, without clerical deep espousal of stewardship, things could not move forward; indeed, the diocese experienced stewardship parish practices grinding to a halt with changes of parish clergy (F2, note 5).

This particular kind of 'power' embodied in the parish priest was also a major feature of the work of the Westminster Agency for Evangelisation (B). The nature of this Agency's work meant that they were often placed between the mandate of the bishop and the realities of parish life on the ground – realities shaped by parish priests in a particular way. Team members spoke of encountering different ecclesiologies and approaches in parishes from their own, which effectively limited or even blocked further work (B1, Cycle 2, Focus Group 2). There was even talk of 'direct conflict' between the understandings of some parish priests and those of the Agency (B3, Agency Team 4), which led to uncertainty around the effectiveness of the Agency's work. The clear, normative theology of priestly ministry held by the (ordained) Director – that priests are obedient to the bishop – was, for all its normativity within church teaching and canons, impossible to 'enforce' in the face of rather different operant theologies of parish ordained ministry (B3, Director). Just as in the Portsmouth experience, the frustrations over the sometimes dramatic changes in parish practice and culture attendant on a change of parish priest were clearly felt (ibid.).

This identification of the effective power of parish clergy to enable and disable practices will not be at all surprising to many who have experienced parish life – although the attributing of 'power' to parish priests is something they themselves often decry. What is important in the learning from practice here is the ways in which the particular powers of *influence* of the parish priest – over parish culture, over what does and does not get to happen, over what communications reach the wider parish – prove to be highly significant not only for lay-led FBAs, but also for dioceses and their bishops. Organisationally, the parish priest occupies an important point in communication flow, and – whether aware of it or not – has enormous potential in transmitting or blocking communications to affect practices across a range of contexts. Both Portsmouth and the Westminster Agency sought to work with clergy, especially pedagogically in the former's case, and yet, the structural and cultural patterns of clergy power and influence seem intractable in organisations where structures of accountability seem difficult to enforce.

Ecclesial structures and embodied normativities

The 'clue' to identifying this third learning point around organisational context comes from the exchange between a Quaker and an Anglican volunteer at Housing Justice (E4). The disclosure here concerned how the different normative practices of worship – even down to the layout of chairs and space – shaped the participation of these volunteers in the research's reflective conversations. Bill, the Quaker, recognised from his embodied normative tradition, something of a worship event in the layout of the focus group, whereas James' Church of England experience of 'sitting in rows' made such a connection more difficult.

What this conversation makes clear is that the normative 'voice' is not necessarily spoken, but can also be – and perhaps is most powerfully – embodied in established practices. If this is true for liturgical practices, it is also the case for organisational practices. Normativity not only has an articulated content (scripture, tradition, doctrine), but also it has a *means* – structures by which its authority is exercised.[26] Such embodied normativity is especially clear in the experience of the Westminster Agency for Evangelisation (B1). Having talked about their experience of tension, frustration and even conflict in relation to their episcopally mandated work and the realities on the ground (B1, Cycle 2, Focus Group 2), the Agency members were still clear that they did not accept the ARCS team's reading of this as being 'stuck in the middle'. Their commitment to the ecclesial structures as a part of their ecclesiology meant that they accepted the reality of episcopal governance and presbyteral ministries as normative – simply "where we are at", making them reluctant to voice any account of this reality as a negative thing or even to question these realities critically (B1, Cycle 2, Feedback Document and Joint Feedback Document Notes). The same appropriation of the bishop's mandate as normative can be seen as playing a significant part in the team's lack of a shared espoused theology of their own (B2).

Similar – though perhaps less problematic – examples of the structural expression of normativity can also be seen in the Portsmouth Diocese and CAFOD projects. The Portsmouth renewal work based on stewardship was also – and necessarily – a work in response to the earlier Diocesan Pastoral Plan of the bishop, *Go Out and Bear Much Fruit*.[27] Making the connection between the bishop's plan and the diocesan process was of particular importance and needed the articulation of the bishop himself (F1). In a rather particular way, CAFOD, too, witnesses to the place of structural normativity. As not only an agency mandated by the Catholic Bishop's Conference of England and Wales but also as a part of the international network of Caritas Internationalis,[28] CAFOD is thoroughly implicated in *ad intra* church structure even as an organisation committed to *ad extra* practice (G4). The importance of Catholic Social Teaching both as a part of the internal culture and as a visible characteristic for CAFOD is the theological key to understanding this ecclesial identity. Commitment to a deeper appropriation of this teaching reflects the impact of the normative structures of which CAFOD is a part, whilst nurturing a more grounded espoused and operant theology than seemed possible for the Westminster Agency for Evangelisation.

Conclusion

In exploring the organisational contexts of our projects, it looks as if there are ways in which the lay-led FBA can overcome many of the limitations experienced in more tightly hierarchically led and implicated practices. At the same time, FBAs will often have a dependency, of varying degrees, on the more ecclesiastical expressions of organisation – especially through the support, cooperation, or not, of the parish priest. The relative success of FBAs may also be related to what Helen Cameron has described as their 'cultural form'.[29] Whilst not exactly fitting any of the five categories identified by Cameron, the FBAs clearly have more in common with the small groups (with their cultural resonances with book-groups and party-plan selling groups), and with some aspects of gathered congregations, (with their resonances with voluntary associations), than they do with parishes (culturally identifiable as 'service providers'). Illumined by Cameron's argument, it may well be that our attention to organisational context has surfaced the ways in which certain, long-established structures simply lack the cultural form best suited to speaking into late modern urban culture.

From this perspective, it is striking that much of the renewal work being attempted by the diocesan practices with whom ARCS co-researched was focused on the development of 'small groups', in common with many other dioceses,[30] suggesting an instinct for the cultural form of the book group (to use Cameron's term) as an effective way of restructuring for renewal. The question is whether, in fact, such a small group culture can be engendered 'from the top-down'. The parish and diocesan structures continue to be the embodied normativity within which such groups take place, and so attention is inevitably returned to those structures even in the attempt to nurture and develop different cultural forms of church engagement. The nature of the FBA's normative structures of relationship presents itself as of particular importance for contemporary church life and mission, and an area for special discernment and care.

Notes

1 So see *Catechism of the Catholic Church* 1554–1571; Church of England *Book of Common Prayer: The Form and Manner of Making, Ordaining and Consecrating of Bishops, Priests and* Deacons: "It is evident unto all men diligently reading holy Scripture and ancient Authors, that from the Apostles' time there have been these Orders of Ministers in Christ's Church; Bishops, Priests and Deacons". The significance of the threefold order for the contemporary Church of England can be demonstrated practically by the requirement for Methodism in the UK instituting episcopacy as a condition of a covenanted

unity with the Church of England. See Church of England Faith and order, *Mission and Ministry in Covenant*, 58. Available at: www.anglican-methodist.org.uk/wp-content/uploads/2019/06/MMiC-areas-for-further-reflection-0619.pdf. Accessed August 2019.

2 Here, the term 'lay' (from *laos* – people) is used in the canonical sense of the non-ordained, rather than to signify the whole People of God of which ordained people are, of course, members. The second Vatican Council's addition to this negative ('non-ordained') definition of lay, in this sense, was complemented by the more positive account of the laity as those who live their Christian life in solidarity with 'the world', and so with a 'secular character'. See Second Vatican Council Dogmatic Constitution on the Church, *Lumen Gentium*, 31. Whilst this idea remains contested – not least for what it might suggest about the ordained state – it will remain useful in this book's discussions for the ways in which frames the realities on the ground which will be described.

3 In Weberian terms: see Max Weber, *The Theory of Social and Economic Organisation.* Talcott Parsons trans. (Free & Falcon's Wing, 1947).

4 There has been some interesting, though sporadic, theological discussion of the possibilities and limits of considering the church as an 'organisation'. So see: Peter Rudge, *Ministry and Management: The Study of Ecclesiastical Administration* (Tavistock, 1968) and *Management in the Church* (McGraw-Hill, 1976); Mady Thung, *The Precarious Organisation: Sociological Explorations of the Church's Mission and Structure* (De Gruyter Mouton, Reprint 2016, orig. Pub. 1976); Clare Watkins, "Organizing the People of God. Social Science Theories of Organization in Ecclesiology." *Theological Studies* 52 (1991): 689–711; Joseph F. McCann, *Church and Organisation: A Sociological and Theological Enquiry* (Associated University Press, 1993); Lyndon Shakespeare, *Being the Body of Christ in the Age of Management* (Cascade, 2016).

5 An account of this complexity, in a business setting, is given by Charles Kadushin, *Understanding Social Networks: Theories, Concepts and Findings* (OUP, 2012): 95–100. See also Kerstin Sahlin and Linda Wedlin, "Circulating Ideas: Imitation, Translation and Editing." Royston Greenwood et al. eds. *The SAGE Handbook of Organizational Institutionalism* (SAGE, 2008): 218–236.

6 This language is taken from the work of Grace Davie, and the debates that flow from it. Grace Davie, *Religion in Britain Since 1945: Believing Without Belonging* (Blackwell, 1994).

7 As well described by Martyn Percy, *Engaging With Contemporary Culture: Christianity, Theology, and the Concrete Church* (Ashgate, 2005): 70–78.

8 *Catechism of the Catholic Church*, 1581–1589.

9 Vatican II Dogmatic Constitution on the Church, *Lumen Gentium*, holds this tension by describing the reference proper communion of church as 'hierarchical': "Communion is a notion which is held in high honor in the ancient Church (and also today, especially in the East). However, it is not understood as some kind of vague disposition, but as an organic reality which requires a juridical form and is animated by charity. Hence the Commission, almost unanimously, decided that this wording should be used: 'in hierarchical communion'". Preliminary Explanatory Note 2. The term hierarchical as used ecclesiologically here is, I would argue, significantly different in its import than its use in sociological and common discussion would suggest. The theological sense of being 'ordered to what is holy' (*hierus*) does not necessitate a 'top-down' account of ordering. The tension held between hierarchy and communion in *Lumen Gentium* is more comprehensible in this reading.

10 For a helpful critical study of Anglican orders, see Martyn Percy, *Clergy: The Origin of Species* (Continuum, 2006).

11 Originally use by Edward Farley, *Theologia: The Fragmentation and Unity of Theological Education* (Fortress, 1983).

12 See note 4 above.
13 Stephen Sykes, *Power and Christian Theology* (Continuum, 2006); Martyn Percy, *Power and the Church: Ecclesiology in an Age of Transition* (Cassell, 1998).
14 This language has been arrived at to describe the usually lay led agencies which worked with ARCS. Initially referred to in our thinking simply as 'agencies' to differentiate them from diocesan or parish practices, they became increasingly in need of a new name, as our discussions around 'agency' understood as the ability to act developed. To avoid confusion between these two senses of agency, I am here referring to Faith-Based Agencies (FBAs). These are somewhat different from Faith Based Organisations (FBOs) – which have become a particular area of study – although there may be some overlap.
15 So see especially: David Goodhew ed., *Church Growth in Britain: 1980 to the Present* (Ashgate, 2012); Goodhew; Staf Hellemans and Jozef Wissink, *Towards a New Catholic Church in Advanced Modernity: Transformation, Visions and Tensions* (LIT Verlag, 2012); Helen Cameron, *Resourcing Mission. Practical Theology for Changing Churches* (SCM, 2009).
16 Here, I am referring more to modern, post-Enlightenment practices than those of pre-modernity or antiquity. Indeed, it maybe that in negotiating the challenges of late modernity it is precisely to the pre-modern and ancient we need to look.
17 Sweeney, op. cit. 159–161, 166–167.
18 For the Fresh Expressions account of its movements see: http://freshexpressions.org.uk. See also: Archbishop of Canterbury (Foreword), *Mission-Shaped Church: Church Planting and Fresh Expressions of Church in a Changing Context* (Church Publishing, 2005), in which the idea of a 'mixed economy' is articulated. For more on the mixed economy see Andrew Dunlop and Anna Brooker, *Mixed-Economy Mission: Collaborative Ministry for Multi-Church Growth* (Grove Books, 2019). It is interesting that these 'grass roots' initiatives have now been effectively taken up by the hierarchy, who now provide funding, training and recognition for many such ventures. Organisationally, this is an ambivalent move which both validates and further enables these initiatives, whilst, arguably, and over time, changing their nature.
19 These 'movimenti' or 'new movements' were especially championed by Pope St. John Paul II. For an excellent account of these see: Massimo Faggioli, *Sorting Out the Catholicism. A Brief History of the New Ecclesial Movements* (Liturgical Press, 2014). For a helpful setting of these movements in context see Sweeney, op. cit. 147ff, esp. pp. 153–154, 161, 167–171.
20 Something of this debate can be seen in Andrew Davison and Alison Milbank, *For the Parish: A Critique of Fresh Expressions* (SCM, 2010).
21 *Code of Canon Law for the Roman Catholic Church* (1983), Cans. 369, 375; in the Church of England ordained ministers are likewise required to take an oath of obedience to their bishop: see Canon C14, www.churchofengland.org/more/policy-and-thinking/canons-church-england/section-c#b59.
22 I am aware that not all Anglican parishes would refer to their presiding minister in this way, and the language of 'Rector' was that preferred by St. Mary's. Here, I take the liberty of using it as a general term to describe this parish role, on the basis that it has some currency and shared understanding between the two ecclesial traditions.
23 See Can. 536. A Finance Committee with lay expertise is, however, a compulsory part of Catholic parish structure; Can. 537.
24 For example, see Church of England Can. C 24.7.
25 James Sweeney highlights the important and 'middle' role that religious orders have played in modern Catholic Church development, owing in no small part

to their specific organisational culture, which is both thoroughly ecclesial and yet also highly participative and more able to change in response to external factors. "Catholicism in Britain: A Church in Search of Its Way." Op. cit. 153–154.

26 This has some resonance with Pete Ward's identification of the "affective gravitational pull of the church", which describes the ways in which, often implicitly, ecclesial traditions and practices shape the reasoning of the Christian: Pete Ward, "Blueprint Ecclesiology and the Lived: Normativity as a Perilous Faithfulness". *Ecclesial Practices* 2, no.1 (2015): 74–90; and in his *Liquid Ecclesiology: The Gospel and the Church* (Brill, 2017): 18ff.

27 Available at www.portsmouthdiocese.org.uk/plan/plan2005.pdf. Accessed August 2019.

28 www.caritas.org.

29 Helen Cameron, *Resourcing Mission, Practical Theology for Changing Churches* (SCM, 2010). For Cameron's five cultural forms and their significance for church, see especially 24–37.

30 Sweeney, op. cit. 166–167.

Part III
Ecclesiological themes

Rationale for Part III

Just as chapters 5 and 6 presented what was being learnt contextually through the research with church practitioners, so now Part III sets out five chapters – again, interspersed with Accounts of Practice – which explore the insights into theologies of church generated from these theological action research projects. In each case, the chapter treats a key theme that has emerged through the meta-analysis of the projects, demonstrating the ways in which the four voices of theology might function to create a renewed approach to church as a theological reality 'disclosed' through our processes. The chapters that follow call the reader to revisit some familiar ecclesiological themes, and engage with them in fresh ways, learning from theological action research's commitment to practice as an authoritative voice.

Chapter 7 takes up the major theme of mission or evangelisation, working with what has been learnt from practitioners towards an essentially outward turning (ek-centric) vision of church. This exploration calls into new question the nature of the church as a bounded organisational reality – a theme that is explored in chapter 8. Following these fundamental ecclesiological explorations, chapters 9, 10 and 11 each testify to questions that emerged powerfully across the projects worked with, suggesting these themes are of lively importance for contemporary ecclesiologies seeking to serve Christian practice. They are, in order: sacrament and sacramentality; orders and the ordering of the church; and tradition, with the questions of normativity that this generates.

These themes in no way exhaust ecclesiological questions, of course, and, indeed, iterative reading of the data could be expected to throw up new and additional ecclesiological themes which might have been chosen. These have been chosen for the strong way in which, together, they authentically reflect much of what is most alive and powerful in the concrete living of church today. As such I offer them as a contribution to the on-going conversations around practical and ethnographic ecclesiology, rather than as an exhaustive account of the data, or a total ecclesiology.

Account of practice C

St. Mary's Parish, Battersea, Alpha course

Project time frame: February 2008–September 2009

Introductory narrative

Given the research project's commitment to exploring church activity as 'outreach', the ARCS team was keen to look at the Alpha Course as a key development in evangelism.[1] Alpha is widely recognised as one of the most successful evangelism processes recently developed and is now widely used across the world. Whilst the process of inviting people for a meal and then presenting material about Christianity followed by small group discussion has been copied by other 'introduction to Christianity courses', none have achieved the global reach achieved by Alpha. The Alpha website recognises that "no two Alphas look the same, but generally they have three key things in common: food, a talk and good conversation". There is a degree of flexibility envisaged, for all that many Alpha 'courses' use the teaching DVDs supplied by Alpha, and so will have a common content. Perhaps unusually, though still within the Alpha 'spirit', the church ARCS worked with when looking at this programme did not use these DVDs, and was rather less traditionally evangelical than is perhaps typical of churches using Alpha.

In order to identify a congregation we might work with and who might be happy to work with us in a theological action research process, we looked at the websites of Anglican parishes in London for any that might be advertising Alpha courses. St. Mary's website conveyed that they were committed to running Alpha and that they had an inclusive ethos seeking to welcome marginalised groups. This congregational context offered a particular context for exploring Alpha – already a much-researched programme[2] – which might offer new perspectives, and which also fitted well with the ARCS project's own intentions. What was, as ever, crucial, was the possibility for developing a research relationship in which the process could be effectively co-owned by practitioners and the ARCS team by 'insider' and 'outsider' groups. On this basis, in March 2008, the team made an appointment with the Rector, to explain the ARCS project and invite participation.

The meeting took place in the church vestry with, in one direction, views into the listed Georgian interior and, in the other direction, the river Thames. The team were learning the importance of the 'insider' agenda and so although we made it clear that an interest in Alpha had taken us to him, we asked what issues he would like to explore in the parish. The issue presented by the Rector concerned the desire to help fringe parishioners become more committed to the church. The commitment to welcoming all and to inclusivity at St. Mary's had been very 'successful' in bringing new people from a variety of backgrounds to the church, but there remained a concern that the core work of welcome and outreach continued to be carried out by the Rector and the small team around him. The leadership were increasingly concerned to understand what might bring people from attendance and enjoyment of the church's hospitality to a committed service from within and on behalf of the church itself.

In order to explore these realities of a successful Alpha, and a congregational sense of a remaining lack of thorough-going involvement by new members, it was agreed that the ARCS fieldworker would conduct a series of eight short interviews with Alpha participants and group leaders. These interviews would gather the stories of the experiences of coming to St. Mary's through Alpha, as well as accounts of what it meant to be part of this community. At the same time, the Rector was interested to carry out his own survey work with attenders, exploring questions of attendance and general demographics. The interviews were transcribed and the ARCS team met to reflect upon the data and then prepare a 'feedback document' sharing their reflections. This was presented to a meeting of the Parish Council along with the survey data. A follow-up meeting with the Rector elicited what was to be done with the insights from this meeting. At a later stage, evaluation interviews were conducted to assess the impact of the research.

Work with St. Mary's was especially helpful for the ARCS team in bringing to the fore questions of community and faith, hospitality and evangelism – themes which were commonly embodied in ecclesial outreach movements, as well as being discussed academically in terms of 'believing and belonging'.[3] Here, we identify five disclosures which cast light on these questions from this particular context.

Five disclosures

1 Hospitality, inclusivity and the journey to commitment

At the warm-up meeting, the Rector had explained that there was a felt need to increase attendance, increase giving and have greater involvement in parish activities among the majority of attenders and those who understood themselves as part of the St. Mary's community. Interestingly, he presented this as being in tension with the inclusive ethos of the church, which wanted to accept people as they are without putting any demands on them.

He felt the parish had a relatively high turnover of membership and so there were constantly new people to be incorporated into the life of the church, presenting particular challenges for the nurturing of a committed and stable core community. In this context, the Alpha course was seen as catechising people into the basics of the Christian faith and bringing them into relationship with other parish members:

> **Tell me about your experience on the Alpha Course?**
>
> I think the social element for me was the most important because it was a chance to actually sit down and have a meal, which most people enjoy doing, and talk in an informal way. But to be there with a purpose. It was more than just going out for drinks with friends. That was the strength of it for me.
>
> (Interview Six, Alpha Course Organiser)

It was the number of quotes like these from the interviews that led the ARCS team to reflect upon the importance of hospitality in the Alpha course and the way in which that developed a sense of belonging for the participants. We summarised our thinking around this in one section of the feedback document, so as to share it with the St. Mary's leadership, and enter into deeper conversation with them around the question the interviews raised regarding this theme:

> **Theology of Hospitality**
>
> - The data shows friendship/welcome/social interaction as key arising themes, and highlights the much-needed theology of such practices – for example, a theology of invitation and friendship.
> - There are strong themes of hospitality, identity, being guests and hosts. Alpha includes a journey to be made from being a guest to being a host. And this is a very strong theme. The data suggests that some may be held as 'permanent guests' – so not necessarily committing to the parish for example.
> - How is the journey to be made from guest to host in this inclusive and mobile (changing) community? How does this link with commitment?
> - In what ways are these hospitable practices related to what we know with Jesus ministry?

At the presentation of the feedback document to the PCC meeting,[4] the language used in the Feedback Document of movement 'from guest to host' was identified as bringing a new framework for discussion within the pastoral theme. It was a language of hospitality 'all the way through' as it were, avoiding the sense that a person moved from being welcomed to having onerous, inhospitable demands made of them. Rather, the community as characterised by hospitality could envision deeper involvement in terms of the intensifying of participation in the celebration to which all were invited. In a follow-up meeting with the Rector, this was identified as a key moment of disclosure, and described thus:

> The Guest to Host language has 'set free' the PCC from the deadlock tensions between commitment and inclusivity, whilst still remaining rooted in scriptures (e.g., Old Testament feasting, Eucharist, heavenly banqueting and so on). This was 'breakthrough language'.
>
> (Notes of Follow-up Meeting with Rector)

This sense of breakthrough language was further affirmed when, in the evaluation interview of March 2010, the curate said that the image of host had been used with new members of the ministry team and found helpful.

2 *Alpha and building belonging: authenticity to a church context*

In the research warm-up meeting, the Rector spent time making sure we understood they were not a typical Alpha using church. He explained that Holy Trinity Brompton (HTB) – where Alpha originated – knew he was using the course and were happy for him to have the banner on display along the River Thames. However, St. Mary's didn't use the HTB produced videos, but rather various members of the ministry team delivered the talks live. Parts of the material that did not quite accord with their beliefs or church culture were omitted or changed. However, they were sticking to the Alpha formula in terms of hospitality through a meal and through getting existing church members to mix with fringe attenders or newcomers in the small groups. The information given at that first meeting was important for understanding the parish's commitment to using Alpha in a way authentic to their own sense of community, especially as characterised by welcome and inclusivity:

> St. Mary's Battersea have run eight Alpha courses. They began two and a half years ago with a group of leaders from the parish going for training at Holy Trinity Brompton. The Rector was very honest about his deep reservations about introducing Alpha into the church, both due to the very liberal catholic history of the church and his own prejudices and upbringing. There was considerable opposition initially by members of the PCC who felt this 'marketed' the church in the wrong way – offering too narrow and conservative an image and teaching. After one course using the DVDs text-book style, the Rector decided to keep the talks clearly structured on the Alpha framework but to do some of the talks himself.... He found the DVDs to be white and middle class and didn't like references to 'holidays in France', or 'just back from the gym'. He didn't like the analogy made of the Bible being like a rule book of a football pitch.
>
> (Notes of Warm-up Meeting)

This adaptation of Alpha to the specifics of the community was reflected in a number of the interviews:

> **Tell me about your experience on the Alpha Course.**
>
> "I think with most of these things, what you get out of it a lot depends on who is on the course with you and for me, the first evening I thought, oh my God, this really isn't going to do much for me. But I think I've learned things that I hadn't expected to learn from Alpha and things Alpha doesn't expect to teach. So more in terms of seeing things from people's different perspectives".
>
> (Interview 3, Participant)

> **How did you organise the talks and topics?**
>
> Oh we were given the topics beforehand. There were booklets that we followed and we prepared the evenings beforehand. Yes, they were all the Alpha headings. They exactly followed the formula. So it is pretty formulaic but then it has to be, otherwise it wouldn't be the Alpha Course would it? But we did change it quite a bit. I found it really, really interesting doing it because the people I met on it have remained quite close friends. Yes, not everyone. But quite a lot of people I got to know really, really well. Not all of them came to St. Mary's beforehand. Others came habitually to the early morning communion, who I never knew due to singing in the choir.
>
> (Interview Seven, Course Co-leader)

In reflecting on this data with the PCC, a moment of disclosure came when it was suggested that the process of Alpha was probably more significant than the content for their church. The impetus for the course was to bring people up to speed on the content of Christianity (and that was a real need), but in fact, the course was a success in that its process brought people into relationship with each other and generated a sense of belonging from which belief could emerge. In keeping with the parish's characteristic commitment to hospitality and inclusivity, the Alpha process had been valued and enacted in terms predominantly of relationship and the building of community and friendships.

3 The struggle to name Jesus

The ARCS research team was conscious that we were learning about our processes as we went along. It was in our reflections on this case study that we stumbled on the significance of feeding back what we didn't see but had expected, as well as what we did see. Here, our surprise at not seeing what we had expected led to us asking a question of the insider team, which can be related to the previous disclosure's sense of the relational rather than the catechetical/educational being the dominant experience of

Alpha for this church. This is an extract from the feedback document presented to the PCC:

> **Where is Jesus?**
>
> - It was noted that whilst people are giving a rich and complex account of personal and human concerns, that people are not talking in explicit faith language. However, it was observed that there is a strong sense of people describing the reality of God in their lives.
> - In the data so far collected, there is little use of language describing personal relationship with Jesus Chris, or little reference to the Gospel.
>
> **Where is Jesus in the process?**
>
> It could be said that there is an implicitly Jesus sense through the table fellowship (which links with the theme of hospitality).
>
> (Feedback Document)

At the feedback meeting, a member of the group responding to these questions commented, 'We're not a very Jesus-centred parish'. This statement met with a laugh of recognition, as insider team members owned this rather paradoxical reality which had been revealed to them through the data. (Laughter often signals a significant disclosure). But if there was some truth in this sense of 'not being very Jesus-centred', this could be seen as in tension theologically with other practices of the community: this was a parish whose main act of worship was a Eucharist and where preaching that followed the lectionary was valued – so Jesus must have been regularly invoked in the liturgy. In addition, the Alpha course around which the research was centred, contains a lot of teaching specifically on Jesus. This leaves both research teams with something of an un-answered question as to why 'Jesus-language' didn't stick, or become a part of the discourse of the relational culture being so fruitfully built up in the parish. It was as if the 'Jesus-content' of liturgy, preaching and teaching was somehow bounded in ways which made its permeation into personal and inter-personal reflection problematic – for all that survey results demonstrated the high value put on liturgy and preaching by church members.

During meta-analysis of the case studies, the ARCS team came closer to some account of this apparent paradox when we reflected that evangelism materials need to connect meaningfully to the culture in which the evangelism is taking place. In a number of the ARCS case studies, people have avoided the name of Jesus for fear of attack by secularists, fear of giving offence to people from other faiths and fear of being seen as a proselytising fundamentalist (the 'wrong sort of Christian'). These concerns can be recognised as related to a broader cultural concern – strong in St. Mary's – that of being inclusive, non-judgemental.

The 'Jesus-question', as it became known to us, was one of the persistent themes affecting the church life and practice at St. Mary's following the research. In an evaluation interview in March 2010, one PCC member summed up the learning like this:

> **What was the most significant thing to have come out of the research?**
>
> You named the things we weren't doing. We are a busy socially active Church but you encouraged us to ask deeper questions about where Jesus was in all that we do. That was challenging.
>
> (PCC Member Evaluation Interview)

4 *Hospitality without conditions*

One of the themes that the ARCS project sought to explore was the way in which Christianity was present in London as a global city, with a population of great diversity and mobility. At the warm-up meeting with the Rector, he had emphasised the challenges of running a parish with a regular turnover in membership, pointing to the phenomenon of people's leaving London at the point they started a family or retired. In addition, many people lived in central London because they had highly mobile and high pressured jobs and so didn't engage with the church regularly. We were interested in whether Alpha would be a mechanism to overcome some of that anonymity and isolation which can be present in the global city. Here again, what was striking was the significance of St. Mary's' commitment to hospitality of a particular open and inclusive kind:

> The only expectation I think St Mary's places on people is to be present in a Church and to celebrate God as you understand him. It's so non-expectational that it's magnetic! I've started staying for coffee with the people from the Alpha Course after Church on a Sunday. Close friendships are now forming out of this group of lonely misfits. . . . I include myself in that. We all have something and we can all be friends.
>
> (Interview Two, Alpha Course Participant)

> **What should be celebrated about St. Mary's Church?**
>
> Well, I think open-minded is, for me, very important. And then I can come here with some of my gay friends and they feel very welcome and I can come here with Catholic friends and they feel very welcome. The only person I haven't got here is my Jewish friend. So that is very important. I think the fact it is such a wonderful community. I love the fact you can walk around Battersea and bump into people you know from Church. I think it does have something that should suit everybody's taste.
>
> (Interview Three, Alpha Course Participant)

Theology of hospitality

> These practices of friendship and welcome can be seen as responses to the 'shadows' of loneliness etc. in our modern, urban context. The Alpha experience highlights what people are yearning for, what the need is in our modern culture. This would link with the Gospel message. (Feedback Document)

We were struck by the genuineness of the invitation – hospitality without hope of payback was magnetic. Reflecting this back to the church made them realise how precious this was and how central to their aim of sustaining an inclusive ethos. However, there was a counter-cultural element in that people were being invited to eat and talk with people who were different from them. They had to acknowledge that they too might be a 'misfit' in some way – indeed, that we are all, in some way, 'misfits' in society. This was seen as fitting with the portrayal of Jesus' table fellowship in the gospels, as he ate with those on the margins of, or excluded from the 'religious' society of his day. Of course, the Gospels speak of Jesus' eating with 'sinners' – language clearly at odds with the contemporary cultural Christian expression of hospitality and inclusivity embodied at St. Mary's. There is a shift in language here, seen as necessary to this outreach of hospitality, which shares some resonances with the theme of 'Jesus-language' noted in the previous disclosure.

5 Parish in the late modern global city

The Church of England parish system is based upon a desire to worship and represent God in a particular place, and for many, there remain residual expectations that people will attend the church in the parish in which they reside. Indeed, this long tradition of the parochial as characteristic of the Church of England has become one of the main themes in debates around Fresh Expressions communities, which seem to base church on less located, geographically delineated social realities.[5] The ARCS team, aware of these debates, were interested in exploring the nature of parish in a global city, and of questioning, in particular, whether and in what ways the tradition of located parish could continue to have any currency in this setting. In the warm-up meeting, the Rector had painted a picture of a mobile population, and this was supported by data from the survey he conducted:

> 22% have attended the church for five years or less
> 12% have attended for between five and ten years
> 25% plan to move from Battersea in the next ten years (Survey Data)

St. Mary's can be understood as a community with a stable core, around which were a good number of people in transition.

We looked at the interview data to see if there was evidence of what motivated attendance at St. Mary's; in particular, how far was this a church which gathered the local population, and how far might it be seen a place people travelled to, choosing it for its own particular character.

What is it about St. Mary's that you like?

Being part of a community, and the people because it is very friendly and the fact that it is a range of ages from young people to the elderly. Yeah, a sense of community. Definitely the prayer and [the Rector] and the sermons. That sort of thing.... I love St. Mary's because we got married here and I'd miss it. We feel so welcome here. It really suits us from the sermons, to the family and I think it's difficult to find that – a Church that ticks all the boxes.

(Interview Three, Alpha Course Participant)

Can you tell me the story of how you first became involved at St Mary's Church?

Right, I went with a friend. She'd heard of it and we'd decided to go. It wasn't the parish church where I lived. I wasn't really aware of parish boundaries in those days.

(Interview Four, Alpha Course Leader)

When I first started coming to St Mary's, I was still working then. I came to recharge my batteries, and I tended to come to the 8am where it was quiet and there were no children, and I didn't necessarily have to talk to anyone if I didn't want to, so it was an oasis! But as the years have gone on, you realise that it is not all about pleasing yourself and that it's also about being part of the body of Christ so that you need to meet and make contact with and understand and be there for other people, not just for yourself, however pleasant it is, so that's the difference.

(Interview Six, Alpha Course Participant)

Well, I came specifically to St Mary's because it was my nearest church and I always have been to church all my life and I also liked it very much as soon as I came. I came from a house in Wandsworth and I bought a boat, which was moored down the river just here. This was my nearest church. I've been ever since. It's very easy when you only live across the road! People I admire are those who travel a long way in. People who move away still come to St. Mary's because it's a very good congregation.

(Interview Seven, Alpha Course Participant)

Summing up our understanding from the interviews on this theme, the ARCS team fed back to the insider team:

Ways of being Church

> In terms of a sense of church, there would seem to be a strong emphasis on the influence of the minister and a focus on relationship and community building. A congregational model of church rather than a larger episcopal sense of church.
>
> (Feedback Document)

One of the espoused theological understandings of the parish system is that each church reflects the diversity of its particular area, bringing together and serving everyone within a particular locality. What we were seeing at St. Mary's was a different kind of diversity – an intentional choosing of diversity born out of a principled commitment to inclusivity. It was this, rather than a sense of parish, that brought people to St. Mary's even if that meant crossing parish boundaries.

Concluding reflections

This case study was the first one where a participant, the Rector, named an insight as a 'breakthrough'. At this stage, we didn't pick up its importance to our emerging methodology, but on-going reflection on the development of theological action research processes helped us recognise this language of 'breakthrough' as key to the revelatory potential of our development of conversation as a theological research instrument. As our sensitivity to the significance of 'epiphanies', 'light-bulb moments' or 'break-through moments' began to contribute to an understanding of theological action research as 'disclosive', so too did our appreciation of feedback and intentional conversation between the ARCS team and practitioner teams become established. The energy generated by feeding back to the PCC was palpable – this was 'where the action is'. This spurred us own to developing ways of better encouraging practitioner reflection and feedback on data, and the development of Joint Feedback meetings and documents more formally.

Notes

1 https://alpha.org.

2 So see for example: Mike Booker and Mark Ireland, *Evangelism – Which Way Now? An Evaluation of Alpha, Emmaus, Cell Church and Other Contemporary Strategies for Evangelism* (Church House Publishing, 2003); Chris Hand, *Falling Short? The Alpha Course Examined* (Day One Publications, 1998); Elizabeth McDonald, *Alpha: The Unofficial Guide. Overview: A Whole New Study on the Alpha Course* (Cambridge: St Matthew, 2001); Paul Tracey, *Spreading the Word: The Microfoundations of Institutional Persuasion and Conversion* (Informs Science; Organization Science, 2016).

3 Grace Davie, *Religion in Britain Since 1945: Believing Without Belonging* (Blackwell, 1994).

4 At this early stage in the ARCS project the practice of separate insider and outsider feedback, being brought together conversationally in a joint feedback document was yet to be routinely established.

5 Most influentially see Andrew Davison and Alison Milbank, *For the Parish: A Critique of Fresh Expressions* (SCM, 2010).

7 Church in mission

Learning ecclesial ek-centricity

> My understanding of Stewardship has changed dramatically since the first meeting. I had completely misunderstood its meaning and importance.... I thought it was based on the need for the laity to become more involved in parish life due to lack of priests and the likelihood of fewer priests in the future ... [but] Stewardship is recognising that everything comes from God and everything is a gift.... How and when we use our gifts will change over time depending on personal circumstances but there will always be a way that what we have can be used to spread God's message.
>
> (Portsmouth Diocese, F3, Questionnaire Response)

The church is "missionary by its very nature".[1] This quote, used by Stephen Bevans and Roger Schroeder to head the first chapter in their highly influential work on mission,[2] identifies a growing consensus in recent decades. As the churches in the post-Christendom West struggle to re-understand themselves in increasingly secularised and religiously plural cultures, Christians have been put back in touch with this central, Gospel truth about who we are, and to what we are called. The growing scholarly literature in missiology[3] has reminded ecclesiologists, in particular, that the Christian community's prime – even single – end is "that each person may be able to find Christ, in order that Christ may walk with each person the path of life, with the power of the truth about man [sic] and the world that is contained in the mystery of the Incarnation and the Redemption and with the power of the love that is radiated by that truth".[4] Such an ecclesial *telos* clearly must have implications for how church is construed for our own times. At the same time, the re-assertion of the *missio Dei* (of which more below) has repositioned church in relation to a mission which is fundamentally *God's*. The missionary church is a church of service to the Triune God whose very being dynamically reaches out to all creation in a mission for its participation in divine life.

The concern for church as missionary is not only a matter for academic theological voices; it has also engendered new outreach practices and ecclesial change. At the structural level of church, both the Roman Catholic Church and the Church of England explicitly set church policy around mission when naming the decade prior to the onset of the third millennium "the decade for evangelisation/evangelism".[5] Arguably this decade's activities did not see much real impact in relation to church growth[6] and served largely to highlight the real struggles ahead for any traditionally structured church in facing the challenge of what Pope John Paul II referred to as "the New Evangelisation".[7] However, in the wake of this experience, and perhaps provoked by the perceived 'failure' of the decade for evangelisation/evangelism, considerable energy was unleashed. This can be seen particularly in the Church of England's exploration of the different ways of being church needed to meet the new missionary challenges – an exploration increasingly shared in the United Kingdom by the Methodist and United Reformed Churches.[8] I refer here to the publication in 2004 of *Mission-Shaped Church: Church Planting and Fresh Expressions of Church in a Changing Context*,[9] and the extensive discussions that surrounded it, and continue as Fresh Expressions and Church Planting practices develop and are researched.[10] I would suggest that the 'new movements' within the Roman Catholic Church, whilst significantly different in their ecclesiology from either Fresh Expressions or Church Planting, nonetheless embody a similar search to respond in new ways to our current contexts.[11]

To take all this seriously as an ecclesiologist is to re-vision church, in its complexity of structures, practices and theological self-understanding. This chapter explores how learning from the ARCS co-researching practices can aid in this task. In particular, what follows argues that the work with our co-researchers evinced a specific embodied theology which speaks particularly to the long-observed tensions around 'maintenance and mission' – the classic and perennial tension of the *ecclesia ad intra* and the *ecclesia ad extra*.[12] What we see is not only the lived experience of this persistent ecclesiological tension, but also demonstrations of the fruits of the tension, as well as its better-recognised problems. What emerges is a re-reading of 'maintenance/mission' in terms of an '*ek*-centricity' in which church is both centred and called out from itself.

The ARCS project determined from the outset to explore specifically sites of practice concerned with evangelisation, understood in its broadest sense. Here, the differentiation between 'evangelisation' and 'evangelism' – so far merely alluded to without definition – is important. Broadly speaking, these different terms reflect Catholic and Church of England/Protestant terminology respectively – hence the different naming of the decade for evangelisation/evangelism by the Roman Catholic and Church of England leaders. Behind this difference of ecclesial usage, however, lies a difference of missionary sense: whilst 'evangelism' has traditionally been seen as the conversions of people to faith, 'evangelisation' has a decidedly wider sense, broadening mission to include the "evangelisation of cultures",[13] situations, and the establishment of the Kingdom through the *consecratio mundi* – the consecration of the world to Christ through human activity within it.[14] This does not in any way exclude conversion of people, of course, but it raises complex questions as to how cultural and structural transformation relates to personal conversion. It is this broad understanding of mission as evangelisation that informed our work in the ARCS project, whilst our awareness of the differing emphases on cultural transformation and personal conversion served to provoke questions as to what was being seen in the varied forms of mission and outreach demonstrated by our co-researchers.

The variety of ways in which this evangelising work can be understood is reflected in the practices we worked with and learnt from. Evangelisation is variously interpreted as work for social justice (A: LJV, E: Housing Justice, G: CAFOD), catechesis (B: Westminster Agency for Evangelisation), outreach to the un-churched (D: Messy Church, C: St Mary's), or renewal of existing church members and structures (F: Portsmouth Diocese), with diverse and complex points of contact and areas of overlap between these interpretations. The contention of this chapter is that the voices from these practices contribute to a fuller understanding of the theology of mission and church,[15] particularly by drawing attention to the difficulties with living out the *missio Dei* within contexts shaped not only by late modern cultural assumptions but also by certain limitations in ecclesial life and tradition. In what follows, this learning is arranged under two headings. First, I use the data to describe what we called 'the *ad intra* pull' that seemed prevalent and significant for the ways in which the well-recognised 'maintenance-mission' tension was experienced in the practices. Building on this, I suggest that the practices have things to teach us about the ways in which this (necessary?) tension can be lived so as better to enable the kind of ecclesial and ecclesiological learning that is needed for the churches to live *ek*-centrically – outwards from their centres. What becomes clear is that ways of real living are needed which do not offer 'maintenance' or 'mission' as alternatives or differentiated tasks; but rather, our understanding of church needs to be construed in terms which newly identify *what* is to be 'maintained' and how, *in order that* 'mission' can be served out from the centre toward the world.

The *ad intra* pull

Ecclesiologically, the focus on mission might be most properly understood as referring us to the church *ad extra* – that is, the church understood in terms of its life and work toward its 'outside', in 'the world'. The motivation and espoused theologies of all the co-researchers in the ARCS project reflected a passion for looking outward, all be it in their varied ways and organisational situations. It was therefore striking to see just how difficult it was in practice for many of these groups to resist a pull back into more ecclesiastical, or *ad intra*, concerns, even whilst maintaining that these very concerns were, nonetheless, a kind of mission. As our reflections developed, we began to refer to this as the *ad intra* pull – the centripetal realities of structural church life which exerted a particular power over the practices of mission and outreach.

As one might expect, this phenomenon was most clearly seen in those practices closely related to diocesan church structures. Indeed, this can be seen as the dominant theme across all the learning points identified by the Westminster Agency for Evangelisation research. As a clerically led team, at the heart of diocesan structures, this Agency demonstrated a vivid living with a "tension"[16] between their evangelistic motivation and the largely catechetical and educational burden of their actual work. The strongly held sense of the Agency as *having* to understand its purpose in terms of "the bishop's work no matter what we think individually" (B2, Director) effectively limited the flourishing of any personally espoused sense of mission. The exchange between Agency Team 3 and the Director set out in B2 is a striking example of how the tentative struggle to name something like a *missio Dei* theology – "something bigger than us" – is met with a strong affirmation of the episcopal mandate, almost as if *this* is the "something bigger". At the same time, as described in chapter 6, this evangelisation team was constantly feeling frustrated by the assumptions from parishes (laity and clergy) that their work was really about sacramental catechesis – the resourcing of sacramental preparation largely for children and young people.

In this case, the practice group worked hard to read their real (catechetical) practices in terms of their evangelising sense of purpose. The pedagogical practices of both catechesis and adult education were construed as ways of "facilitating evangelisation at a local level" (B4, Agency Team 2), equipping people for the works of mission in their own contexts. Shared scriptural reflection by the Agency Team on the Road to Emmaus story (Luke 24:13–35) enabled a constructive sense of their work as simultaneously pedagogical and evangelising, as they sought to "meet people where they are" (B4). Especially intriguing is the team's suggestion of a possible reading of the Emmaus disciples' return to Jerusalem as a proper *ad intra* "return to church" which had its own missionary necessity and purpose (B4). Here, we glimpse a dynamic of 'in-and-out', coming-and-going, with regards to church and outreach, which goes some way to mitigating any unhelpful polarisation or division of the work of mission in relation to church structures.

That being said, the Westminster Agency's experience highlights the difficulty, particularly for ecclesiastically structured initiatives, in breaking open practices of church maintenance to more radical practices of mission 'in the world'. This can be sharply identified in the Portsmouth diocesan stewardship process, where, from the beginning, the internal concerns of the Pastoral Plan around falling numbers of clergy and anticipated parish closures were in some tension with the more missionary extensive vision of church expressed through the adopted stewardship process (F1). The espoused intentions of stewardship – to renew the life of laity in the world of work, family and the 'ordinary' – were consistently felt as something for which neither clergy nor lay people themselves were equipped (F3). Indeed, many of the parish audits of "gifts and talents" shared with the ARCS team fell into the familiar patterns of asking what gifts people might bring to parish life, rather than encouraging the naming of graced living "Monday to Saturday",[17] and the gifts exercised in the home, workplace and the day-to-day patterns of life.

The Portsmouth practitioners were, perhaps, more ready than their Westminster colleagues to surface this tension as a real difficulty for them. As a result, their responses shed a little more light on the underlying dynamics of this *ad intra* pull. In part, it was seen as related to differences in ecclesiology.[18] The stridently expressed account of the diocesan Head of Finance and Property (F3) witnesses to there actually being quite distinct understandings of church operative in the diocese, which read the question of ordained and lay participation in mission rather differently. If, like him, we adopt an ecclesiology which is predominantly about the mission of lay people in the world (*ad extra*) served by a few clergy, the tendency toward any *ad intra* pull can be quickly recognised as improper and responded to as such. However, another ecclesiological position is identified, counter to this, which is typified here as Jesus wanting the church "to run like a well-oiled machine". This – often implicit – ecclesiology will tend to valorise the organisational work and life of churches, suggesting that lay people are called to serve these realities as the number of ordained men diminish. Here, the *ad intra* pull can be seen as something to be welcomed – often at the expense of mission energy and activity. A fundamental ecclesiological question is identified: how, *in practice*, does the community and organisational life of the church, with all its demands, relate to the ends of mission? As theological action researchers committed to serving Christians in their living of an evangelising faith, we must face the concomitant challenge as to what might be learnt from practice-engaged theology about how the churches might resist any *ad intra* pull which militates against their stated aims of mission and evangelisation.

Something like this question is raised in the Portsmouth practitioners' reflections on the formation needed for an *ad extra* way of being church. The question of formation for both laity and clergy is raised in F3 as the diocesan pastoral team identified through the research process this central question for their work:

> How to shift focus of stewardship away from over emphasis on 'churchy' things towards a 24/7 living out of discipleship?

The difficulty in responding to this question can be acutely felt in the pastoral team's accompanying recognition that "we have not equipped people.... we have been inward looking, not outward looking" (F3). The kind of formative resources and practices that enabled laity to expand their notions of stewardship (F3, Questionnaire), and freed ordained men to rediscover and celebrate their own gifts and talents (F2, Parish Priest Interview) appear as important, if elusive, keys to any resistance to the *ad intra* pull. Yet, as the experience of the Westminster Agency showed, this could not simply be a matter of putting on more courses; rather, it requires an appropriation of an ecclesiological shift, a change in church culture, which enables a formation-in-ordinary of laity and clergy such that 'the worldly' is truly lived as *the* place of grace, and the work of the Spirit. It is this, the Portsmouth data suggests, that freed people up to live evangelistically (F3 Questionnaire; F2, Parish Priest Interview).

To make these observations is not simply – or even – a criticism of these diocesan agencies whose work was clearly effective and enabling of many groups in their areas. Rather, we refer to the experiences of these two as explicit examples of a wider, we might even say all-pervasive tendency to collapse evangelisation into the *ad intra* work of the church. The parish priest's desire to make the Housing Justice initiative "more religious" (E1, Clergy Interview 1), and the tensions around what belonging to church might look like for the Messy Church mothers (D2), indicate that this centripetal ecclesial understanding was at work, in varying degrees, for many, if not all, of these outreach practices. The data makes clear that the immediacy and familiarity of the more 'maintenance' focussed work almost inevitably dominates the practical day-to-day activities of those involved. The Westminster Agency team was aware of a certain anxiety as to whether what they were doing was really evangelisation. The "usual context" was one where "people present themselves for sacraments" (B4, Agency Team 4), eliciting a catechetical response from the Agency. The sacramental routine – whilst in some sense evangelising itself – can also be recognised as a deflection of energies away from bringing Christ into people's lives who have not known him before – a major part of the self-understanding of the Agency's purpose. The risk is that 'sacramentalising' takes the place of evangelising, and a theology of the routinisation of God's grace becomes operant – all be it unwittingly.

There is, in all this, an outstanding learning point, drawn from the experiences of the (even unsuccessful) struggle to be *ad extra* in our living of church. Both the Westminster Agency's re-visioning of their work as "facilitators of evangelisation", and the Portsmouth diocesan team's growing emphasis on stewardship as extra-ecclesial, and characteristically lay, suggest a first ecclesiological insight: that mission as such is most effectively carried out from the *ad extra* places of church, the places of lay living, of Christian discipleship in the world. Diocesan bodies' very nature as structurally *ad intra* seems to limit their effectiveness as primary evangelising agencies, This work is more fully embodied and worked out from the world, where the church lives its lay apostolate.[19] The ecclesiological paradox is that, in practice, this apostolate in and for the world both depends upon *and* is hampered by the structural, organisational life and demands of the churches.

Hard lessons in *ek*-centric church

This paradox of *ad extra* and *ad intra*, with its practical tendency of the former being pulled back into the latter, shapes the many lessons to be learnt from the co-researching practitioners' experiences of struggling to be missionary, evangelising. However, this is a more complex tension than might be resolved by simply cutting 'lay' initiatives off from the structural churches. As we shall see, the experience of being simultaneously 'held' by the centred church community and compelled out into God's bigger world was often painful but also fruitful. It is here that the language of *ek*-centricity comes into play, as my attempt to describe a practical ecclesiology in which church life is simultaneously centred and yet centri*fugal* in its energies.

One of the places we saw this painful yet fruitful holding of the *ad intra-ad extra* tension was in the Messy Church research.[20] Here, the breaking point of the conversations, leading to significant disclosures around Messy Church as "church lite", or "a church of the (as yet) unknown God" (D2), lay in the way that the data confronted the Messy Church leadership team with realities which failed to match what they had hoped, worked and prayed for. In fact, the data offered a different account of church, faith and conversion than that commonplace in their *ad intra* experience. What was evident was not a community clearly centred on Jesus or the Gospel – despite the vibrant and important relationships being built at Messy Church. Indeed, for some respondents the structural links to Christian church were problematic: "In my perfect ideal world there would be an equivalent of this that was not necessarily religious" (D2, Interview Six). For the majority, it seemed that the fact that the organisers "don't go overboard on religion" (D2, Interview Seven), and that "it's not really focused on religion" (D2, Interview Eight) was a definite positive. The mothers really appreciated and valued Messy Church – but precisely *because* it was on the edges of religion, church and explicit faith.

One of the things going on in this Messy Church story is that the leadership in the church – themselves committed Christians and "Sunday church" people – were effectively exercising their instincts around hospitality, welcome and lack of judgment, discussed in chapter 6 above. They know that, culturally and contextually, a certain reserve about faith and church was necessary in order to foster the community of Messy Church as successfully as they had. At the same time, both the Messy Church practices of worship and Gospel-based play and activity, as well as the evangelising hearts of the leadership team, sought to centre Messy Church on those same things which are central to "Sunday church" life. The outreach of Messy Church depended upon the *ad intra* life and practices of the hosting and facilitating church. At the same time, the difference between these two ecclesial expressions – Sunday church and Messy Church – was initially experienced as worrying, disappointing, challenging by our co-researchers. Ultimately, it led to a 'stretching' of the notion of church, for both practitioners and eccleisologists,[21] in which the ecclesial graces present in Messy Church could be rightly celebrated and fostered as such, whilst – and through – holding them in relationships with the explicit community of faith. The graces *ad extra* are recognised, named and nurtured from the *ad intra* life; but in doing so, the *ad extra* experience reshaped the *ad intra* understanding of church life, outreach and its purposes.

Coming from quite a different ecclesial tradition, St. Mary's Battersea's experience of welcome and outreach nonetheless holds at its heart a similar set of challenges as found in Messy Church, Croydon. Similarly to Messy Church – and a number of other of our practice groups – hospitality, welcome and inclusion, had been highlighted as central to St. Mary's mission (C1, C4). Here we see the importance of the ways in which especially lay expressions of the church's *ad extra* mission were appropriately instinctive about cultural realities and assumptions.[22] However, what became clear, even in the 'success' of such generous hospitality (for example, C4, Interview 2), was that there were certain lacks – of being centred on Jesus (C3), of movement from guest to host (C1), and of a clear sense of what people were being welcomed into. The conversations highlighted the need to accompany welcome and inclusion with an answer to the 'into what?' question – a question which, in the context of this chapter's argument, can be recognised as a practical expression not only of the tension between *ad extra* and *ad intra* living of church but also of their mutual dependence.

Similar holding together of the *ad extra* and *ad intra* can be glimpsed elsewhere across the projects. Perhaps most vivid was the LJV experience of having the often demanding and even distressing experiences of living faith alongside those on the margins 'held' and made life-giving through the return to a community and embodied tradition. Through this *ad intra* formation it became possible for volunteers to "see God present in your life every day" (A5, Outsider Feedback Document, p1). The volunteers at Housing Justice also worked *within* the tension of *ad intra* and *ad extra* church, recognising – even if in complex ways – that both liturgical celebration of the Eucharist and being with the homeless guests were ways of embodying that "you love God" (E3, Richard). Arguably the CAFOD reflection on the difference between the "fig-leaf" of the "pope quote" and the deep appropriation of the flavouring "bay leaf" of Catholic Social Teaching (G1), also reflects not only the difficulty of relating out-reach to mainstream, organisational church but also the potential in keeping that relationship alive and vibrant. The challenge was, for all practitioners, how to remain true to their missionary, culturally sensitive instincts whilst still enabling their *ad extra* practices to be vivified by the explicit and organised faith community of church.[23]

Conclusions: discerning the *missio Dei*

Learning from our practitioner co-researchers about living church outwardly has been framed in this chapter by the perennial tension between mission and maintenance, *ecclesia ad extra* and *ecclesia ad intra*. I have argued that in theologising with faith-full practices, we learn not only about the problem with this tension but also about its necessity and fruitfulness. For where these groups were able to embody a dynamic of exit and return in relation to church and find ways of 'stretching' understanding and insight across the within and without of church and faith, practice and mission can be seen as enriched and revivified, as can the organisation of church. Church is not simply lived *ad intra* on the one hand and *ad extra* on the other, but rather *ek*-centrically, as the centre holds fast, whilst at the same time ecclesial dynamics work centrifugally, compelling energies out from the centre itself.

I want to suggest that the practical living of this tension might also be helpfully construed as the discerning of the *missio Dei*. In using this term I am referring to what has now become one of the key theological themes for missiology, transforming understanding away from ecclesial agency and activism in mission, toward a focus on the agency of God in all true mission (and indeed, in all true church).[24] For the ecclesiologist, of particular note here is the way in which this way of thinking has thrown into relief a certain differentiation between the *missio Dei* and the *missio ecclesiae*, with significant ecclesiological implications. For once this differentiation is made, it raises the question as to how far 'church' – especially understood as structural or institutional – does, and even *can*, serve this mission of God. Indeed, some come close to regarding church as most often an obstacle to God's mission[25] – a deeply challenging position which is not without its practical resonances as we have seen. Nor is such a position, as might first be assumed, a radical Protestant position: Pope John Paul II, having named mission as "the single end" of the church, goes on to speak of how "Jesus Christ becomes, in a way, newly present, in spite of all his apparent absences, *in spite of* all the limitations of the presence and of the institutional activity of the Church".[26] In the terms explored in this chapter, might it be that the *ecclesia ad intra* hopelessly obstructs the missionary intentions of the *ecclesia ad extra*, even to the extent that the describing of faith-full life in the world as *ecclesia* needs to be abandoned as too ecclesial, preferring, instead, a non-ecclesiological account of *missio Dei*?

How such a question is responded to will, in large part, depend on one's ecclesiological tradition and commitment, of course. However, even within this highly contested relationship of church and *missio Dei*, it seems to me that our practice-based reflections offer a particular insight: that the *ad intra* realities of church life are most helpfully patterned when they are enabled to serve the *ad extra* as a source of discerning divine agency in the world. The need for all faith-full work *ad extra*, toward, in and for 'the world' to respond to the divine agency of the *missio Dei*, requires that we know how to discern that divine agency with wisdom and humility. In the following chapters, we will see a little more of what has been learnt from these practices concerning the importance of certain gifts – of community, sacrament, service, scripture and church traditions – that the church *ad intra* can bring to this on-going work of discerning what the Triune God is doing ahead of us in the world. The challenge is how to live ecclesial practices and shape ecclesiology in such ways as to be true to such an account of centrifugal *ek*-centric church.

Notes

1 Second Vatican Council's Decree on the Mission Activity of the Church, *Ad Gentes* 2.
2 Stephen B. Bevans and Roger P. Schroeder, *Constants in Context: A Theology of Mission for Today* (Orbis Books, 2004).
3 A number of such works will be referenced, all be it briefly, in this chapter, though the literature is far more extensive. Of particular note are: Stephen Bevans and Roger Schroeder, op. cit; David J. Bosch, *Transforming Mission: Paradigm Shifts in Theology of Mission* (Orbis Books, 1991); Darrell Guder ed., *Missional Church: A Vision for the Sending of the Church in North America* (Eerdmans, 1998); Leslie Newbigin, *Trinitarian Faith and Today's Mission* (John Knox Press, 1964); Leslie Newbigin, *The Open Secret: Introduction to the Theology of Mission.* Rev. ed. (Eerdmans, 1996); Cathy Ross and Stephen Bevans eds. *Mission on the Way to Emmaus: Constants, Contexts, and Prophetic Dialogue* (Orbis Books, 2013); Cathy Ross and Colin Smith eds. *Missional Conversations: A Dialogue Between Theory and Praxis in World Mission* (SCM, 2018); Robert Schreiter ed., *Mission in the Third Millennium* (Orbis Books, 2001); Andrew Walls, *The Missionary Movement in Christian History: Studies in the Transmission of Faith* (Orbis Books, 1996). In this chapter I am especially indebted to Bevans and Schroeder, op. cit., whilst having some critical reservations about their typology.
4 John Paul II's Encyclical, *Redemptor Hominis*, 1979, 13. The assertion of this mission as the church's "single end" set the tone for this pontificate in which the Vatican II emphasis on evangelisation came powerfully to the fore.
5 John Paul II, Encyclical, *Redemptoris Missio*, 1990; Lambeth Conference 1988.
6 See, for example, the evaluative study carried out by Leslie Francis, University of Warwick, "Growth or decline in the Church of England during the Decade of Evangelism: did the churchmanship of the bishop matter?". Available at: http://wrap.warwick.ac.uk/2877/1/WRAP_Francis_0673558-ie-170210-decade_of_evangelism_mla.pdf. Accessed August 2019.
7 The term "New Evangelization" was especially coined to refer to mission within those countries previously recognised as "Christian" – a response to the effects of rapid secularisation and increasing pluralism in the West. More profoundly, however, the challenges of the attitudes and instincts of the 'ordinary Christian' needed addressing as much as cultural change. So see: Phillip Knights and Andrea Murray, *Evangelisation in England and Wales: A Report to the Catholic Bishops* (London, Catholic Communications Service, 2002).
8 So see: www.methodist.org.uk/our-work/our-work-in-britain/evangelism-growth/new-places-for-new-people-starting-christian-communities/fresh-expressions/; and https://urc.org.uk/our-work/fresh-expressions.html.

9 Mission and Public Affairs Council, *Mission-Shaped Church: Church Planting and Fresh Expressions of Church in a Changing Context* (Church House Publishing, 2004).

10 Proximate to the original report are: Sally Gaze, *Mission-Shaped and Rural: Growing Churches in the Countryside* (Church House Publishing, 2006) and the critical response, John M. Hull, *Mission-Shaped Church: A Theological Response* (SCM Press, 2006). Significant thinking and study around Fresh Expressions and their challenge to practical ecclesiology – critical and affirming – has taken place: Mike Booker and Mark Ireland, *Evangelism – Which Way Now? An Evaluation of Alpha, Emmaus, Cell Church and Other Contemporary Strategies for Evangelism* (Church House Publishing, 2003); Stephen Croft ed., *Mission-shaped Questions – Defining Issues for Today's Church* (Church House Publishing, 2008); Andrew Davison and Alison Milbank, *For the Parish: A Critique of Fresh Expressions* (SCM, 2013); Louise Nelstrop and Martyn Percy eds., *Evaluating Fresh Expressions: Explorations in Emerging Church* (Canterbury Press, 2008); John Walker, *Testing Fresh Expressions: Identity and Transformation* (Ashgate, 2014).

11 See Massimo Faggioli, *Sorting Out Catholics: A Brief History of the New Ecclesial Movements* (Liturgical Press, 2014); and the same author's *The Rising Laity: Ecclesial Movements Since Vatican II* (Paulist Press, 2016).

12 The language of *ad intra* and *ad extra* was adopted in our ARCS conversation, and has its immediate provenance in the debates surrounding the Second Vatican Council. This Council uniquely offered not only a Dogmatic Constitution on the Church (*Lumen Gentium*) treating classic themes of hierarchy, laity, and the nature of the church understood as the Body of Christ, People of God and so forth; but also promulgated a second ecclesiological text, the Pastoral Constitution on the Church in the Modern world (*Gaudium et Spes*). Cardinal Josef Suenens is generally credited for using the language of *ad intra* and *ad extra* in describing these two 'faces' of the Council's account of Church, and the terms were quickly picked up and became established.

13 Pope Paul VI's Apostolic Exhortation, *Evangelii Nuntiandi* (1975): 20.

14 See Vatican II, Dogmatic Constitution on the Church, *Lumen Gentium*, 34.

15 I am indebted to conversations with and insights from James Butler, whose unpublished PhD, *Exploring the Lived Theology of Small Missional Communities: Uncovering Charismatic Practices and Beliefs to Enable Sustained Engagement in Social Action* (Durham University, 2017). Available at: http://etheses.dur.ac.uk/12849/. Accessed August 2019, shares a number of similar concerns to those expressed here, all be it in rather different contexts.

16 A word, we should note, that they were uncomfortable with – see B1, Agency Team 2, at least in so far as it might convey restraint, or being 'caught'.

17 I borrow this phrase form the Church of England's *Setting God's People Free* project. It is striking that this very recent initiative is recognising the struggle to effect a fundamental "culture change" in that church which enables lay living of faith "in the world" to be privileged and surfaced, in the face of a tradition of emphasis on "clerical" leadership (both ordained and non-ordained). See www.churchofengland.org/SGPF. Accessed August 2019.

18 One of Bevans' and Schroeder's missiological constants, we should note. These 'constants identify for these authors the significant nodes of theological debate for missiology. What one believes about one's ecclesiology, Christology, anthropology and so forth fundamentally shapes missionary practice.

19 The use of the word 'lay' here is not exclusive of ordained people. Rather it refers us to the primary baptismal calling of Christians to live their faith 'in the world', in a 'secular' or 'lay' context. For the understanding of 'lay' as characteristically

'secular see: Vatican II, Dogmatic Constitution on the Church, *Lumen Gentium*, 31. This was later helpfully elaborated by John Paul II, Apostolic Exhortation, *Christifideles Laici* (1988): 9.

20 This was subsequently written up and published: Clare Watkins and Bridget Shepherd, "The Challenge of 'Fresh Expressions' to Ecclesiology. Reflections from the Practice of Messy Church." *Ecclesial Practices* 1 (2014): 92–110.

21 This is illustrated in more detail in the article cited note 20 above.

22 See the discussions of hospitality in chapter 6 above. Human Culture is another of the missiological constants – or fundamental theological themes – identified by Bevans and Schroeder, op. cit.

23 This is an important and ongoing discussion within Pioneer Ministry. For example, see Clare Watkins, "Ek-centric Ecclesiology: Innovation, Agency and the Holding of Tradition." *Anvil* 35, no.3 (2019).

24 Bevans and Schroeder give a very helpful account of the growth of this move, highlighting its rootedness in the fundamental revelation of God as Trinity – the God who goes out from Godself in mission to humanity. Ibid. 286ff. Here the earlier Trinitarian insights of Karl Barth and his influence in mid and late twentieth century Protestant missionary thought, and the growing Trinitarian sense of Church developed in twentieth century Catholic ecclesiology, notably and authoritatively through the Second Vatican Council, are foundational. The resurgence in Trinitarian theology in the 1980s onwards further enriched this deepening of missiology's Trinitarian roots and self-understanding in terms of the *missio Dei*.

25 Johannes Hoekendijk, see Bevans and Schroeder, op. cit. 291.

26 John Paul II Encyclical, *Redemptor Hominis* (1979): 13. My emphases.

Account of practice D

Messy Church, Croydon

Project time frame: January 2010–December 2010

Introductory narrative

At the time of the research, Messy Church was one of the fastest growing networks of Fresh Expressions with well over a thousand registered groups, broadly based both ecumenically and geographically, and it remains one of the most widely adopted forms of Fresh Expressions.[1] Begun in 2004, its founders sought to create church for local families who were unable or unwilling to attend church on a Sunday morning. In response, they offered imaginative Bible-based craft activities for parents and their children *to do together* on a week day evening, followed by a short informal service of prayer and thanksgiving and a sit-down meal. This became a powerful magnet for attracting new families to the church, giving church people opportunities for creating new Christ-centred community.

This chapter recounts the story of ARCS working with Messy Church at Emmanuel Church, South Croydon. This was a large, lively evangelical Church of England parish in the South London affluent commuter belt, which proclaimed its identity boldly in its motto: 'All for Jesus – Jesus for all'.[2] This parish's Messy Church began as a pilot project in 2008 instigated by the curate with six families; six months later, it had grown to 130 people. At the time of the research, this Messy Church met once a month on a Monday afternoon from 3.30 to 5.30 for a short, all-age service based on a Bible story, followed by games and crafts on the theme of the story, and ending with a meal for the children. Messy Church Extra had also been introduced, meeting monthly (in the intervening fortnight) for a shorter service in the church with no meal. The leadership team of women who ran this Messy Church had had professional careers and were now taking time out for family. They were a committed group of Christians who longed 'to be and make disciples'.[3]

Following a meeting of an ARCS team member with Lucy Moore, the national co-ordinator of Messy Church, it became clear that the ARCS research and Messy Church's own desire to research its practices could be the basis of a fruitful co-researching partnership. It was agreed that a London Messy Church could be included in the ARCS project, and the curate at Emmanuel Church was approached and responded enthusiastically to the idea of engaging in a participatory action research project. Two warm-up meetings were held in the homes of women on the Messy Church organising committee. These meetings involved two ARCS team members perching on the sofa, taking minutes on the coffee table, with small children running around the room. It soon became clear that making time for reflection was a new experience for this group. These were can-do mums, accustomed to non-stop action, ideas and creativity. They initially found the theological action research methodological process difficult to grasp and the ARCS team later learned that the research-trained curate had to engage in a degree of one-to-one follow-up, encouragement and translation of the ARCS language to get the project off the ground. Yet the mothers' commitment, curiosity and passion for Messy Church shone through and they were soon united behind a burning research question: how does Messy Church make disciples? Already in the raising of this question, certain things were becoming clear: firstly, that the bringing of people to follow Jesus Christ was a real desire on the part of Messy Church leaders and that, at the same time, the practices they experienced were casting a new light on what such discipleship might look like.

The decision was made to collect data both through participant observation, carried out by members of the Messy Church team, and through interviews with participating parents, carried out by the ARCS fieldworker. Some 15 participant observations were made, and eight interviews were carried out. Participant observations followed a pattern of standard questions – how many people were in attendance, how people appeared to be interacting, how people appeared to be reacting to 'religious' activities etc. – which were responded to by members of the leadership team.

Before the interviews were conducted and an interview schedule drafted, the insider team of mothers and two members of the ARCS team reflected upon the participant observation data. This opening exercise was important, especially for the Messy Church leadership team, challenging as it did certain assumptions they had had – for example, around the Bible story being assumed as an 'awkward moment' for families in the sessions. 'Soft' features of the Messy Church gathering were recognised, including thoughtful hospitality, welcome, and 'ordinary' conversation building up relationship:

> I overheard a mother sharing a story about her health problems to another mother – they weren't discussing their journey to the

> Lord, but nevertheless it was an important point of support and relationship.
>
> (Messy Church Team Participant Observer)

Indeed, the leadership team began to see many of their assumed practices in a new light through these observation exercises:

> How can we avoid our prayers being a list of needs for God to meet? How do we nurture in the children a relationship with God and a knowledge that they are loved?
>
> (Messy Church Team Participant Observer)

It is perhaps worth noting that acting as observers was, for some members of the team, a rather difficult and unsatisfactory process. This may reflect a need for greater training for such work, but also highlights questions around the nature of relationships existing between the leadership of Messy Church and the participants – relationships which are often primarily friendships forged between mums in the same situation, whilst also, in this context, having something of a pastoral quality. Something of this complication lay behind the decision made by the Messy Church leadership team to invite the ARCS Fieldworker to carry out in-depth interviews with eight new mothers. The mothers leading the group felt understandably uncomfortable about interviewing friends about explicitly faith-based questions; the sensitivities around friendship and the ways that perceived proselytising might affect that friendship were keenly and often justifiably felt. Once again, a cultural sensitivity around explicit naming of evangelism/evangelisation can be discerned.

None of the interviewees selected attended Emmanuel Church on a Sunday morning. One mother attended a Baptist church regularly, one was a lapsed Catholic, another a non-practising Muslim and the rest had no present-day connection with a church outside of Messy Church. The leadership mothers took enormous care to ensure that interviewees felt comfortable and unthreatened by the experience with details in place such as a fresh brew of coffee, pastry and the offer of free childcare during the interview. Yet despite these efforts, when the fieldworker touched upon personal faith identities, the body language of some mothers indicated that this was an unwelcomed inquisition.

Both the ARCS team and the Messy Church team reflected on the data generated from the interviews which was rich and layered. Whilst using somewhat different approaches in these reflections, the two teams were able to share reflections and produce a Joint Feedback Document, enriched by the active interest and involvement of the vicar of Emmanuel Church and Lucy Moore at the Joint Feedback Meeting. Something of the findings from the research were subsequently published.[4] Below, we work with five themes as our disclosures, focusing especially on the ecclesiological learning that was experienced for both teams.

Five disclosures

1 Discipleship: a long and complex journey

It was the 'making of disciples' that was the heartfelt focus of the research for the insider team, and it was here that a significant learning for both teams took place. First and foremost, what became apparent from the interview data was the huge range and depth of attitudes of attending mothers towards faith, together with the length of time it took to build trusting relationships given their wariness of church. The disclosure for both insider and outsider teams was that growing in discipleship was a longer and more complex journey than had been supposed. Here is just one example:

I: Since coming to Messy Church, has it changed in any way your view of the church?

R: Yeah, it has a little bit actually. I think for a long time I was very much an atheist and I think coming to the church has made me slightly more agnostic. I just feel a little bit more connected and I really love the feeling of the community and the feeling of support and it's made me, you know, kind of almost doubt some of my previous beliefs a little bit, you know. So I think it has changed. And I think it's also made me more willing to be more flexible with my own children and say "well, you know, if they want to be part of this then that doesn't bother me". Or maybe in years to come, I might change a little bit. I don't know. I'm a bit, you know, the jury's out, kind of thing.... There definitely has been some kind of softening and I think before I saw [the Church] as a little bit more of a kind of institution and a bit more perhaps dictatorial, and I think, through attending Messy Church, I now see it as something that's a bit softer than that.

I: And how about your views of God?

R: Yeah it has, it has affected my views of God. I don't really know how; I think I'm just a bit more open to it. I think before, it was very much a closed book for me because I come from a non-religious family and almost a slightly anti-religion family, not only non-religious, almost slightly anti-religion. I think that's sort of what I was brought up with and that's just really what I followed (Interview One).

The Insider Team reflected upon this quote as follows:

> If the first stage of making disciples is turning people around – from being anti-God and anti-faith to a position of openness – then the

> first stage has been successful in the case of this participant. So if we define disciples as someone who says 'I turn to Christ', this is a turning!
>
> (Insider Feedback Document)

The Outsider feedback document also tried to bring together the different views in the interviews as follows:

> **Discipleship involves a very long journey**
>
> This data firmly illustrates that discipleship involves a very long journey from people's initial contact with church to people coming to faith. The current figure in some literature for this journey is thought to be about three years. This figure matches the time for catechesis in the early church. However, this data demonstrates that there are many different shades of experience along the journey to faith and Messy Church has a challenging task of discerning how best to address everyone's needs and deal sympathetically and reflectively with people's prior experience of Church. In the data, you find evidence of people in transition from atheism, through to tolerant agnosticism, through to people feeling comfortable with their nominal Christian identity through to those explicitly wanting to explore faith further. These transitions are complex and often guilt is a stumbling block for people. What is clear is that Messy Church is clearly touching some of these parents in quite deep ways and this is leading them to ask questions about faith.
>
> (Outsider Feedback Document)

We illustrated these observations with some direct quotes from the interviews, which portrayed ambivalent, but often 'opening up' positions:

> I'm basically very agnostic really.... I'm not quite sure what, if anything, I do believe.
>
> (Interview Four)

> I would like to have that faith that they [the Messy Church leaders] do but ... I think you can just be a nice person and do what are perceived to be good Christian things without being part of a church. I think that's kind of where I am.
>
> (Interview Three)

> It's made me think about [faith] more. It is something that I hadn't thought about for a long time and it's made me think about it more and coming here and seeing there's a big sense of community, I can see that it is something that would be very nice to be involved in. It is very attractive and I do want to come to church but ... I think this

> is too full on. I think I probably need to ease in gently before I could cope with this.
>
> (Interview Six)

Other mothers were very clear that it was for the children that they came to Messy Church for – but "they were okay, thanks". The insider team reflected that some mothers appeared content with being passive recipients rather than active participants/disciples, perhaps embracing Messy Church as a good activity for their children, but not feeling any further need to explore for themselves. At the same time, as we shall see in disclosure four below, the relationship of family, parents and children militates against so clear a division.

2 *'Jesus-less community', 'Church of the unknown God' and Church-lite'*

The complexity of personal views about faith also translated into a complexity of views about the extent to which mothers associated Messy Church with an ecclesial community. It became one of the most challenging questions for both research teams, as to how and in what way Messy Church could see itself as truly 'church' – a major question for Fresh Expressions more generally.

One of the most powerful themes coming through the data was that of community – Messy Church being a welcoming and hospitable place 'to meet up with friends' and 'reconnect with neighbours'. But on reading the interview transcripts, it became clear that these networks of friendships could operate and even be self-perpetuating without any reference to Jesus. Could it be, the Messy Church team found themselves asking, that rather than enabling church as such (as is the goal of a Fresh Expression), the organisers were in fact creating Jesus-less community? The following quotes provoked much discussion and debate amongst the insider team:

> In my perfect ideal world, there would be an equivalent of this that was not necessarily religious where people could come together and discuss all sorts of important issues and stuff in a nice and fun and friendly way that wasn't necessarily religious. However, that's not what church is for.
>
> (Interview Six)

> *In response to the question: Does the idea of Messy Church being in a church put you off?* It doesn't phase me at all. Why would you be against your child going to a local activity, meeting local people and enjoying themselves and it filling an entire afternoon? Because when you're a mum, that's what it's about; it's about filling your week, because if you're at home day in and day out with your children, you do go a bit mad.
>
> (Interview One)

> There are some people I know who are quite active within the church and always attend obviously not just the fun Messy Church bits but seriously and religiously attending [on a Sunday]. And then some I suppose are more like me and they come in and you meet more as a playgroup with added benefits, educational benefits and the church and community feel. So there's a mixture of people who attend.
>
> (Interview Three)

> So my children enjoy the singing and the action to the songs in church. It makes church fun rather than it being religious, dull and sitting down.
>
> (Interview Three)

> I don't find I'm ever at Messy Church and we talk about religion. I don't find that that happens. Maybe it does if people go to Sunday service and have coffee afterwards and they might have taken on board some of the messages, I don't find that the conversations veer around that. But it's just a really nice opportunity to catch up with other mums and just, you know, 'what's going on?' their concerns and if you haven't seen somebody in a month it's just a really nice way to do it.
>
> (Interview Seven)

> They don't go overboard on religion, and I think that people feel comfortable.
>
> (Interview Seven)

> I don't put much on the religious element. Yes, they pray and they sing the songs, but it's not really focused as religion, if you see what I mean?
>
> (Interview Eight)

The idea that 'all' that was being achieved by Messy Church was another mother and child arts and crafts group could have been a cause for some dismay for the insider team especially. However, building on their instinct for what was happening at Messy Church as a real ecclesial grace, the group were able to reflect on these realities through a turning to scripture: Acts 17:23. In this passage, St. Paul uses the altar to 'an unknown God' at Athens as the basis for preaching and evangelism. In a similar way, perhaps, the Messy Church leadership might come to understand their work as properly ecclesial, allowing people to attend a 'church of the (as yet) Unknown God'.[5]

Another response to this question of ecclesial identity was taken up from one of the interviewee's own comments – Messy Church was a kind of 'church lite':

INTERVIEWER: *Do you feel that you're going to church when you come to Messy Church?*

R: A bit like church lite.... It's so kids focused. To me, church is a bit like you sit down and you have the sermon and you sit quietly and you sing your hymns and it's so full on and whatever, not happy and ... It's just I like a proper what I call old church and it is lots of sitting quietly and praying and stuff. No, I wouldn't see [Messy Church] as the same as coming to church. It's something that the church does and I can see it's religious but I don't view it as going to church.
(Interview Six)

This, and testimony from other interviewees, made clear that there is a prevailing sense that Sunday church is 'proper church'. Messy Church is seen instead as church for beginners – a diluted-to-taste, 'church lite' version of the 'real thing'. One mother explains that she brings her children along 'to give them an introduction into the church and religion'. Another says 'I want my children to have exposure to it but I don't want it to be too full on'. Messy Church is appropriate for those who are new to public worship as 'you don't have to worry about being quiet in church'.

Interestingly, again, the insider team picked upon this language and thinking and interpreted it positively, likening these Messy Church experiences with learning to swim in the shallow end of a swimming pool. Messy Church is a place where beginners can be fully immersed in church, where they can explore, play, learn and build confidence, but still keep their feet on the bottom. The opportunity is there to progress deeper should people want to, or simply to enjoy splashing around in the shallow water.

3 'Ecclesiological overflow' – church beyond church

In exploring the data, especially around this vexed question of what it meant to be 'proper church', the outsider team identified a theology of grace implicit in the practice and conversations of the Messy Church team. A key aspect of this was what we named 'ecclesiological overflow'. This was the term the ARCS team began using for those occasions where the data suggested that elements of Messy Church were finding their way out of the explicit ecclesial practice and into the homes of those who participated – through things like stories or songs, or incorporating things made at Messy Church into play or family meals. Most frequently, this osmotic process happened through the children themselves. So, one mother reported being told by her daughter: "Mummy you're not in charge. God's in charge" (Interview 2); and another related how her son didn't like her saying "God" or "Jesus" in a disrespectful way at home (Interview 3). Stories and songs from Messy Church were being picked up through the children at home:

> I think the bits I like most is when we've had the bible stories we go home and I remember X once, when they were having their bath and he said 'I'll be Jesus and the big storm's coming. So you splash waves

> at me'. So it carries on and it just goes to show that he's listening and I can see his face intently listening in church and he gets cross if he can't see what's going on. I think he really does take it in. He calls himself Jesus. 'I'll be Jesus. You be somebody else'.
>
> (Interview Three)

> On the way home, [my child] asked me questions about the stories she'd listened to, you know, and she asked me about.... they had a story one week about, walking past people when they needed help and how one person did stop and help and she was asking me about that and about how when someone's sick you must be nice to them.
>
> (Interview One)

These examples illustrate the very porous nature of the family or household as a place of grace and evangelisation. Friendships developed between mothers at Messy Church, which could also be seen as ecclesiological overflow. The ecclesial grace of Messy Church affected the mothers' wider sense of connectedness within their locality. A number of those interviewed spoke of recognising and chatting to others they passed in the street, or met at the school gates, as a result of their being part of Messy Church. The community of Messy Church seemed to have a clear impact on this 'natural' community of mothers with similar age children living in the same area. However, it would be an oversimplification to see this overflow as one way (from Messy Church into the local community); it was also clear that Messy Church was building on a "natural gracedness" of a community of parents, with their shared concerns and experiences, quite apart from any faith dimension.

This is outlined in the Outsider Feedback Document:

> **Affectivity and interconnectedness**
>
> We were also surprised by the effectiveness of the relationships and interconnectedness of the mothers and their families. This is to do with the fact that they all knew each other outside of Messy Church. They didn't get a sense of community simply because they got together but they had a sense of community because Messy Church actually affected their relationships with mums at the school gate and people they passed in the street. This was really interesting. So their connections extended well beyond the more physically focussed activities of Messy Church and into their wider lives. As well as the 'ecclesiological overflow' of Messy Church into participants' home lives there is a similar rippling out into their relationships in the locality.

Mothers commented upon their extended social networks as a result of attending Messy Church:

> My networks have extended and I know probably about, I don't know, eight to ten people now in the community, more, than I did a year ago. So that's quite a lot of people really.
>
> (Interview One)

> It's nice that I know some extra people that come from her class, from other schools and from down our road. In fact, our neighbours go. So that's one thing where I can talk to my neighbour, meanwhile the children are all occupied and we can have sensible chatting.
>
> (Interview Two)

These networks between Messy Church mums extended back to their homes especially on the Messy Church Extra days when there was no meal, when they might invite each other back for something to eat and drink:

R: Yeah. So we take turns and we go back to each other's houses and we just do, you know, sandwiches and whatever for the kids.
I: So actually your friendship and activity extend back to your own houses?
R: Oh yeah, absolutely. There are four or five of us mums and we just, you know, go back to each other's houses on those days and do it there (Interview One).

Not only did the data suggest that Messy Church was building a network of relationships and communication but also that these friendships were often built on a common experience of ecclesial practices, story and song – elements especially kept present by the children themselves.

4 *Suburban isolation and the attraction of belonging*

We were struck by the way in which the common separation of the father's work place from the family's home imposed so much by way of lifestyle on the women and children attending Messy Church. South Croydon is an affluent South London suburb where family life often follows the pattern of a woman at home with small children whilst the man commutes into central London for a long-hour, high pressure job. The global city brings great rewards, but they come at a cost to family life, as a number of the interviewees testified:

> If you are a mum on your own, it is a very lonely life if you're the one at home with the baby, first baby as well, very lonely. And every mother will go through their insecurities, their lows and their ups, and if you go to groups like this, you talk to other mums and you find that other mums are also going through the same thing as you. And it's not the end of the world and I think it's very good for people who might be on the border of post-natal depression. … You can have the support,

> you can get advice, you can give as well, I think that's very important because you're just stuck in your four walls, your husband's out at work, he's not sharing your doubts and your worries with you.
>
> (Interview Eight)

> I think it's nice being able to walk along your road and be able to go, 'Hi, hi', as you're going along rather than just walking around and not knowing anybody. I think that's so much what has happened nowadays. People don't know the people who live around them. They don't know the people on their street. People just exist, go to work, come home, close the door and they don't know people around them and I really feel that since coming onto Messy Church, it's made me realise how many people in this community are part of this church. I never knew it. I never really was part of it or knew about it or appreciated. It really kind of opened me up to a new world. And that actually they're normal.
>
> (Interview One)

> I think it's harder for younger mums, because I think they are definitely more isolated, the pre-school ones. They have social contact there, but I think just in general they go through the whole day and if there's a problem or if they've got anything, marital problems or they're stressed about something going wrong in the house or their child is playing up or anything like that, I don't think they have much of a support network for pre-school mums.
>
> (Interview Seven)

The ARCS team reflected this back in our Feedback Document, as we described the sense we had gained from those we had met and spoke with:

> **Isolation and loneliness**
>
> The data gives real glimpses into the isolated lives of some of these mothers. At times, there was an unspoken sense of loneliness and insecurity in people's lives which was almost tangible.... The journey of discipleship begins with the breaking of isolation into personal relationships and friendships. Messy Church is making a huge contribution to this. The popularity of Messy Church does indicate the cravings of human beings to belong to community.
>
> (Outsider Feedback Document)

In reflecting on this, it became clear how well this Messy Church fitted the 'type' identified by Helen Cameron as a 'magnet church',[6] providing as it does a 'safe space' for these families to experience something of Christian practice. This type of church attracts these families because of the focus on providing professional activities suitable for them, in ways transcending of denominational or faith backgrounds. What was striking was the Messy

Church team's often un-named commitment to providing this real level of support and hospitality for parents and families, often more or less tacitly recognised as struggling to live happily and connectedly in their context:

> **Theology of welcome: a magnet church**
>
> The ARCS team were genuinely amazed by the effectiveness of the welcome and hospitality operating at Messy Church in South Croydon. Time and time again, the interviewees expressed appreciation and gratitude to the organisers for their care and attention to detail in this welcome. This point is especially valid when one takes into account the sheer numbers that Messy Church is dealing with and the way it is tapping into parenting social networks in the community in such an effective way.
>
> (Outsider Feedback Document)
>
> The importance of hospitality was noted – and the little things that make a difference in the welcome. E.g., the coloured cups. To help with a personalised welcome, it was decided to have an extra person on the welcome desk, and a middle person to help escort families around the Church.
>
> (Joint Feedback Document)

In a community where isolation is a common experience, a welcoming church able to cater for children has a magnetic appeal that has little to do with parish boundaries. At the same time, there were hints at how, as with St. Mary's Battersea, the journey from welcome guest to participating host is not straight forward. Indeed, the question might be raised as to how far a permanent 'guest' can really belong to a community:

> I don't get a massive sense of belonging because I'm not part of the actual ... you know, if I was let's say, contributing every week and doing something then I think I would feel more a sense of belonging. So I don't think I have a sense of belonging to it, but I think I'm a supporter. I'm just a massive supporter and I spread the word but I don't get a sense of belonging, I have to say. To me, it's about community really; it's about community and it's about fun. That sums it up for me; it's about community and fun and I come because of those reasonings. But belonging, no, no, I wouldn't say that's probably the right word for me, to be honest.
>
> (Interview One)
>
> I really want to get fully involved like some of the mums are and I just can't. So I feel I belong in the fact that I know the other mums and the social aspect of it, but the religious side of it, I don't, even though I would like to.
>
> (Interview Six)

5 Choosing church

The Messy Church leadership could be said to be working with a received notion of discipleship in which the notion of commitment is strong and central. With this in mind, it was striking that the language of the mothers interviewed was less about commitment and more about freely choosing, as happier to keep their options open on matters of faith. The theme of choice in relation to faith and church comes up a lot in the data. "It doesn't bother me; I want it to be my child's choice" was a typical response. Other examples eco this attitude:

> It's made me more willing to be more flexible with my own children and say well you know, if they want to be part of this then that doesn't bother me. Or maybe in years to come I might change a little bit. I don't know I'm a bit, you know, the jury's out, kind of thing.
>
> (Interview One)

> I just really want it more to be their choice. I didn't want (baptism) to be something we do just because that's what expected and I'm not quite sure why.
>
> (Interview Three)

> I want my children to have exposure to (faith) but I don't want it to be too full on. I kind of think that they should grow up and make their own decisions.
>
> (Interview Seven)

When it came to reasons why, given this strong sense of leaving children free to choose, the mothers had chosen to bring them to Messy Church, one recurring theme was that of 'morals' or 'values'. Many were prepared to accept that faith could be a vehicle for morality and so wanted their children to be involved in Messy Church as a way for children to engage with moral issues:

> I like the way that the Bible stories all have morals in them, which are very important.
>
> (Interview Six)

> We just want to expose the kids to as many religions as possible. They all aim for one thing.
>
> (Interview Eight)

> It doesn't bother me that there's a religious element to it at all because if my child turned around to me and said, 'You know mummy, I want to learn more about the church'. Fine, I'd never discourage it. Just because it's not my belief, I don't then think that I have to put that onto my child. If they choose that they want to, you know, believe then that's

> up to them. You know, I would never stop that. So it doesn't bother me. And also all the stories are really about morals anyway. A lot of the bible stories are about morals and decency and kindness to others, so why would you not want to encourage that?
>
> (Interview One)

This cultural emphasis on choice extended to the clear sense that church – and any particular church community – was itself a matter of personal choice, based on one's own taste or felt needs. Such comments indicated that the mothers still saw other churches as unattractive, adopting an approach to church rather like that of deciding which supermarket to shop at: the one you go to is a good one, but you need a reason not to go to the other ones:

> I think it's encouraging me more and part of me thinks I would like to be part of a church, but part of this church, not part of any other church because I like the way this church, or from what I've seen of this church, is run. I like the way it has an emphasis on family and community and fun and its inclusive and it's got everybody. It's not the image of the other church I remember from being at school where it was all quite formal and serious.
>
> (Interview Three)

> It's probably made me think that were I to start attending church I would certainly consider Emmanuel. . . . I very much like the approach and the fact that they're very informal and the way they treat young people; it always strikes me.
>
> (Interview Four)

Concluding reflections

The research carried out with Messy Church was one of especial significance for attending to ecclesiological themes 'on the ground'. The perennial question of "what makes church 'church'" was never far from the reflections, and the particular realities of contemporary suburban life challenged all involved to think differently about previously assumed positions. So, the Messy Church leadership began to re-vision their understanding of 'discipleship' and, specifically, their sense of what 'becoming a disciple' entails. There was also significant ecumenical learning within and across the teams. On the one hand, the Messy Church leaders recognised the ways in which the ancient practices of catechumenate might helpfully inform their understanding of contemporary journeys into discipleship. In doing so these Evangelical Christians were also introduced to contemporary Roman Catholic practices which are based on the catechumenate. On the other hand, one member of the ARCS team (the present author) saw her own Roman Catholic normative assumptions about 'proper church' challenged, and renewed, by the lived ecclesiology of grace encountered in this Messy Church.

Notes

1 www.messychurch.org.uk.
2 www.emmanuelcroydon.org.uk.
3 Clare Watkins and Bridget Shepherd, "The Challenge of 'Fresh Expressions' to Ecclesiology: Reflections From the Practice of Messy Church." *Ecclesial Practices* 1 (2014): 92–110.
4 Ibid.
5 This idea is further developed by Bridget Shepherd in Watkins and Shepherd, op. cit.
6 Helen Cameron, *Resourcing Mission: Practical Theology for Changing Churches* (SCM, 2009): 34–37.

8 Identifying church

Edginess and edgeless-ness

> I think it's nice being able to walk along your road and be able to go. 'Hi, hi'. As you're going along rather than just walking around and not knowing anybody.... People just exist, go to work, go home, close the door and they don't really know the people around them and I really feel that since coming onto Messy Church, it's made me realise how many people in this community are part of this church.... It really kind of opened me up to a new world. And that they're actually normal.
>
> (Messy Church, D4 Interview One)

> Tonight, I wasn't quite sure who was a volunteer and who was a guest. And there's no particular dividing line.
>
> (Housing Justice, E3, Chris)

When I read much contemporary ecclesiology, I am increasingly troubled by what seems to me a 'management paradigm' in the reading of what church is. By this, I mean that tendency to assume that: first, we can speak about 'church' as if we know what that is and, secondly, that when we speak of it, we are referring largely to something of a bounded, organised, observable reality, all be it one with a transcendent or mysterious aspect, and a missionary activity. 'Church' quickly becomes identified – more or less – with ecclesial structural institutions, all be it in various ways. Even when it is the subject of the church's identity that is being discussed, there is all too often an assumption that we know the 'thing' whose identity we are concerned with. So, for example, Paul Avis in starting with the primary sense that "the church's identity is derived, not only from how it understands itself but also from its *locus* in culture and society, the prevailing image of the church in its environment"[1] assumes the fact or reality of something called 'church' even whilst recognising the contested nature of its identity. The church is a self-evident phenomenon, with an inside and an outside, and some kind of relationship with its environment. It is, in short, an organisation. It seems to me that, in this way, academic ecclesiologies have their own version of the *ad intra* pull that the previous chapter identified for practices.

What is important here is not, in fact, this common, unquestioning use of the language of 'church' in ecclesiology. Indeed, it is hard to see how even the most open, fluid and liberationist understandings of church can avoid such a starting position: 'the church' is what we are thinking theologically about in ecclesiology, and its accepted fact is a foundation for the discourse to exist at all. What is significant, however, in my beginning with a question about such a self-evident focus for the ecclesiologist is that it surfaces a certain kind of learning of my own: it is only since the experiences of working closely with practice-based co-researchers that my own sensitivity to the inadequacy of such a commonplace position in ecclesiology has developed. Increasingly, through such engagement with practice, I have found myself reaching for the kind of liberation ecclesiology set out by Leonardo Boff in which he suggests that the church might helpfully be understood not only in institutional or historical terms but, radically, as "grace, liberation, the irruption of the Spirit, the new creation, the heavenly Jerusalem and the kingdom of God".[2] Karl Barth's starting place in responding to church also rings true here: "Today, there is rather too much than too little said about the Church. There is something better: let us *be* the Church!"[3] The ARCS research, in a particular way, unsettles the ecclesiologist, and confronts us afresh with the classic question: what *is* the church?

This is not, of course, a novel question. Modern ecclesiology, in particular, has frequently felt the need to define 'church' early in its discussions, in part to distinguish them from a popular and/or sociological readings. Roger Haight's definition can stand as an especially typical example:

> The church is the institutionalization of the community of people who, animated by the Spirit of God, live in the faith that Jesus is the Christ of God.[4]

As Haight himself observes, this statement carefully holds together "the historical and the theological, the dimension of transcendent faith in God's presence and operation in the church and the human, historical and social character of the community".[5] This account is also, significantly, followed by a statement of this church's purpose as missionary.[6] These ingredients of visible-invisible, human-divine, historical-eternal are the mainstays of ecclesiological discussion, as this volume discussed in its opening chapter. I have no argument with this as such; but the ARCS research has left me thinking that, when ecclesiologists talking of the human and historical, we tend more to an unquestioning identification of church with organisational structures than with the just-as-historical and concrete practices of the faithfull Christian in the world.

A notable exception to this tendency to read church 'managerially' comes with Pete Ward's *Liquid Ecclesiology*,[7] which builds on his earlier account of 'Liquid Church',[8] so as to offer a reading of church as culturally expressed, and so more fluid in its identity and accounts of itself. This notion of liquidity, based on Zygmunt Baumann's critical account of late modern shifts in social cultural forms,[9] offers ways of understanding human life and sociality beyond the gathered and structured. This provides, as Ward recognises, a particular gift for ecclesiology, opening up a logical and theological space for engagement with practices as precisely cultural expressions of church which need to be attended to and discerned.[10]

Although, ultimately, my own ecclesiological sense of the gathered and continuous church is somewhat more concrete than Ward's liquid church, it is nonetheless in something like this spirit of liquidity that I turn in this chapter to explore what the ARCS project might teach us about the nature of church, as lived and made historically present in the realities of contemporary culture and society. This learning is already shaped by the intentional selection of co-researching practices that were engaged, in some way, with mission or outreach. This leads to a particular kind of attention being given to the experience of church *ad extra*, and the struggle to enable such experience to be heard with the authority it truly has within an ecclesiological discourse where, traditionally, a great deal of what is said theologically about the church is articulated from 'within'. Both the normative voices of church teaching and traditions, and, as I've suggested, the formal voices of academic ecclesiology give accounts of church which have already an 'object' in mind – whether that is (as most often) an institution, a specific organised tradition, a historical reality or a theological ideal. For the lived church caught up in the dynamics of mission, culture and *ecclesia ad extra*, there are, I suggest, different readings of what church is.

In particular, what kind of 'community' the church might really be, and how this relates to 'the world', receive particular fresh illumination from our ARCS practitioner groups. Developing these emergent themes, this chapter takes up in a practice-informed account the question of church identity at a radical (*radix*, root) level of what 'church' is. I argue in what follows that, learning from 'the grounds' of church life, church emerges as more of a verbal than noun-al reality. It is a doing of life in Christ (what Pete Ward might refer to as an 'abiding'[11]), which is characterised as essentially edgeless (unbounded) whilst at the same time thriving on the (perceived) ecclesial edges of the organised, structured church itself. Frequently, indeed, the 'edginess' is expressed by the ways in which Christians are called to the marginal places – the 'peripheries'[12] of society. Whether ecclesially or societally, the practical living of church seems to find a vibrant home on the edges, away (though not apart) from the perceived centres of political and religious structure. The reality of church which is revealed here is that of a church in mission, in the world, which knows itself as – in these senses – both edgeless and 'edgy'. It is an ecclesiology based on a particular pneumatological understanding in which participants begin to know church as a living into which they are continually called, rather than something they possess or objectify – let alone manage – themselves. In order to demonstrate this, I will explore what can be learnt from the Accounts of Practices under two headings: 'the world' and 'community'.

Church, world and overflow: church on the edges

The church-world relation is a theme which is perennial in ecclesiology and basic to any response to the question of the church's identity. It has a roots in a reading of scriptural accounts of 'the world' – notably in the Gospel of John[13] – which appear to present 'the world' as in some kind of antipathy or opposition to the Christian community. One need only think of passages such as John 15:18–27, which speak of the world's 'hatred' for Jesus and subsequently for his followers, to see the seeds of counter-cultural accounts of church, which separate Christians from the rest of society. In such a reading church emerges as an alternative to worldly social forms. Alongside such a tradition of church-world opposition – intensified at times of persecution and in some responses to modern secularisation – there has also run a more complex account which recognises the inevitable intermingling of church and world. For Augustine this famously results in his sense of church as *corpus permixtum*,[14] in which the church's world reality causes us to recognise that the identity of the church over and against a 'world' of sinners cannot be clearly discerned in this life; church is thoroughly enmeshed in world, with all its social, cultural and even sinful realities. The identity of church becomes complexified. However, if it is true that the church cannot escape the world, it is also the case – though perhaps less frequently recognised – that the world cannot escape the Spirit who is the church's fundamental life. God's missionary Spirit is already active in the world, and the structural church, as "the primal and fundamental sacrament" is entrusted with the task of publicly or 'officially' holding and embodying God's Word such that this work of the Spirit can be discerned, named and celebrated.[15] It is this ecclesiological perspective – perhaps best articulated academically by Karl Rahner and his theologies of church, history and grace[16] – that informs the reading of the practice accounts in this area.

As self-identifying evangelising initiatives, the ARCS practices already locate their work in ways which are especially oriented to 'the world'; they are, variously, already interested in the working of God in wider society, into which they feel called to act as followers of Christ in some way. This 'worldliness' takes different forms and is shaped by differing accounts, influenced not least of all, as we have seen, by the location of the initiative in relation to ecclesial organisation. However, in these different locations, each Practice struggled to live church 'on the edge': as lay-led activities reaching out to the margins of society (LJV, CAFOD, Housing Justice); as parish-based initiatives going out form themselves into the wider community (Messy Church and St. Mary's Battersea); or, more problematically, as diocesan-led movements for facilitating greater engagement with those beyond explicit church structure and life (Portsmouth Diocese and the Westminster Agency for Evangelisation). We have already suggested, in chapters 6 and 7, that the particular structural location of diocesan initiatives can be seen as constraining the 'edgy' aspiration of these last two practices – and this will qualify their contribution to these reflections. Nonetheless they stand, at least, as testimony to the desire to nurture and encourage church from its everyday and dispersed realities – the ecclesial peripheries of lay living (B4, F3). These 'edgy' expressions of church communicate a fresh theology of the church-world reality and help the ecclesiologist to see in embodied form an emerging theology of church-and-world for our own time.

A first point here relates to the argument of the previous chapter and can be briefly identified: that church on, and oriented towards, the edges still draws on and is nourished by the (perceived) centre. We have seen that the challenging experience of LJVs in moving from gathered church to work in places of profound marginality and suffering was made possible and sustainable through the group's being held in a parish and wider religious community, and within the practice of a spiritual tradition. In similar ways, the work of both Messy Church and Housing Justice can be seen as enabled by gathered, structured communities of faith. The energy for the particular type of engagement with the world beyond their immediate experience, came – for the practitioners – from their sense of belonging to 'church', as a stable, more or less defined reality in their lives. The 'edgy' church depends on a sense of 'centre' for its effectiveness on the edges.[17]

However, there is something more that needs to be recognised in these Practices' experiences in and of 'the world': fundamentally, what is experienced by the church-on-the edge, is that ecclesial graces exist beyond the church's visible boundaries; and that, indeed, the church can draw from these *ad extra* graces for its enriching in gifts of the Spirit. This is something which, through working with the Messy Church data, we came to describe, in a kind of short hand, as 'ecclesiological overflow'. Here, the naming of the Gospel story and its graces could increasingly be seen as shaping and naming realities beyond the gathered ecclesial practices of Messy Church. The mothers, whilst not being explicitly converted to Christ, nonetheless were able to tell of how conversation and play in their (non-Christian) homes now included language, stories and songs learnt from Messy Church (D3, Interviews 2 & 3). Perhaps more profoundly still, Messy Church had enabled better relationships within the community more widely, contributing to more supportive friendships for these mothers (D3, Outsider Feedback Document and subsequent interview quotes). The 'edgy' practice of Messy Church taught, in embodied and formative ways for both practitioners and the ARCS team, an ecclesiology of extensivity beyond both the structural boundaries of the parish, and, as we shall see, the implicit belief-boundaries of the Messy Church leadership. Living church in edgy places highlights the expansiveness of God's grace.

Something similar can be seen in the LJV's experience of working both on the edges of church structure and in the marginal places of society, as they took on volunteering with non-church agencies, sustained by Igantian practices of prayer and discernment in small groups. What emerged in this edginess was a clear sense of the thinness of the dividing line between 'us' and 'them', in relation to those they tried to help (A4, Reflective Writing 2), accompanied by an account of the overflowing of grace into their ordinary lives (A2, Sarah). One volunteer wrote powerfully of this, reflecting that "seeing love working where you do not expect to find it is a blessing" (A4, Reflective Writing 2). Church in this kind of edginess makes itself open to such unexpected blessings.

This last point reminds us that the notion of 'ecclesiological overflow' doesn't just (or even) describe a gifting from church to world, as if they were separate entities. Rather, what these practitioners seem to be describing is a *recognition* of something of church which they discover in the world through their living of church on an edge of one kind or another. In this sense, any overflowing is mutually experienced by those explicitly inside or outside any structural expression of church; it is an over-flowing of grace, of the Spirit, encountered in historical and contextual forms, which exposes the extent of church as in and for the world, even ahead of its concrete and explicit expression. The being of church on the edges allows the language and grace of ecclesial life to find new homes and places of expression in world much in need of them; but, at the same time, this edginess learns to recognise that there are already 'whispers of church' through the activity of the Spirit in the world. So, the volunteer work engaged in by LJV is not ecclesial itself; and the building on the need for hospitality and sharing of food in Alpha at St. Mary's, and, in a different way, at Housing Justice, is not developing exclusively Christian ways of relating. The experience of Messy Church in South Croydon also recognised the ways in which 'natural' friendships and common patterns of life form the basis of their growing ecclesial community.

In all these cases, the practitioners demonstrated an instinct for the work of the Spirit in the world, building on these as activities appropriate to the edginess of their endeavours. In doing so, they expressed a theology of world as the proper place in which God's church is coming to be, whilst at the same time reminding the more structural, non-edgy elements of church life of the unexpected blessings that this world has precisely for the more 'centred' church. To respond fully to these insights, however, requires of ecclesiology a particular learning about the nature of ecclesial community and communion.

Community, communion and edgelessness

Communion – or *koinonia* – is an ecclesiological theme which dominates contemporary talk about church, whether from the academy, in ecumenical dialogue, or in pronouncements from church bodies.[18] It is a term which, as one scholar puts it, "has all but swept the board"[19] in ecumenical ecclesiology and ecclesiology more widely. There are good reasons for this: the language is rooted in scripture, and has also been understood in terms of the fundamental Christian doctrine of God as Trinity. The language of communion fits well with both ecclesiological and cultural concerns with unity-in-diversity, and accommodates late modern preoccupations with community and relationship.[20] Communion/*koinonia* is a widely accepted way of answering the fundamental question of this chapter: what *is* church?[21]

One of the difficulties with this language, which I have drawn attention to elsewhere,[22] is the tendency to elide too easily the language of communion/*koinonia* with 'community'. They are, of course, related, but not (necessarily) identical. In particular, the theological notion of communion as applied to church might reasonably be required to include expression of what has been called the 'vertical' element of communion[23] – that is, communion in Christ. Readings of communion which are too uncritically understood as community not only risk failing to incorporate that essential ecclesiological ingredient of the divine-human dynamic but also – perhaps paradoxically at first sight – give rise to more bounded, self-defined ecclesial groupings; human communities are inevitably places of belonging, and so of non-belonging, however inclusive their intentions. The question is, given these realities, what forms can ecclesial communion in Christ concretely take in our world, which are not simply replicating human community?

Learning from the Practices helps us understand the practical realities of such questioning. First of all, the instinct toward gathering communities is pervasive and strong, with many of the initiatives described seeing the embodiment of community as the most effective expression of mission. For St. Mary's Battersea, hospitality and social life was a key component of their outreach and development as a parish (C1, Interview 6; C2 Interview 7); for Messy Church, too, responding to isolation and the need to belong was key (D4). In contexts where alienation and loneliness are common experiences, and where the desire of identity in a diverse and plural setting is keenly felt, the opening up of community is profoundly attractive, and there is a proper Christian call to enable the formation of "close friendships ... out of this group of lonely misfits" (C4, Interview 2).

However, the experiences of these Practices also draw attention to a certain dissatisfaction with building communities as such, mirroring something of the academic and church questioning of the relating of community and communion. For Messy Church, this dissatisfaction was expressed through their concerns that all they were doing was building a "Jesus-less" community (D2), which failed to live up to their own sense of church as grown out of discipleship, following Jesus. A similar apparent "Jesus-lessness" was identified for St. Mary's Battersea (C3), as they came to see that their emphasis on inclusivity and hospitality enabled an experience of 'community' in which, however, formation toward moving from being guest to host was lacking. For both Practices, a deeply practical reality of the tension between community and communion-in-Christ was experienced and in troubling ways.

What can be learnt for our practice-engaged ecclesiology, however, lies in the ways in which these practitioners responded to these experiences. The Messy Church team, in particular, through its extended theological reflection, began to work with a more 'stretched' understanding of church, beyond not only its gathered social reality, but beyond, too, the explicit belief assumptions of the team. The aim of bringing people to know Christ remained; but such was the encounter with 'something of the Spirit' even among the 'non-believers' who made up most of Messy Church – that the leadership felt they had to find ways of speaking of the integral connection between the 'Sunday' and 'Messy' church communities. Here, beginning to see terms such as 'church lite' (D2, Interview 6, 2nd) and the 'shallow end of church' as positive indicators of ecclesial grace beyond the structural boundaries of church was experienced as liberating (D2, final paragraph). Theologically, this experience was re-discovered and rooted by the group biblically through reflection on Acts 17. This scriptural testimony to a natural theology which might underpin evangelism enabled movement beyond a sense of tightly bound church community, which the Christian had to get people to join toward something unbounded, as the (as yet) Unknown God was recognised as at work in the lives of an apparently Jesus-less community. The edgelessness of church, when seen in this way as continuously stretched into the Spirit's presence in the world, gives a fresh and liberating perspective to the work of mission. The Messy Church leaders' move to this position reframes the language of 'community' in ways more in keeping with 'communion in Christ' as the expansiveness of divine love shatters our own human and limited sense of community and relationship.

There is something to be learnt from the ARCS Practices which challenges any ecclesiological tendency to valorise the gathered, stable community. For, whilst depending on some such community existing, these practices nonetheless witness to a more fluid, less concrete experience of Christian community which finds its basis less in togetherness as such, and more in the shared experience of missionary action on the one hand and spiritual support on the other. For the Housing Justice volunteer, the call to service of the homeless guest might even disrupt the commitment to the gathered community, as he chooses the community/communion of the kitchen serving the homeless over the communion of the Mass (E3, Richard). The Housing Justice community of loving action spilled over into the wider community, as actions of kindness from others became focused on their work – the local pub, the parishioners and those with no church connection (E2; E3, Linda). Senses of bounded community became blurred or lost as the expansivity of such loving response took over (E3, Chris).

None of this is to say that some kind of gathered community was unnecessary to these Practices. All of them, though in different ways, depended on such stable groups for their functioning. It is more that the witness of these practices suggests that such gathered communities are not so much ends in themselves, but rather communities of service toward the edges, witnessing to the edgelessness of God's love in and for the whole world. What then becomes important is not the gathered community as such, but rather the extent to which it is orientated to this service. The simple responses of thanks from parishioners to Housing Justice volunteers – "This is what the church should be doing" (E2, Matilda) – their donation of amazing "puddings" (E2, Johnny, 2nd) hint at the gathered community finding its meaning in going beyond itself, beyond any sense of hard-edged identity.

Indeed, the LJV's experience also suggested that Christian community, rooted in practices of scripture reflection and prayer, might be quite different from that expected in more traditional, stable, parish-type communities and still be effective for mission. Reflecting on the fragmented nature of his own 'fading' LJV reflection group, Joseph makes a telling comment:

> there doesn't have to be a tomorrow for there to be some community today. So I guess there is some sense of community, of sharing with others, of thinking with them, praying with them and just being with them without there necessarily being stability.
>
> (A3, Joseph)

The experience here suggests that practices – of love and of prayer – themselves constitute Christian community as communion in Christ and his mission, every bit as much, and often even more, than any stable, gathered – and so bounded – community in itself.

Conclusion: edgy, edgeless and still church?

Working with the ARCS practices taught me, as this chapter has tried to describe, that when ecclesiology attends to the living of church 'in the world' rather than in ecclesial organisation and structures, a distinct and powerful account of church is glimpsed. It is as if we were seeing, at the places on the edge, new kinds of centres for church break open; and when they broke open, it was expressions of church without hard edges that were expressed. It is this that has led me to struggle to describe the edgelessness of church, centred on ecclesial structural edges.

The great risk of recommending an ecclesiology of church on the edges and without edges itself is that it lays itself open to the misunderstanding that it is nothing to do with the institutional church. Indeed, this is a view which has its voice in the theological tradition, classically in Emil Brunner's ecclesiology.[24] However, the ecclesiology lived out in these practices not only speaks of the essential liveliness of edgy and edgeless church, but also – and at the same time – of the dynamic relating of that edginess to a structural centre: a centre which exists to serve the edges (which then, in some sense, become the central concern!). To celebrate one's membership of the visible, traditioned church is what enables the Christian disciple to recognise, beyond the visible bounds of the ecclesial organisation, 'the church of an (as yet) unknown God' – a place where the Spirit is at work bringing people to the Father, through Christ. Learning this lesson 'on the edges' is what can enable us to review our institutional centres as places of service to that work of the Spirit, rather than as some static tabernacle of 'the true Church'.

The church thus lies ahead of us as vocation, every bit as much as it is present to us as identity, community, structure and ritual. As such, it is not something to be possessed, managed, envisioned or strategically planned. That this has significant implication for how structures, and especially authority and ministry work is clear. It also has enables a renewal of understanding of the churches' sacramental lives in ways which break open our liturgical and ritual practices to the realities of world and boundary-less Spirit. It is to this we will turn in chapter 9.

Notes

1 Paul Avis, "Ecclesiology and Ethnography: An Unresolved Relationship." *Ecclesiology* 14 (2018): 322–337. See 323.
2 Leonardo Boff, *Ecclesiogenesis: The Base Communities Reinvent the Church* (Collins, 1986): 47.
3 Karl Barth, *Dogmatics in Outline* (Sixteenth Impression, 1988; SCM, 1949): 141.
4 Roger Haight, *Ecclesial Existence: Christian Community in History* (Continuum, 2008): 36.
5 Ibid. 36–37.
6 The normativity of this kind of definition of what the church is and what it's for can be seen in the way that a similar approach is taken in *The Church: Towards a Common Vision*. Faith & Order Paper 214 (World Council of Churches Publications, 2013).
7 Pete Ward, *Liquid Ecclesiology: The Gospel and the Church* (Brill, 2017).
8 Pete Ward, *Liquid Church* (Wipf and Stock, 2013).
9 Zygmunt Baumann, *Liquid Modernity* (Polity Press, 2000).
10 Ward, *Liquid Ecclesiology*, op. cit. 34–36.
11 Ibid. 184–199.
12 Pope Francis' well-recognised use of this language of 'peripheries' is given interesting treatment by Pasquale Ferrara, "The Concept of Periphery in Pope Francis' Discourse: A Religious Alternative to Globalization?" *Religions* 6 (2015): 42–57.
13 For example, John 15: 18–19.
14 For a helpful contemporary discussion of Augustine's ecclesiology here, see Roger Haight, *Christian Community in History Volume 1: Historical Ecclesiology* (Continuum, 2004): 259–264.
15 Karl Rahner, *The Church and the Sacraments* (Herder, 1966): "The Church is the official presence of the grace of Christ in the public history of the one human race.... [it is] ... the primal and fundamental sacrament." 19.

16 Karl Rahner, *Foundations of Christian Faith: An Introduction to the Idea of Christianity* (Crossroad, 2000).

17 This language of centre and edge, like all spatial language used theologically, needs a little chastening, not least of all because of the ways that 'centrality' refers both to structural centre and value or importance. The playful use of edgy centres, and being centred on edges, in this chapter does, I hope, make the limitations of these spatial terms clear.

18 Most influentially, the language of *koinonia* and communion in relation to church is set out by John Zizioulas, *Being as Communion: Studies in Personhood and the Church* (Darton, Longman and Todd, 1985). See also Nicholas Sagovsky, *Ecumenism, Christian Origins and the Practice of Communion* (CUP, 2000). The importance of this language in ecumenical ecclesiological discussion is described in Clare Watkins, "Objecting to *Koinonia*. Why Communion Isn't the Answer." *Louvain Studies* 28 (2003): 326–343.

19 Sagovsky, op. cit. 18.

20 For a discussion of these points see Watkins, "Objecting to Koinonia", op. cit.

21 The dominance of this image can be recognised in the place it holds in World Council of Churches Faith & Order Commission Paper 214, *The Church: Towards a Common Vision* (World Council of Churches Publications, 2013).

22 See note 18 above.

23 See Congregation for the Doctrine of the Faith, *Letter to the Bishops of the Catholic Church on Some Aspects of The Church Understood as Communion* (Vatican, 1992).

24 Emil Brunner, *The Misunderstanding of the Church*. Harold Knight trans. (Lutterworth Press, 2003. Orig. German *Das Missverstaendnis der Kirche*, 1951).

Account of practice E
Housing Justice

Project time frame: February 2008–March 2010

Introductory narrative

Housing Justice[1] is an ecumenical charity that supports local churches and church-based projects that want to take action on homelessness. It campaigns for affordable housing, raises awareness about homelessness and inadequate housing, seeks to represent the voice of the churches to government and within the voluntary sector and promotes innovative Christian responses. One aspect of the charity's work concerns working with groups on the ground to secure night shelter accommodation for homeless people, especially during the winter months. In particular, the 'rolling church model' has become widely used as a way for a group of churches in a locality to provide shelter seven nights. Seven churches in a local area co-ordinate the work, with each opening up their facilities for one night a week. This is a particular church-based outreach as well as an ecumenical effort across Christian communities in one place. Researching with volunteers working with this model gave the ARCS team the opportunity to explore with practitioners themselves the theological significance of this grounded, practical and ecumenical work. This was a particularly fruitful example of working with a practitioner group over two cycles of theological action research (winter 2008 and winter 2009).

The theological action research process was aided by the fact that the charity itself had a long-standing interest in and some experience of theological reflection and was looking for a project that would enable it to fulfil that interest. When the opportunity to take part in ARCS came along, they were eager to participate, and, unusually, initiated the research collaboration. Two warm up meetings took place in late 2007 between ARCS team members and representatives from Housing Justice, from which it was agreed that the action research could be rooted in the work of a cold weather shelter in one London borough (Islington), where – following the rolling church model – seven churches in the same locality each provided a night's food and accommodation for people sleeping rough in the months of January to March.

The identification of a research question involved both Housing Justice and the particular Cold Weather Shelter. In the first cycle, the question that arose concerned how participation in the shelter scheme affected the theological outlook of the churches concerned, as well as a secondary concern as to how such an integration of *ad extra* practice and ecclesial identity might be enabled:

- How does the parishes' involvement in the Cold Weather Shelter influence the theological outlook of the churches and the faith practice of individuals involved?
- How might ways be developed of enabling the churches to reflect theologically on the impact of their involvement with the Winter Shelter?

(Remit Document)

To work with the ARCS team, an insider team of reflectors was drawn from members of Housing Justice and the coordinator of Islington Churches Cold Weather Shelter. The first cycle of research involved recording conversations from focus groups of volunteers, in two groups, one from a Catholic, one from an Anglican parish; and 'guests' (those sleeping and eating at the night shelters) in another. In addition, there were interviews with church leaders and the night shelter co-ordinator. The data was shared for reflection by both the ARCS team and Housing Justice team – a practice by this time established as part of the theological action research process – and the two teams fed back to each other on their reflections. This material from Cycle One was rich in a number of ways, as illustrated below, but it raised a particular question about the use of religious language, or the naming of faith, which whilst prevalent among the guests, was shied away from by the volunteers. It seemed that the guests generally took a more explicitly Christian understanding of the work of the Shelter than did the volunteers. This led to a Cycle Two of the process, in which excerpts from the original guests' focus group were discussed in focus groups of Volunteers, so as to explore further their motivations and their relating of faith with their practices as volunteers. There were also additional interviews with clergy from the participating churches at this stage.

This project was an especially rich one for deepening our theological understanding of the theological and ecclesiological significance of *ad extra* church work. Not only were Housing Justice familiar with theological reflection and so more immediately in tune with theological action research but it also became clear that there were particular advantages in working with a small, entrepreneurial, faith-based agency because of the flexibility and creativity of the organisation. More of this is said below. Learning from this ARCS project helped to improve training programmes and hospitality practices at borough shelters across London, as Housing Justice developed their approach in response to the theological action research process. At the same time, this was a project that led to a significant publication,[2] as well as a highly successful piece of post-graduate research form the ARCS Fieldworker.[3]

Five disclosures

1 Naming faith – or not?

As recorded above, one of the most striking features of the data gathered in Cycle One was the identification of interesting variations in the accounts given by guests and volunteers, with guests appearing very much more willing to be explicit about these connections. For example, a number of guests used explicitly Christological language to describe their encounter with the church:

> Tell you what, it's like God has let you into his house. If you want to look at it in a deep way, it's like God has said come into my house and get out of the cold. That's if you want to look at it in a deep spiritual way.
>
> (John, Guest Focus Group)

> I am finding it interesting that despite the difference of the churches here – being it a this or a that church – actually they're coming together as a body, as it should be, in the Body of Christ and actually working together and establishing some sort of unity and strength in unity together to help the outside. I'm finding it really interesting that they are working together instead of going against each other.
>
> (Stephen, Guest Focus Group)

On the other hand, some volunteers at the night shelters, most but not all of whom were church members, expressed explicit reluctance to connect their motivation to volunteer with their faith. This was based on a sense that they "were no better than other people" and that they were simply making a human response to human need. Below are typical responses:

> Even though I've got faith, I'd be quite wary of pushing my faith or anything to do with it onto people who are quite vulnerable, who are here to get out of the cold and they just want to come in to have a bit of freedom and a bit of space and not have to worry about – am I going to get beaten up tonight. I don't know about the rest of you, but I'd be quite reticient about pushing [my faith] forward!
>
> (Jenny, Volunteer Focus Group One)

> I guess for me, I don't think you have to be Christian to volunteer because it's just something that I think most people with good values, whether they're Christian or not – I say good values because that's my view – but most people would have values, want to

help people and try and be kind and so on. But it's the Christian way as well.

(Sarah, Volunteer Focus Group One)

There was almost a sense that naming faith in relation to their volunteering work somehow made the work vulnerable to misunderstanding. This reluctance seems closely related to an ambivalence around explicit evangelism and a concern not to appear 'pushy', exploitative or even un-caring of present practical needs.

This difference in the data led, in Cycle Two, to further probing in this area. Transcripts from the guest focus group of Cycle One were circulated to volunteers to explore their reactions to such explicitly Christian naming of what was being experienced. Volunteers reacted with surprise, but still with no energy to draw personal faith connections:

JESSICA: Those responses were much more interesting than ours.
FIELDWORKER: What surprises you about these quotations?
JAMES: They were a lot more religious than I thought, but that maybe reflects on what we were saying earlier than we don't see it as an overtly Christian thing, but they are very conscious of being in a church, much more than we are.
PATRICK: Going back to the question, does it make a difference if it's in a church? Very clearly to them it does. It matters much more than for us.
JESSICA: That is why they do ask us theological questions. They are seeing us as people who are.... (*unheard*)
(Focus Group Two, Anglican Parish)

One of these volunteers was a Quaker – Bill. Like the others, Bill was reluctant to highlight faith language or motivation, preferring to draw out political and social explanations for the guest's responses. He felt the important thing was to offer a 'place of equal encounter' to homeless people irrespective of the host faith community:

> Bill: There are big structural questions about housing which need to be addressed here. They are political questions about redistribution of wealth and many things that I could talk about but that plays out in people's lives by being treated like shit. That doesn't happen here and the fact that it doesn't in places like this, I don't think it's because it's a church per se – I think it happens in other spaces of equal encounter.
>
> (Ibid.)

The implication seems to be that this powerful practical outreach was, in the volunteers' minds, distinctly different from any 'evangelising' type of ecclesial work; indeed, it came across as a matter of principled importance that his work was *not* primarily a work of faith but rather a work of common human goodness. The separation implied remains a matter of interest sociologically, and – especially – theologically.

Another perspective on this question of the relation of faith to these social justice practices was gained when one of the clergy interviewed seemed to regret a lack of more explicit 'religious' identity in the work:

> Part of our relationship is to feed them and it is an opportunity to talk about God and what Jesus means to us. Now, one of the things I would want to talk about with [. . .] the coordinator, is the religious side of things. How do we bring people beyond the physical aspect of coming to the Church and giving or coming to the Church and receiving, to coming to realise and accept that this is what Jesus has asked us to do? And in turn how can the guests help each other?
>
> (Clergy Interview One)

Given the explicit faith exploration of the guests, there is something of a paradox here in this clergy person's reading of the situation. Nonetheless, in its own way, this perspective also raises the question of the (lack of) integration between faith and the work being carried out by the churches in this scheme.

2 *The transformative potential of* ad extra *work*

Despite the above differences, data from both guests and volunteers unveiled the potential of cold weather shelters to act as an *ad extra* expression of Christianity in local neighbourhoods. As such, we were also aware of their potential as bridges between *ad intra* church activities and the outside world in a global city. What was striking were the complex ways in which volunteers described the relation of their *ad intra/ad extra* ecclesial practices. One female volunteer below, for example, identifies a clear distinction and even disconnect between the *ad intra* and *ad extra* witness of her church. In addition, she articulates a strong commitment and sense of responsibility to tackling local injustice in Islington and doing the 'Lord's work'. This is a practical ecclesiology being wrestled with in action:

> I've had people [from the church] saying to me: 'Thank God you are doing this. This is what we should be doing'. People do feel that this is what church should be. . . . we are a high Anglican Church with a lovely sung Mass and not much else – so through no fault of anyone, we have become more and more insular. So people are enjoying that opening up of the doors. . . . Almost everybody that I have come into contact with doing this work . . . have had their attitudes to the homeless seriously changed. . . . I have lived in Islington all my life for about 40 years and I have always felt very angry that the community is so polarised. . . . I do feel very privileged to be alive on this earth, and I

> can only call it muscular Christianity, it's what the Good Lord put us on the earth to do.
>
> (Matilda, Volunteer Focus Group One)

What we saw were vivid examples of volunteers experiencing something transformative in their work with the Shelter. Above all, a powerful operant theology of compassion, and coming alongside those on the margins of society was being embodied:

> When I first came here, there was this guy called X who was an alcoholic, he smelt, he was dirty, he had bad feet, he couldn't walk properly, he almost had his toes cut off and he was sitting here one Sunday and he was just telling me this story of how he was married but he'd split up, and he had a pub and that was taken away from him and I sat their looking at this guy who was in his 40s but looked like he was in his 70s, and I got up and hugged him and he said, 'Do you know what, it's the first time I've been hugged in 8 years'. It was so touching. Just that physical contact. I don't even know why I'd done it. A couple of years ago, I would never have done it, you know, go up to a total stranger who smelt and had no teeth in his mouth. That didn't mean anything to me. I just had to hug him. That just sums it all up for me. It's lovely.
>
> (Margaret, Volunteer Focus Group One)
>
> **Is there any impact on your own faith or spirituality?**
>
> It makes my faith stronger definitely just because you see humanity expressed so overtly here.
>
> (Jonny, Volunteer Focus Group One)

This volunteer went on to draw links with the wider community and the church, which had arisen through the work of the Shelter:

> Then you look at the link with the local pub which brings a really nice joint of beef and organic juices over, and the local parishioners who bring over the most amazing puddings.

There are strong parallels to be drawn here with findings from LJVs (Account of Practice A above). Social justice volunteering, when fully integrated with the Christian tradition (and this is the challenge), can bring a wholesome and healthy sense of mission to the local church and the local community. The transformative power of these practices were not restricted to the volunteers, or the guests, but had an effect beyond their immediate locus of practice, within their wider church communities and beyond.

3 Hospitality and Sacramentality

'Hospitality', we came to realise, was a key theme across a number of the projects participating in the ARCS research. In the case of Housing

Justice, this gained a particular enrichment through the reflections on 'sacramentality' that emerged.

When reflecting on the data articulating their practice, a key learning point for Housing Justice and the Cold Weather Shelter was that they were providing more than a bed and a meal; they were providing hospitality. They realised the value of the personal encounter which the shelter made possible. This can be seen in these examples from Cycle One focus groups with volunteers:

> Occasionally, Louis will ring me up to say can you come down here early because we're short of numbers. I will just miss Mass, or come out of Mass early. I could stand there through the Mass and I enjoy Mass and I'm there for different reasons and values but I'd much sooner do this if I had the choice between the two – in terms of the importance. It's all very well saying you love God but if you're sat upstairs knowing that down below they are rushed off their feet in the kitchen that would just be ridiculous.
>
> (Richard)

> At St. James, we are lucky that we have a big kitchen. That is also part of it – elements of the communion – with the cooking, with the sharing, with the breaking of bread, so there is a lot of symbolism around that which we all share in. A lot of volunteers who come here feel that this is what Christianity should be about; they may not want to call it Christianity or may not want to go to Church. In fact, we are finding that we are getting people volunteering and enjoying the community who have no wish to go to Church.
>
> (Linda)

> I've done quite a lot of the cooking this year and it's just really nice for people to be appreciative of your cooking! Because I've have three children and I don't get that response from them! These guests come back for seconds. Just to be alongside with them at the table and eat with them, and be on their level with them. We've tried to integrate and mix. I think that's really good. It's good for them and it's good for us.
>
> (Sally)

> Tonight, I wasn't quite sure who was a volunteer and who was a guest. And there's no particular dividing line. That's what is so lovely sitting around that table. People are just being there together. It's an unthreatening and warm environment.
>
> (Chris)

For the outsider team, coming from a more explicitly theological context, there were clearly sacramental resonances in this material which led to further thinking about the relationship between sacrament and sacramentality.

These went on to bear fruit in the published paper mentioned above, (n.1) and will be further discussed in the present volume in chapter 9. However, here it is important to record that when these sacramental links were pointed out to the volunteers in the second cycle of research, once again, the reception was mixed:

FIELDWORKER: *A re-enactment of the Last Supper, do you make that kind of connection?*
HENRY: Sorry, I totally missed that point!! (a lot of laughter)
PRIEST: Let us break bread together, you know, that's something of it, that we break bread, that I am breaking my bread. People are bringing food.
CHARLOTTE: I don't make that connection.
BERYL: I don't think about it. I mean yes, it's through my church but I don't automatically link it with the Eucharist.
CHARLOTTE: You're not doing it because of the church; you're doing it because you want to do it?
(*Several agree*) (Focus Group, Catholic Parish)
SALLY: Do you make any questions between communion and volunteering at the shelter?
JENNY: Sharing the meal.
LAURA: Oh yes!
JENNY: Sharing the meals, sitting down and everyone is kind of equal together. Everyone sat together in the evenings.
SARAH: The fellowship aspect. Yes.
JAMES: I was about to say that communion in Church is seen as rather detached from what it was based on anyway. I mean, you could say something like the Last Supper is much more of a meal that happens downstairs whereas communion always seems a rather artificial and rather detached from that, because of the process it goes through, it doesn't feel like a meal and sitting down and being in community together. Maybe that's why there's not such an obvious connection in our minds
(Focus Group, Anglican Parish)

Again, what we were seeing seemed like a sense of disconnect between *ad intra* liturgical and sacramental practices and their *ad extra* work with the homeless. In reflecting upon this outcome in the joint meeting with the Housing Justice team, one person from the insider team suggested that for Roman Catholics, the Eucharist is 'special' and 'sacred', and so to associate it with something as mundane as preparing food for homeless people could be seen as disrespectful. Whilst not being able to verify such a remark, it highlights a certain tendency in the data to work with an implicit (operant) theology of sacred and secular as separate realms of action and meaning. The sacramental perspective taken up in the outsider team, in contrast, was reflective of the desire to make connection, to integrate ecclesial work across all its loci.

4 *Different normativities and their potential*

One over-arching question for the ARCS team, as we developed our research methodology and learning, was the place and effect of what might be considered 'normative' within a particular church group. This normativity would usually be identified in scripture, liturgical practice or ecclesial teaching. In fact, this has proved a problematic question, and it has often been difficult to find explicit discussion of the tradition and its effect on practice. It is as if that belongs to a language of theology that is not accessible – or, better perhaps, desirable – to ordinary church participants. This Housing Justice project, for all its fruitfulness for all concerned, was also characterised by a resistance to explicit faith or theological language relating to practice, as we have seen.

However, one advantage of turning speech in research into text is that it is possible to revisit it and ask fresh questions as thinking and sensitivities develop. In a meta-analysis session, when the outsider team were preparing the materials for this book, we revisited the following off-the-cuff exchange at the end of a volunteer focus group in Cycle Two of research.

BILL (QUAKER): I just wanted to say before we end that when I came up earlier this evening I thought, this is silly, you shouldn't do this now, but actually it felt a little bit to be like a worship sharing space and I didn't expect it to be like that at all, but people were quite open, so thank you for that; that's a sense of where spirituality is, just a little bit, and there was a moment there where people were talking quite honestly and people were listening quite honestly. It was great.

JAMES (ANGLICAN): You are probably more used to this from a Quaker tradition, you know, this sort of set up. We all tend to sit in rows in church! *(Laughter)*

(Focus Group Two)

After the research with Housing Justice took place, we became more aware that disclosures are often present in laughter or interruptions or at points when the session isn't 'official'. This conversation, just as a focus group session is closed, is such a moment of disclosure. On one level, what we are seeing here is how the Christian tradition is transmitted in two different communities – Quaker and Anglican. What is striking is how it becomes clear that these different normativities affect the volunteers' reading and experience of participating in the research. Bill discerns the focus group as being like a meeting for worship and so having the potential to disclose what is of God in everyone. The focus group is a kind of spiritual experience. The Anglican response is to refer back to the liturgy as the point of normativity; for James, it is in this more formal, ritual setting that God might be expected to make himself known. As researchers and reflectors, our normative experience shapes the very ways in which we participate and converse.

What is especially notable here is that it is the expression of the 'outsider's' normativity that highlights the learning. As a Quaker, Bill is the outsider in this largely Anglican group, and it is precisely from this place that he is able to articulate something of what they have shared together. For the ARCS team, this insight mirrored our sense that the guests as outsiders were more easily able to articulate the theological significance of sleeping in a church than were their hosts.

5 An agency working ecumenically

A final significant aspect of this project was its intentionally ecumenical nature. The deliberate selection of an ecumenical project enabled both Anglican and Roman Catholic views to be included in a single case study. Something of the fruitfulness of this can be seen in the disclosures already described in this chapter. However, a further significant feature of Housing Justice was that it was an agency that, as ecumenical, worked in a particular way across local churches. In particular, access to the parishes involved seemed more straightforward than when we were working with dioceses and their agencies. Reflecting on this, we surmised that the Shelter coordinator, as an agency worker, had less complicated relationships with the parish clergy than if he had been a part of their respective hierarchies. Furthermore, there was a sense of parishes having a real pride in the work that was being done and so an eagerness to share it through research and reflection.

The final evaluation interview with Housing Justice also suggested that it may be that ecumenical settings create the expectation of difference and therefore better enable reflective learning. Such a culture within the agency opened people up to the possibility the research process:

> A couple of years ago, when HJ was involved with the national Justice and Peace conference on migration, we wanted to give everyone an experience of being a stranger, so we deliberately gave everyone an experience of different worship – and 60 people came to the Quaker meeting and the only Quaker there was the guy leading the meeting and we'd laid out maybe 12 chairs, 8am before breakfast, thinking not many people would come, but they kept arriving and we increased the size of the circle until, in the end, people were spilling over into the pews behind the circle – the nuns loved it, they were ministering, we couldn't shut them up!! It ends with everyone shaking hands.
>
> (Final Evaluation Interview)

Concluding reflections

From the point of view of the ARCS team, the work with Housing Justice was not only rich in theological learning, but also significant for the development of our methodology. Journeying with them for two years and carrying our two cycles of research, together with the agency's own commitment to theological reflection and learning, enabled refinement of feedback processes and the identification of shared – and not shared – learning between the teams.

This was also a project in which recurrent themes gained a particular focus: hospitality; sacramentality in *ad* extra work; the integration of 'sacred and secular' – all these resonated with learning from our other projects. For Housing Justice, too, the language of hospitality which emerged has had an on-going significance for the organisation, enabling it to define the Christian distinctiveness of the service provision it supports.

Notes

1 www.housingjustice.org.uk.
2 Clare Watkins and Helen Cameron, "Epiphanic Sacramentality. An Example of Practical Ecclesiology Revisioning Theological Understanding." Chris Scharen ed. *Explorations in Ecclesiology and Ethnography* (Eerdmans, 2012): 71–89.
3 Catherine Duce, "Church-based Work With the Homeless." MA Dissertation Heythrop College (University of London, 2011). Winner of the British and Irish Association for Practical Theology Dissertation Prize 2012. Later aspects of this work was published as: Catherine Duce, "Church-based Work with the Homeless: A Theological Exploration of the Practices of Hospitality." *Practical Theology* 6, no.1 (2013): 87–103.

9 Sacrament and sacramentality

Celebrating the peri-liturgical sacramental[1]

> communion in church is seen as rather detached from what it was based on anyway. I mean, you could say something like the Last Supper is much more of a meal that happens downstairs [the meal with the homeless], whereas communion always seems rather artificial and rather detached from that, because of the process it goes through, it doesn't feel like a meal and sitting down and being in community together. Perhaps that's why there's not such an obvious connection in our minds.
>
> (Housing Justice, E3, Focus Group, Anglican Parish, James)

A picture is beginning to emerge of the ways in which co-researching with the ARCS practices led to a renewed ecclesiological understanding of fundamental questions of church *ad intra* and *ad extra*, gathered and dispersed, concretised and expansive. The gracedness of the world beyond the visible boundaries of church, together with a strong sense of the connectedness of that *ad extra* grace to the life and liveliness of the Christian community, is clearly embodied in these Practices, and has found deep resonances with other witnesses from the tradition. This emerging sense of church arises, notably, from working with traditions (Anglican and Catholic) which can be described as 'liturgical', with a strong emphasis, at least at the level of ecclesial normativity, on sacrament, and particularly Eucharist. Yet the ecclesiology of expansive grace and worldly church that has been disclosed so far might be seen as in some tension with this sacramental commitment. Certainly it has particular implications for the centrality of sacrament for church and what this might mean in the light of an account of church from the edges, from mission, from a lay ('secular'[2]) perspective.

In fact, as the Accounts of Practice demonstrate, reference to sacraments as such (in their liturgical sense) was rare among the ARCS Practices – a point interesting in itself, given the traditions from which they sprang. However, where it does occur – or is hinted at – there were striking lessons to be learnt, not so much about Baptism or Eucharist, but more about the understanding of church and 'sacramentality' more broadly which, all be it implicitly, seemed to inform the practitioners. They remind us, this chapter will argue, of the wider reading of sacrament beyond the ritual, which is, in fact, an essential part of the Christian tradition. As such, the disclosed theology of sacrament within the expression of church *ad extra* makes a valuable contribution to the existing discussion of sacrament, church, sacramentality and mission, opening up fresh insights on how sacramental life and practice might better serve and be of a piece with the life and mission of the church in the world.

Reflecting on the ecclesiology outlined so far in this section's chapters, we can see how questions of grace, Spirit, church and world shape our discussion. The central 'problem' of ecclesiology – of the church as both human and divine, in the Spirit and an institution – has a recognisable resonance with the theology of sacrament. For both the church traditions with which we worked, 'sacrament' is understood in terms of 'effective sign' – a ritual practice in which the materiality of creation is celebrated as the place where the Risen Christ becomes present for God's People. As the Anglican Catechism puts it, a sacrament is:

> an outward and visible sign of an inward and spiritual grace given unto us, ordained by Christ himself, as a means whereby we receive the same, and a pledge to assure us thereof.[3]

There is here a strong sense of divine presence in the material, which has persisted in the Christian understanding of sacrament from earliest times, though variously interpreted and understood.[4] In a particular way, sacraments speak of the characteristic dynamic of church as human and historical, whilst at the same time, the People of God, living in the Holy Spirit. Sacraments "are actions of the Holy Spirit at work in his Body, the Church. They are the 'masterworks of God' in the new and everlasting covenant".[5] This understanding and its repeated performance in the regular celebration of Eucharist makes clear that sacraments are not only ecclesially important as "actions of the Holy Spirit at work in the Church," but also for the way in which they proclaim a profound Christian belief in the way in which God comes to meet God's people which can shape a 'culture' of understanding the world. Through the Paschal Mystery of Christ's death and resurrection, and in the power of the Spirit's action in the church, Christians are enabled to meet God in our very bodiliness through effective signs and symbols drawn from God's creation. The incarnational, determinedly non-dualistic nature of Christian faith, is here intensified. Indeed, it has been argued that the celebration of sacraments at the heart of Christian life in these traditions enables the formation of a 'sacramental imagination'[6] – a distinctive way of seeing the gracedness of the world around us.

However, this sacramental way of knowing has not been without its difficulties, especially when considering the practice and understanding of the church as missionary. To illustrate this, we can refer to the comments of

Avery Dulles in his highly influential book *Models of Church*.[7] Commenting on the Second Vatican Council's use of the language of 'sacrament' to describe the church,[8] Dulles not only criticises this 'model' as ecumenically problematic,[9] but also – and significantly for the discussion here – argues that it is antithetical to a missionary understanding of church.[10] The argument is that sacrament refers us to something ritual, exclusive and inexorably *ad intra*. The notable absence of extensive discussion of sacraments among the Accounts of Practice may well reflect this sense of the sacramental as liturgical, and more to do with the church's inner life than its outreach and mission in the world.

A closer look at the normative sources for Dulles' identification of the church as sacrament does, however, suggest something rather different. Positively this language seeks to integrate the human-and-divine nature of the church and militate against any temptation to separate the institution from the community of the Spirit. So the Second Vatican Council speaks of the church as "like a sacrament or as a sign and instrument"[11] as one of the foundations of its ecclesiology, developing from this a highly incarnational sense of church as the Body of Christ, and the Spirit filled People of God.[12] This conciliar theology was both influenced and developed by Karl Rahner's account of the church as the 'foundational sacrament', continuing the presence of Jesus Christ in the world, and from which all the sacraments as such flow.[13] But a further look at the context of this language makes clear that this church which is a kind of sacrament,[14] is – by virtue of this very nature – also missionary:

> Since the Church is in Christ like a sacrament or as a sign and instrument both of a very closely knit union with God and of the unity of the whole human race, it desires now to unfold more fully to the faithful of the Church and to the whole world its own inner nature and universal mission.[15]

The language of sacrament here speaks not so much of the static or passive sacredness of the church body, as of its needing to be given to the whole world in response to God's saving love and will for all people.

There is a small and rather fragmented literature which has tried to extend the theology of sacraments in terms of mission,[16] ethics,[17] and most notably – liberation.[18] Eastern Christianity has long held a theology of 'the liturgy after the liturgy' which would, in principle, develop a more *ad extra* account of sacrament.[19] Something like this is reflected in Pope Benedict XVI's Apostolic Exhortation on the Eucharist, *Sacramentum Caritatis*, which moves from the theology and liturgical practice of Eucharist to the "living" of Eucharist in the world.[20] These more extensive readings of sacrament are, however, largely overshadowed by the *ad intra*, liturgical emphases of theological textbooks and church practice. What working with the ARCS Practices made clear, however, was the crucial importance and pertinence of these more under-explored accounts of sacrament and mission, justice and life in the world, as they enabled us to catch glimpses of an often implicit living-out of a sacramental – and specifically Eucharistic – theology in their outreach work. In this way, they bring significant learning to this area of ecclesiology, allowing the operant theology to call us back to some more neglected aspects of the normative and formal accounts.

For all the ARCS Practices Eucharist was, in some way, central to their tradition, and attitudes towards this sacrament provide a fruitful locus for exploring their embodied theology of sacrament and sacramentality in relation to church and mission. In what follows, two main features of this theology will be observed. The first illustrates the ways in which the apparent tension between sacrament and mission is perceived and operant on the ground, as 'the problem of sacrament for mission' is addressed. However, the learning from our practices did not stop there. Deeper reflection on their experiences disclosed a pervasive sense of sacramentality, in which grace or the presence of the Spirit, was both identified in some way with the celebration of sacraments, whilst at the same time being perceived and powerfully encountered outside the liturgical, and even beyond the visible bounds of church. This embodied instinct for sacramentality 'in ordinary' gives rise to the possibility of a theology of the 'peri-liturgicial sacramental' – a specific learning for me from working with these practices.

The problem of sacrament for church in mission

It has already been observed that – somewhat surprisingly – there is little explicit reference to the Eucharist, or sacraments as such, from the practitioners with whom we worked. LJV was based in a Jesuit-run parish, and centred on prayer and Bible reflection, but there was no substantial referencing among the volunteers to their worshipping, liturgical life as Catholics, which, for most, would have centred on the celebration of Sunday Mass. Where reference to Eucharist did occur, it was within the context of a specific Volunteers' gathering, in which, notably, the Mass was celebrated with particular symbolic reference to the volunteers' practices (A2, Joint Feedback meeting p2). St. Mary's was a parish deeply committed to daily celebration of Eucharist; but whilst preaching and hospitality were clearly named as important to members, the sacramental life of the community did not surface as strongly. More striking still is the way in which Housing Justice volunteers, when a connection between Eucharist and their feeding of the homeless was suggested, were resistant to the idea: "You're not doing it because of the church; you're doing it because you want to do it?" (E3, Charlotte). The supposed tension between sacrament and mission, the difficulty of relating one to the other, seems born out in these accounts.

What the Accounts of Practice also allow us to see, however, is more detail around why these connections between Eucharist and outreach work might be so difficult to make effectively. Among the Housing Justice volunteers there is, first of all, some sense that attributing their work to something theological or religious somehow undermines it, or holds their motivation in question. In contrast to the guests, the volunteers are hesitant about using faith language (E1), in part because of not wanting to be seen as 'pushing' faith onto the guests, but also through a sense of being "no better than other people". It was the human goodness that was affirmed, rather than anything distinctly Christian (E1, Sarah). It may be this reluctance to draw on faith language which informs the resistance to the ARCS team's reflections, which sought to link the feeding of the homeless with the Eucharist, and certainly appears to be the case with the Catholic Parish Focus Group (E3). There is another hint here that it is the very ritual nature of the Eucharist itself which masks the connection between it and the feeding of the homeless. As James points out, "communion always seems rather artificial and detached" from a meal, making links difficult (E3). The final paragraph of this section of the Account of Practice E references a sense that it was the highly 'sacred' nature of Eucharist that militates against its begin associated with something as mundane as cooking, washing up and feeding the guests.

What we seem to be observing here is the way in which the ritualisation of sacraments risks their integration with wider Christian life. Sacraments are, in these traditions at least,[21] properly understood as liturgically celebrated and (for the Catholic traditions especially) effected, but there may be a price to pay if this is the only way in which they are understood, as the rituals risk exhausting sacramental meaning and encounter for participants and making it difficult to speak of and understand the grace and presence of Christ outside the sanctuary. We were reminded of the liberation theologian Segundo, who challenged the 'success' of the liturgical movement in the second half of the twentieth century, by highlighting a "pagan insistence on the altar" which took congregations away from work for justice in the world.[22]

A different kind of tension between the centrality of Eucharist and the call to mission can be seen in the understanding of the two diocesan teams with which ARCS worked. In the Westminster Agency project (B), the ARCS team felt there was a tension between the vision and heart for evangelisation and the day-to-day demands of sacramental catechesis (B4). On the ground, in parishes, evangelisation might well be theoretically recognised as important, but presentation for sacraments took over all the energies in practice as the "usual context" (B4, Agency Team 4). Catechesis for sacraments, likewise, was generally easier for parishes to accept than adult formation, whose purpose was less clear – presumably because it was not associated with a sacramental 'end' (B5, Director). Here, the familiar, even routine practices of liturgical celebration of sacraments seems to pull congregations back from the less certain and troubling demands of mission and evangelisation. A liturgical reading of sacramental life has the advantage over the missionary emphasis in that these are things that can be 'done'; within a broadly Catholic sacramental tradition, the emphasis on sacramental power working *ex opere operato*,[23] offers a divine assurance of the presence of God when we simply do certain things in certain ways, with the right intention and people. Our understanding of mission can feel a lot less clear, and is often accompanied by less clearly assured outcomes.

For Portsmouth diocese (F), the sacrament-mission tension is more structurally experienced. A key feature of the renewal process that the diocese was undergoing, and the ARCS team working with, was the coming together of the bishop's Pastoral Plan and the move toward stewardship as a diocesan characteristic and practice (F, opening narrative). To both of these, the falling number of clergy and the need to cluster parishes was a crucial backdrop, to which the Pastoral Plan offered structural, largely *ad intra* responses whilst the stewardship vision took (in principle) a more lay-centred, *ad extra* approach. In fact, as noted in chapter 7 above, the tendency was to interpret stewardship in terms of ecclesial ministry, pulling the missionary back toward the maintaining of the existing church community.[24] The Pastoral Plan is clear in asserting the availability of Sunday Mass to all in the community as a fundamental commitment, and in many ways, the urgency of this concern is what shaped the stewardship processes and accompanying learning in the diocese. However, as the diocesan team worked in conversation with the ARCS team the potential for a more missionary account of Eucharist began to open up: "you have *become* the Body of Christ. You are going *out* to do the work of Christ" (F5, Diocesan 2). The beginnings of an *ad extra* theology of sacrament, and of Eucharist in particular, began to emerge.

One learning point considered by the ARCS team, which left a particular impression on me, was the possibility that liturgical sacraments could actually 'get in the way' of encountering the grace of Christ's presence elsewhere. The material discussed here certainly could support such a view, as we remember how the eucharistically centred parish of St. Mary's could still see itself as "not very Jesus-centred" (C3), and the 'sacredness' of the Mass could resist links being made to feeding the homeless (E3). We were reminded of an account given in an earlier piece of theological action research, carried out with a Catholic youth group.[25] Arriving late at the youth retreat where Adoration of the Blessed Sacrament was a permanent feature, other than when Mass was being celebrated, a young woman lamented that she had missed Adoration that day, and only made it in time for Mass. This meant, in her own words, that she couldn't "be with Jesus" until the next day. Here, Jesus' presence is not only identified with a liturgical event but with a more reified expression of sacrament still, oddly obscuring, rather than enabling, possibilities for encounter with Christ beyond the ritual and highly ecclesiastical. The risk is that the *ad intra*/*ad extra* tension in church understanding and life, particularly distorted by the *ad intra* pull, leads to a disconnection between sacrament and mission – and so the breaking of the coherence of church life at its very heart. In order to learn more constructive lessons of sacrament from the Practices, we needed to receive in fresh ways what they revealed about the 'sacramental' beyond the liturgical.

Before and after liturgy: the peri-liturgical sacramental

For all that the well-rehearsed tension between sacrament and mission seems evidenced in our Practices, there are strong signals that there is something more complex going on. An initial indicator of this would be the frequent recourse to meals and community as practices of church-in-mission that we have seen here: Alpha's emphasis on the shared meal and its impact (C2), Housing Justice's practices of sharing food with those in need (E3) and Messy Church's recognition of the importance of eating together (D, Opening narrative) all stand as typical witnesses to the pervasiveness of fellowship meals, something akin to Eucharist.

Beyond these practices themselves, the reflections on the data also add to our learning in this regard. So, whilst the Housing Justice volunteers themselves were reluctant to describe their work eucharistically, the connection for the ARCS team remained vivid and powerful as part of our learning. In part, this was due to the disclosive dynamic of the conversation across traditions, as my own highly sacramental tradition came into challenging engagement with the non-liturgical – some would say non-sacramental – tradition of Helen as a Salvationist. A key moment revolved around the interpretation of Richard's observation (E3) that he would miss Mass if help was needed in the kitchen. He reasoned, "it's all very well saying you love God, but if you're sat upstairs knowing that down below, they're ruched off their feet, that would just be ridiculous". For Helen, this was an example "of a realised eschatology when in the enactment of the kingdom on earth as it is in heaven, the need for the temple falls away".[26] For myself, on the other hand, there was a desire to see this as an embodying of connection between the grace of Eucharist and the grace at work among the volunteers and homeless. It is in the nature of theological action research conversations such as this that the interpretation does not need to be resolved; nether view had to be named as 'right'. Rather, the energy of conversation around this question indicated that something was struggling to be disclosed – something about the lively relationship between Eucharist and work for justice, Christian life in the world.

This instinct for a missiological account of Eucharist was persistent, informed not only by this conversation and the learning from Portsmouth (above) but also by the reading of both academic theology and church teaching which – in different ways – opened up possibilities for such interpretation. Reference has already been made to many of these sources.[27] They can be summed up by Benedict XVI's observation that:

> There is nothing authentically human – our thoughts and affections, our words and deeds – that does not find in the sacrament of the

> Eucharist the form it needs to be lived to the full. Here we can see the full human import of the radical newness brought by Christ in the Eucharist: the worship of God in our lives cannot be relegated to something private and individual, but tends by its nature to permeate every aspect of our existence.[28]

What working with the Practices did was remind us of these traditions and ways of thinking and so help us to return to them with a new and sharpened awareness of their importance for the living of church in the world. Once these connections had been made, wider possibilities for understanding the sacramentality of the Practices opened up.

Here, the naming of encounter with Christ is significant. For all the reluctance of the Housing Justice volunteers, it was precisely such a naming that was dominant in the focus group with the guests, who spoke of the Housing Justice work as an action of "the Body of Christ" (E1, Stephen). As another guest described it, "it's like God has said come into my house and get out of the cold" (E1, John). There is a naming of presence here which resonates with the language and understanding of sacrament. In a similar way, the London Jesuit Volunteers spoke of meeting Christ in those with whom they worked. For the ARCS team these connections seemed vivid and important. In part, this was informed by a growing sense of 'divine presences' or the expansivity of grace as a feature of the church in mission we were encountering. This is particularly clear among the LJV reflectors, where there is a sense of meeting Jesus afresh through their outreach work, with the sick and marginalised especially (A5) – experiences that help volunteers "reflect and decide to see Jesus Christ in others when I am not in really great situations, specially in the bus" (A5, Reflective Writing 5). Indeed, this world encounter with grace threw new light on their ordinary living – the washing of dishes, decisions about clothes (A2, Carla's story). There is a sense that sacramental language of grace, presence and transformation lie just below the surface in these accounts.

One response to this sacramental sense 'in the world' would be to develop a sacramental theology which was critical of, or even apart from, the liturgically celebrated sacraments – in something like the way that Segundo does.[29] Such a move would be well supported by, for example, a Salvationist reading of sacrament and Kingdom, as expressed by Helen's comments recorded earlier. However, to do this would be to fail to recognise that, for these practitioners at least, the Eucharist was a central part of their Christian faith. It is precisely the Eucharist that lies at the heart of the Portsmouth diocesan reforms (F5), and the Housing Justice volunteers, too, seem routinely connected to Eucharistic practices (E3). Such liturgical practice is evident, if not dominant, in the Accounts of St. Mary's Battersea (C5) and the Westminster Agency (B4), and can be assumed in the LJV context.[30] The issue is not so much whether sacrament is interpreted *either* liturgically *or* in terms of encounter in the world but rather, why is it that these different 'sacramentalities', or experiences of grace, were not better related in the thinking of the practitioners?

In part, the answer to this question is clearly given by James from the Housing Justice group when he suggests that the very ritual nature of the liturgical celebration of the Eucharist militates against its being connected to their practices in any lively, immediate way (E3). Here, it is as if a dominant operant ecclesiology which emphasises the distinction of *ad intra* and *ad extra*, comes into play so as to shape assumptions about what kind of connections can be made between practices defined in these ways. The sacramental becomes the liturgical, and so is defined as *ad intra*, making the sacramentality of things outside the structural life of church difficult to discern. Yet, as we have seen, the sense of encounter with *Christ* in the world, and specifically at the margins, is vividly attested to; surely it is such an encounter that theologically really connects the liturgical and in-the-world experiences of grace. It is in this nexus of graces that the learning around what I have called the 'peri-liturgical sacramental' came to light as a way of expressing simultaneously the centrality of Eucharist as ecclesial sacrament and the 'edgy' centrality of the encounter with eucharistic living in the world. It is reflection on this concept that may help to develop ways of sacramental thinking and practice which better enable living and powerful connections between the liturgical and the worldly graces of Christian life to be made.

Conclusions: exploring the peri-liturgical sacramental and its implications

The shape of the sacramental theology that is emerging here is distinctive in its desire to bring together liturgical sacrament with 'worldly' experience and practices of 'sacramentality'. In this, it echoes something of the ecclesiological shape that has so far come to light – of a church-in-and-for-the world which is 'held' by its smaller but more structured centre. By naming this theology as 'peri-liturgical sacramental', I am struggling to draw attention to the importance of holding together the *ad intra* practices with the living of church *ad extra*. Referring to the encounter with Christ's presence in the world as 'peri-liturgical' emphasises the ways in which these graces are centred in a sacramental reality which can be explicitly and assuredly recognised in the ecclesial practices of liturgy. Christian life in the world draws us to Christ's presence in the Eucharist, where we join our lives and service to his own, and from that celebration we are compelled out to the world to meet him there afresh.

However, the language of 'peri-liturgical', the concept itself, cannot entirely enable living connections to be made between liturgical sacramental and the sacramentality of daily living. What seems to be indicated is further reflection on what formative initiatives – in relation to both liturgy and lay living and social action – might be needed to enable such mutual enlivening.

There are hints of this already in the data – whether in the question of the rather formal and ritual nature of liturgy (E3, James), or in the sense that the liturgy itself (and attention to it) can proclaim the sacramentality of wider Christian life (A5, F5). Here, ideas of being ourselves "bread broken for the world", and being *sent out* from Mass to be "the Body of Christ" indicated that such liturgical proclamation concerning life in the world was possible and valuable.

Perhaps the most powerful formative influence, however, lies in the practices themselves, and the reflection on them which enabled practitioners to articulate encounter with Christ and his saving grace in their work in the world. This experience has the powerful potential to unlock the sacramental from any overly rigid confinement to the ritual, and in doing so, breathe new life from embodied theologies into the normative notion of the lay priesthood as called to "consecrate the world to Christ".[31] How such a peri-liturgically sacramental work of laity is to be understood in relation to the ordained priesthood, and how it, and its supporting ecclesiology, might affect the lay-ordained relationship is the discussion to which we next turn.

Notes

1 This chapter is indebted to the earlier article Clare Watkins and Helen Cameron, "Epiphanic Sacramentality: An Example of Practical Ecclesiology Revisioning Theological Understanding." Christian B. Scharen ed. *Explorations in Ecclesiology and Ethnography* (Eerdmans, 2012): 71–89.
2 See comments on the secular identity of laity, as set out 103, n.2 above.
3 Quoted by John MacQuarrie, *A Guide to the Sacraments* (SCM, 1999): 4. In the Roman Catholic Church a close parallel to this can be found in *Catechism of the Catholic Church* 1127–1129.
4 For a reliable history of sacraments and their development, see Joseph Martos, *Doors to the Sacred: A Historical Introduction to Sacraments in the Catholic Church*. Rev. and Updated ed. (Liquori/Triumph, 2001).
5 *Catechism of the Catholic Church*, §1116.
6 This idea was made especially popular through the report *On the Way to Life* (2005), authored out of the Heythrop Institute for Religion, Ethics and Public Life. Available at: http://cbcew.org.uk/plain/wp-content/uploads/sites/3/2018/11/on-the-way-to-life-2005.pdf.
7 Avery Dulles, *Models of the Church*. 2nd ed. (Gill and Macmillan, 1987).
8 Vatican II Dogmatic Constitution on the Church, *Lumen Gentium*, 1: "the Church is in Christ like a sacrament or as a sign and instrument both of a very closely knit union with God and of the unity of the whole human race".
9 Dulles, op. cit. 55–67.
10 Ibid. 67.
11 See note 8.
12 *Lumen Gentium*, op. cit. chaps. 1 and 2.
13 Karl Rahner, *The Church and the Sacraments* (Herder, 1966): 19.
14 *veluti sacramentum*, *Lumen Gentium*, 1.
15 Ibid.
16 Ion Bria, *The Liturgy After the Liturgy* (WCC Publications, 1996).

17 So see: Enda McDonagh, "Fruit of the Earth – Work of Human Hands." Mary Grey ed. *The Candles Are Still Burning: Directions in Sacrament and Spirituality* (Geoffrey Chapman, 1995): 22–31; and Bernard Haring, *The Sacraments in a Secular Age: A Vision in Depth on Sacramentality and Its Impact on Moral Life* (St Paul Publications, 1976).
18 Juan Luis Segundo, *Theology for Artisans of a New Humanity (vol. 4): The Sacraments Today* (Orbis Books, 1973); Tissa Balasuriya, *The Eucharist and Human Liberation* (SCM, 1979).
19 See Bria, op. cit.
20 Benedict XVI, Apostolic Exhortation, *Sacramentum Caritatis*, 2007. Available at: http://w2.vatican.va/content/benedict-xvi/en/apost_exhortations/documents/hf_ben-xvi_exh_20070222_sacramentum-caritatis.html.
21 It is significant that the learning in this area for the ARCS team was enabled by conversations between Roman Catholic and Salvationist traditions. See Watkins and Cameron, op. cit, note 1.
22 Segundo, op. cit. 8.
23 See *Catechism of the Catholic Church*, 1128: "From the moment that a sacrament is celebrated in accordance with the intention of the Church, the power of Christ and his Spirit acts in and through it, independently of the personal holiness of the minister".
24 See 122–126 above.
25 This was research carried out with Youth 2000 during the ARCS project.
26 "Epiphanic Sacramentaility", op. cit. 77.
27 Notes 16–18 above.
28 *Sacramentum Caritatis*, op. cit. 71.
29 Note 18.
30 It is interesting to note here that Dr. Susy Brouard's subsequent theological action research project at CAFOD, building on that recorded in this book, concluded that there was a Eucharist 'shape' to CAFOD's work, even as an organization made up of people with a variety of faiths, and none. See, Susanna Brouard "Using Theological Action Research to Embed Catholic Social Teaching in a Catholic Development Agency: Abseiling on the Road to Emmaus." Unpub. Prof. Doc. (Anglia Ruskin University, 2015). Available at: https://ethos.bl.uk/OrderDetails.do?uin=uk.bl.ethos.669009. Accessed August 2019.
31 *Lumen Gentium*, op. cit. 34.

Account of practice F

Roman Catholic Diocese of Portsmouth

Project time frame: February 2006–March 2009

Introductory narrative

Two of the ARCS team – Clare Watkins and James Sweeney – had already worked with agencies of the Roman Catholic Diocese of Portsmouth in an earlier research project exploring Catholic responses to the call to evangelisation.[1] The Diocese had been experienced as one with particular energy for renewal as well as structural change, led, at that time, by a bishop committed to fresh visions for the church and an open, collaborative and participative leadership style. When the ARCS project was established, the diocese expressed enthusiasm for continuing research work and so became one of the earliest projects with whom we worked. This latter fact explains why much of the data referred to in this chapter is rather dissimilar from our other accounts of practice: as our theological action research methodology took shape, processes for participation, and practitioner reflection were established which, at this early stage, were still very much in embryo. Indeed, one of our disclosures below (4) is precisely concerned with the sharp learning around the needs for a genuinely participative theology.

The Roman Catholic Diocese of Portsmouth covers a geographically large area – Hampshire, the Isle of Wight, the Channel Isles and parts of Berkshire, Dorset and Oxfordshire – and was at that time seeing church numbers in certain areas grow through the large number of Polish workers coming to the south of England. Like many dioceses, faced with falling clergy numbers, financial difficulties and the call to mission in an increasingly secular world, the diocese had received from its bishop a pastoral plan – *Go Out and Bear Fruit* (2005).[2] The plan aimed to address the shortage of priests by grouping parishes into Pastoral Areas with a number of priests serving each area. Whilst this strategy had the advantage of keeping many parish communities running, it changed the relationship between priest and parish, and potentially – as well as actually, in some cases – lessened the availability of a priest to a particular community. The traditional model of parish and parish priest was challenged, raising both theological and canonical[3] questions as well as practical, pastoral ones.

Furthermore, it was evident that this way of working would need to be accompanied by greater lay involvement. In recognition of this, one strand of the pastoral plan was to support the development of 'stewardship', calling on all members of the community to recognise their gifts and responsibilities for their local church and parish. The plan puts it as follows:

> We are stewards of the gift of creation and all that life brings: our time, our treasure our talents and one another. Therefore, we have a duty to ensure that we make the best use of all we have, and that we do this in a way which respects the dignity of every person and promotes the common good.

This strand was picked up with particular energy through the implementation of a 'stewardship process'. In this, the diocese drew inspiration and help from the 1992 Pastoral Letter of the United States Conference of Catholic Bishops, *Stewardship: A Disciple's Response*,[4] with further inspiration being drawn from attendance by diocesan personnel from Portsmouth at the annual conferences of the International Catholic Stewardship Council. People returned to the United Kingdom spiritually renewed and passionate about implementing the process in local parishes. The bishop recognised the potential of this vision, and encouraged it as an important part of the implementation of the Pastoral Plan.

Accordingly, across the diocese, structures were established to support the stewardship process: a Pastoral Plan Implementation Steering Group, the Diocesan Trustees Stewardship Committee, a part-time Advisor to the Clergy on Stewardship, a Schools Stewardship Group and a full-time Advisor for Stewardship and Collaborative Ministry in the Department for Pastoral Formation. Pilot stewardship parishes were selected to establish the process in local areas and discover the best ways to roll out the plan across the diocese.

The ARCS team worked with the Head of the Department for Pastoral Formation along with other members of the Pastoral Plan Implementation Steering Group to explore the theology of Stewardship over two cycles of theological action research. The initial research aim which emerged from preliminary meetings was:

> To describe and reflect upon the practice and theology of the Stewardship Pilots with a view to influencing the full implementation of Stewardship in Pastoral Areas.

Fundamental to the project was the need to define the concept of stewardship in terms of theology and ecclesiology. These questions naturally led into consideration of the local settings in which the initiative was trialled:

- Which pilot sites were chosen and why?
- How were the parish stewardship teams trained or formed for the task and what resources were used?

- What was the impact of the project? This included theological reflection and reflection on ecclesiological implications for the parish and the wider community.

In the first cycle of research, the implementation of stewardship was explored in five pilot parishes. A volunteer co-researcher from within the diocese carried out in-depth interviews with key personnel at diocesan level: the Head of Finance and Property, a part-time Advisor to Clergy on Stewardship, a parish priest and active lay woman at two different pilot parishes. Cycle one also included notes from a clergy stewardship workshop several months into the pilot, which raised key theological themes. Theological materials were collected and reflected upon by the outsider team. One of the members of the ARCS team then undertook a grounded theory analysis on this data and a theological paper was prepared and fed back to the Implementation Steering Group, the heads of department and the Trustees Stewardship Committee. As can be seen, this first cycle does not follow what was later established as the theological action research process, which requires participation in reflection on the data from the practitioner, insider group as well as the outsider team. This reflects the learning that was done by the team as the research proceeded.

The outsider theological reflections were received enthusiastically by the Portsmouth Diocese. They named issues that the diocese were wrestling with and offered food for thought. They touched upon the following themes: Eucharist, Christology and Stewardship; issues of ecclesial structure and order in church life; organisation and community; and how to put into practice issues raised in theological reflection. Questions were raised, both in terms of method or process and ecclesiology, which were to provide the impetus for the second cycle of research.

This second cycle involved more data collection by the volunteer co-researcher in individual worshipping communities and pastoral areas. These congregations were explored using three parish questionnaires and two in-depth interviews with parishioners, as well as collecting further parish resource materials over several months. The purpose was to explore whether and how practice and theological thinking had been influenced by the first cycle of research. Subsequent to the second cycle, and as a way of increasing participation in the research for the diocesan teams, a capacity-building workshop was held with the Diocesan group overseeing the stewardship programme, led by members of the ARCS team. Here, major themes from the research were explored in more depth, as well as formative input and exercises being given so as to build confidence in theological reflection as integral to the work of the diocese.

Compared to later projects of the ARCS research, the processes employed here were often lacking and tended to be unclear as regards participation. Nonetheless, the conversations between the diocesan and ARCS teams, which were minuted in detail, together with the research data, can provide an effective witness to some significant learning. Five especially enlightening points are set out in what follows.

Five disclosures

1 Effecting renewal: diocesan plans and processes

Pastoral reorganisation is a common theme in many denominations as churches work to catch up with significant and rapid demographic changes – both those particular to their church, as well as those prevalent in wider society. In episcopally led denominations, the bishop has a central role in determining how that reorganisation takes place, although how that authority is enacted may vary. The approach in Portsmouth at the time of the research was to hold a review of the diocese before the Pastoral Plan was developed, and then to give substantial discretion to parishes in its implementation with the role of the diocesan officers being that of support and encouragement. This reflected a culture of collaboration, participation and the shared ownership of change and response. The outsider team felt that once the new structure of pastoral areas was largely in place, attention shifted to stewardship as the main aspect of the plan. This may have been because representatives from the diocese were attending stewardship conferences in America and coming back with ideas and enthusiasm for implementing stewardship. The structural narrative suggested that the emphasis on stewardship came after the Pastoral Plan, and that in the processes accompanying stewardship the links to the Plan were not always clear.

Something of this concern was attended to in the materials used in 'Stewardship Formation Sessions' in parishes, where the link between the Pastoral Plan and Stewardship was explained with the following quote from the Bishop:

> As we seek to implement the Pastoral Plan in response to the call we all receive from Christ to 'go out and bear fruit', we need to respond as His true disciples. I am convinced that Christian stewardship will enable us to do that. . . . The commitment that Portsmouth will become a 'stewardship diocese', that is, one where the principles of Christian stewardship will have an important place in our lives, is an important step for us all. . . . As Pastoral Areas develop and we begin to work together, what better way than to look at these changes in the diocese through the eyes of a good steward.
>
> Let's ask ourselves questions such as
>
> - What do we have in our Pastoral Area to give special thanks for?
> - What are the talents and gifts of everyone in our worshipping communities?
> - Do we recognise and value these gifts? Do we need to spend time and discover them, together with the talents, which God has given to each of us?

> Through the eyes of a good steward, everything we do, no matter how humdrum we may find it, can be a means to give praise to God.

The outsider team suggested that through theological reflection, a deeper and more consistently owned narrative needed to be recaptured that enabled parish priests and lay people to see the connection between the wider agenda of the pastoral plan and the specific focus on stewardship. To some extent, the two cycles of theological action research contributed to this, although questions for reflection remained for the diocese.

2 *The changing role of the parish priest*

The creation of pastoral areas with teams of clergy looking after a number of parishes signalled a different relationship between priest and parish, as already noted. Within Roman Catholic Canon Law, the parish is defined in a way which makes the existence of a parish priest integral to its identity:

> A parish is a certain community of the Christian faithful stably constituted in a particular church, whose pastoral care is entrusted to a pastor (*parochus*) as its proper pastor (*pastor*) under the authority of the diocesan bishop.[5]

Whilst this canon may not be widely known by the lay faithful, the longstanding culture of parish which it sustains is, nonetheless, a powerful formative reality for both lay people and clerics. In particular, the diocesan clergy would – explicitly or not – generally understand their working lives in terms of being a 'parish priest', with 'his own' parish community.

Perhaps this ecclesial understanding lies behind the research finding that the focus on stewardship felt to at least some priests like a focus on the laity at the expense of their distinctive roles. This sense that stewardship might undermine the parish priest's role can be further illustrated by the experience that the stewardship process in two out of the five pilot parishes "ground to a halt" when there was a change in parish priest. It became clear to both insider and outsider teams "that the leadership of the priest is key to the entire enterprise"[6] – a learning point which became an important one for the diocesan team as it developed ways of working with clergy and their particular questions and concerns. A Clergy Advisor on Stewardship was appointed to work specifically with the priests of the diocese, and his reflections on his experience became an important part of the project data. In particular, he found that some parish priests found it "difficult to be open with their people because of their own training and shaping. Until the priest feels comfortable with it, it cannot really flourish".[7] The stewardship process, with its sense of collaboration and lay participation in mission and ministry required communication and relationship skills and gifts which many clergy may not have felt they needed to nurture and develop in their ministry to date.

At the meeting of ARCS researchers with the diocesan team at the end of Cycle One, the Clergy Advisor was able to report on his work, identifying a number of concerns and questions from the priests with whom he had worked:

> **Role of Clergy Advisor on stewardship**
>
> [Clergy]Advisor is specifically visiting pastoral areas (PAs) and speaking to the clergy in the parishes/PAs. Giving a brief outline of stewardship and trying to root it theologically and ecclesiologically. His input has been received generously. Some questions arise about the terminology – is "stewardship" a Catholic word? Is there some diocesan hidden agenda? Once this is out of the way there is an opportunity for deeper reflection; to affirm the personal 'commitment' of the clergy (how their faith journey has affected their lives). He has visited 15 PAs to date.
>
> (out of 24)
>
> Speculatively – [the Clergy Advisor] expects all Coordinating Pastors [one per Pastoral Area] to be *au fait* with Stewardship as it's the vehicle that is to carry forward the pastoral plan. Expect the co-ordinating pastors to go to the international conference – 1 or 2 each time, so it 'infects' the diocese. Ultimately, stewardship should also be included in clergy formation, especially for newly ordained and new people in the diocese. Stewardship part of a communication vocabulary. This is part of lifting it up to the next level.
>
> There is a need to clear the ground. Ecclesiological jargon and scripture based language which priests are familiar with, conversation shared from their own experience – that is key.
>
> [. . .]
>
> There is concern over change in Mass times. Sense (amongst clergy) of waiting for someone to get on with it; a need to practically re-think i.e. mass times/Eucharistic communities. Need to get an understanding and communication (including with parishioners) that pragmatic considerations are part of Stewardship.
>
> (Cycle 1, Notes of Feedback Meeting with Diocesan Representatives)

This account witnesses to the real need for formation in stewardship for the clergy themselves, if the process and vision was to be fully embodied on the ground. We can note the language of 'infection' as suggestive of something that needs to be 'caught' and thoroughly permeate communities, and, in this metaphor, the clergy are seen as significant 'carriers' of ideas and language. It is also clear that a level of 'personal conversion' to stewardship was needed for clergy to be effective in the diocesan plan. This, in turn, was making demands on the reflective capacities of priests, not all of whom would have received a formation which leant itself to such processes. For all this, there was also evidence of some priests in the pilot parishes finding the stewardship concept liberating. One of those interviewed responded with a sense of personal growth through stewardship:

> There is a need to engender a joyfulness or celebration about a priest's role. It's [the stewardship process] giving priests the opportunity to celebrate who they are/rediscover their gifts/talents; a way of coping with an extremely stressful job, living life like a stretched elastic band.
>
> (Parish Priest Interview)

Still, it was striking that the difficulties of sustaining stewardship in parishes after a change of clergy personnel, together with the rather *ad intra* anxieties around Mass times and their implications, spoke of both a lack of felt agency among clergy, and a real structural power located in the ordained leaders as crucial *loci* for the enabling or not of stewardship. Anxieties, both theological and practical, continued to impede notions of shared or 'collaborative' mission and ministry as this conversation excerpt from the feedback meeting shows:

DIOCESAN 1: Stewardship is not the "least-worst option". I'm much more positive than this. It is a good time in the church when the laity can become fully empowered. I don't see the need for a clerically led church; lay people can share collaboratively with the priest in the leadership of the Church. Difficult as notions of collaborative ministry are embryonic.

CLERGY ADVISOR: Collaborative ministry an important issue with priests. Collaborative ministry is not a shift of power; there is also a lack of training, the laity needs to be trained and resourced. Some collaborative ministry has pushed the priest out. Need to provide formation for both clergy and laity in this regard.

3 *Laity and the* ad intra *pull*

As is clear from the opening narrative to this chapter, the laity are central to the stewardship process, both in principle (theologically) and in practice. A priest working in one of the pilot parishes recognised this early on:

> When the pilot started, I found the best people to speak to the people were the people. When celebrating the gifts, the best thing was [for] the people, including the retired, to speak of their ministry. Why am I performing this ministry? This had a tremendous impact to have that different voice speaking the language and not overtly theological jargon.
>
> (Cycle One, Clergy Workshop)

Here a lay person speaks about their experience of coming to understand stewardship:

> My understanding of Stewardship has changed dramatically since the first meeting. I had completely misunderstood its meaning and importance.... I thought it was based on the need for the laity to become more involved in parish life due to lack of priests and the likelihood of fewer priests in the future ... [but] Stewardship is recognising that everything comes from God and everything is a gift.... How and when we use our gifts will change over time depending on personal circumstances but there will always be a way that what we have can be used to spread God's message.
>
> (Questionnaire)

What we see here is a bigger vision of lay vocation, which is not simply an *ad intra* necessity to 'keep the show on the road' but rather seeks to embrace lay living in its authentic entirety, beyond simply ecclesial activities for the parish organisation.

However, the process of implementing the stewardship programme highlighted tensions in the understanding of the role of the laity, particularly in relation to that of the priest:

> Some think they are being very trendy when they say that the shortage of priests is providential; it's the Holy Spirit telling lay people that they need to take more responsibility for the life of the church, I think that's rubbish actually. I think that JPII's [Pope John Paul II's] statement that a church without vocations is a sick church is right. It is not the vocation of the lay faithful to be running the church; it's the vocation of the lay faithful to be converting the world. Jesus Christ did not come so that the church would run like a well-oiled machine and the reality is we have 85 active priests in the diocese and maybe another 10 religious priests and there is no way they can be missionaries to the whole world, but they can be missionaries to their own communities who can then be missionaries to the whole world. Scriptural precedent for this Christ chose 12 men who chose other people until at least third of the entire population of the entire Roman Empire in 300 years were converted. Asking people to be disciples of Christ, not to be stirring the ecclesiastical pot!
>
> (Interview, Head of the Department of Finance and Property)

What is being struggled with here is the perennial question of lay and ordained vocations in the church – a question thrown into sharp relief by the diocesan Pastoral Plan, and its attendant vision of stewardship.

One especially complex factor in this common-enough issue of lay-ordained collaboration was the way in which stewardship seemed rhetorically to encourage an *ad extra* mission of the laity, whilst in practice, coloured by the strategic concerns of the Pastoral Plan, tended to turn rapidly into calls for laity to 'do more in the parish'. This was acknowledged in the ARCS review meeting with Portsmouth Diocese in 2008, in which the second cycle was discerned. Here, one of the key challenges identified following waves 1 & 2 of the stewardship pilots was:

> How to shift focus of stewardship away from overemphasis on 'churchy' things towards a 24/7 living out of discipleship?

Comments from the clergy workshop also highlighted this question, suggesting that there had been a formative emphasis on the *ad intra* for both laity and clergy, which impeded a fresh emphasis on the *ad extra*:

> It is difficult to inspire people about stewardship as some see it as just another project.
>
> We have not equipped people for the world of work or marriage or youth etc. We have been inward looking, not outward looking.

This difficulty was reflected back and debated at the capacity building workshop:

> **Living in the ad intra/ad extra tension**
>
> The ecclesiological tension between *ad intra* and *ad extra* ways of understanding and being church is perennial in our ARCS research, and very much a feature of the Portsmouth processes. In particular, the universal (?) tendency for the *ad intra*, maintenance demands of church to pull us away from the *ad extra*, missionary call needs to be brought to the fore-front of our reflections. The call to theological reflection is call to openness to the prompting of the Spirit, and a vocation of the *laos* – the whole people of God. Theological reflection cannot be done by a church group on behalf of everyone else; nor can it be a vehicle for particular agendas. The challenge, then, especially for diocesan leadership (inevitably an *ad intra* group in emphasis), is how to communicate a culture of openness, and *ad extra* call, to a *laos* whose proper living of discipleship is *ad extra*.
>
> (Capacity Building Workshop, ARCS Team Member Reflections)

Discussion of these ideas exposed the need for the thorough espousal of a theology of orders which differentiated the purpose of each order and its role in the life of the church and the life of the world, and their interrelationships. This is matter taken up in chapter 10 of the present volume, informed by learning in this area across the projects undertaken by ARCS.

4 Whose theology? 'Outsourcing' and participation

In a project that has proceeded by way of a multitude of shared conversations, there are nevertheless phrases which stand out and act as a defining moments. This disclosure focuses on one such moment, when the diocesan team received the ARCS reflections as an 'outsourcing' of their theology:

> **Feedback [ARCS theological reflection] paper**
>
> Immensely valuable to have an outsourced theological reflection on stewardship and the process of its implementation. We would like this conversation to continue.
>
> (Minutes of Insider Meeting, Jan 2008)

The insider team had made notes in preparation for the feedback meeting at the end of the first cycle, from which this observation is drawn. This observation was picked up again at a later meeting: and recorded in the notes of the meeting.

> Financial Secretary of Portsmouth Diocese commented it has been "extraordinarily useful to have outsourced our theological reflection externally". He emphasised the trustees were committed to the research and open to advice from ARCS.
>
> (Joint Meeting May 2008)

Our method was still in the early stages of development at this point, with no developed understanding of the importance of the dynamics between insider and outsider teams, and this response marked a significant moment in our methodological thinking and practice. This was, in fact, a 'negative epiphany'. What was intended as a compliment by a member of the insider team actually evoked a powerful and instinctive reaction from the outsider team that they – and the processes they had hoped to engender – had been misunderstood.

Our response as an outsider team was to realise that the co-ownership of action research had been missed and that we were being portrayed simply as outsiders bringing expertise into the organisation – expert consultants, perhaps.[8] It was seductive for the team to fall into that role, but we realised how important it was to prioritise the insider reflections and to put them alongside any reflections from us as outsider team, in order to be faithful to our understanding of 'whole theology' and the processes of action research (see chapters 3 and 4 of the present volume). This disclosure also helped us realise the depth of the stereotype of what constitutes theology – that it comes from outside the everyday life of the church in the hands of experts who advise. This realisation needed to inform our approach to future projects and encouraged us to develop our communication of, and – where possible – training in and for theological action research, as well as more clearly establishing norms and processes for insider team reflections and shared feedback between teams.

5 Eucharistic communities: promise and risk

A final observation from this project may be briefly made. One of the concerns for the diocese in its restructuring – as for many Roman Catholic dioceses facing a shortage of priests in relation to its parish numbers – was for the maintaining of Eucharist as central to communities. Arguably the canonical insistence on a parish being identified as under the pastoral care of a particular parish priest is a product of the strong sense that a parish community as a 'Eucharistic community' that regularly gathers around the altar for the celebration of the sacrament of communion. The Pastoral Plan makes this commitment clear as a part of the rationale for the development of Pastoral Areas:

> Sunday Mass is central to our identity and mission. The whole community gathers to listen to the Word of God and to give thanks and praise with Jesus to the Father in the Eucharistic Prayer of the Mass. As we eat and drink the body and blood of Jesus in Holy Communion, we become more fully the Body of Christ, sent into the world to continue Jesus' mission to transform the world.... This Diocese wants to ensure that Sunday Mass continues to be celebrated as widely as possible by as many people as possible (*Go Out and Bear Fruit* p6).

Strikingly, the processes around stewardship and the Pastoral Plan were drawing the diocesan team into reflections about the Eucharist understood in a missionary, or *ad extra* mode, as can be discerned in these notes from the Joint Reflection Meeting:

In response to being asked about the lack of Christological focus by ARCS member:

DIOCESAN 2: "Christ" is a "given" in the Eucharistic focus. Who is Christ for me? – not explicitly drawn out. Church is expressed. Holy Spirit not explicitly expressed – room for development there.

DIOCESAN 3: Being created and being gifted. God is the giver; we have responsibility this is a profound insight.

DIOCESAN 2: And Redemption – Pascal mystery. "We are bread broken for the world". PP mentioned "No genuflection at the end of Mass" because you have *become* the body of Christ. You are going *out* to do the work of Christ.

ARCS 1: Power in being told to "Go" rather than "The Mass is ended".

There is a glimpse here of a sacramental or eucharistic theology of *ad extra* Christian living – a theme further explored in this book's chapter 9.

Concluding reflections

A perennial challenge for all involved in theological reflection is how to make the step from reflection into practice. In the diocesan context, the theological, as well as practical, understanding of structure is of particular significance; as an episcopal church, the Catholic diocese of Portsmouth was not only dependent on the vision and enablement of their bishop but also – in sometimes more conclusive ways – on the participation and ownership of diocesan clergy. In all theological action research, and practical theological work more generally, when something comes to light through our theological thinking together, there is a quite proper (and difficult!) question that will follow: what does it take for this to be embodied in our church? Where and how is this to happen? What structures/processes need to be put in place to bring this about? The nature of the structural context and its theological significance will be what shapes our response to these questions.

These realities were particularly played out in this project not only during the research, but in the years following, when the change of bishop and subsequent departure of many of those in the original diocesan team significantly changed the culture of renewal, and effectively ended the stewardship process. In the later capacity-building projects that ARCS ran, a smaller team from a Pastoral Area within the diocese did take part, inspired by what they had heard and seen in the ARCS project with the diocese. However, one of the striking features of this project must be how difficult it is to renew an ecclesial culture through theological reflection 'from the ground up', especially in the context of uninvolved or unsupportive clerical leaders.

Notes

1 James Sweeney and the present author.
2 www.portsmouthdiocese.org.uk/plan/plan2005.pdf. Accessed August 2019.
3 The Canons make clear the nature of the parish as a territory whose care is entrusted to an ordained priest: Can. 515/1.
4 A summary of the document can be found at www.usccb.org/beliefs-and-teachings/what-we-believe/stewardship/index.cfm. Accessed August 2019.
5 *Canon Law of the Roman Catholic Church* Can. 515 §1.
6 Update from Portsmouth Diocese for ARCS team meeting 29th January 2008.
7 Clergy Workshop 21 September 2007, cycle one, 2.
8 See Elaine Graham, "Is Practical Theology a Form of 'Action Research'?" *International Journal of Practical Theology* 17, no.1 (2013): 164.

10 Orders and ordering

Life together in the power of the Spirit

> Collaborative ministry is an important issue with priests. Collaborative ministry is not a shift in power; there is also a lack of training, the laity needs to be trained and resourced. Some collaborative ministry has pushed the priest out.
>
> (Portsmouth Diocese, F2, Clergy Advisor)

> Isabel feels bad. . . . She often feels frustrated about her inability to do more for the people she tries to support . . . and needs to remind herself that finally it is God who does these things through her.
>
> (London Jesuit Volunteers, A4, Participant Observation 3, Isabel's Story)

In the previous chapter, the ecclesiology being disclosed in our four voices approach enabled a reading of sacrament that was more missiological, more *ad extra*, than that usually found. The challenge of this chapter's theme is how the reading of edgy-edgeless church might renew that most *ad intra* of concerns – 'orders': ordination, lay living and the practicalities of power in the life of the community. This theme was an unavoidable reality encountered in various ways working with the practitioner groups, whether these groups were lay led within hierarchical ecclesial cultures, or whether they were themselves located in the more clerically led, structural expressions of church life.[1] For both the church traditions with which we worked – though in different ways – there is an established patterning of the community around the ordained/laity distinction, with a historic emphasis on the ordained as leaders and as possessing authority rooted not only in expertise and through training but also in sacramental understanding. This ecclesial tradition generated a culture where these patternings of power and power relations were pervasive and formative. As well as the sociologically well-recognised significance of power, power-relations and authorities,[2] the theological legacy concerning these issues is fraught. It is not for nothing that power and orders was one of the first areas of contention experienced by Christians; we need only remember the arguments between the brothers James and John (Mark 10:35–45) and the in-fighting evident in Corinth to recognise that questions of power and authority are deeply human, relational and so deeply ecclesiological. Arguably, the (inevitable) codifying of roles and gifts through ordination[3] and the establishment of different ministries in relation to one another (hierarchy) has further complexified these human struggles by freighting them with theological meaning and significance. Martyn Percy identifies the resulting church difficulties well, lamenting a certain 'divine blueprint' approach to ministry and ordination which results in what he terms 'fundamentalist' and 'creationist' accounts of ordained ministry.[4] As he comments:

> the majority of theologies that inform studies of ministry are primarily deductive in character. That is to say, Christianity's uniqueness and validity are treated as being simply given, a priori.[5]

This reference to Percy's important work in this field also prompts the need to be clear about this chapter's holding together of the themes of power and the structuring of the church around authorised and ordained ministries located in a community in which the vast majority are 'lay'. Like Percy, I would argue that it is crucially important – practically *and* theologically – to reflect on the practicalities of authority, leadership and ordination in our churches within a context which is informed by a reading of the complexity of power. Too often, studies of ordination and of laity-clergy relationships have spoken of power and authority in overly simplistic and ultimately unhelpful ways, in terms of those with or without power/authority, where power is something basically understood as power *over* somebody else.[6] Those of us speaking about these things after the work of Arendt and Foucault, who in different ways draw attention to a greater complexity of power, need more authentically layered understandings of power – as 'power with', 'power to', and 'power relation/dynamic'[7] – if we are to be adequately equipped to offer an appropriately nuanced account of power and its embodiment and practice within Christian community.

In fact, we are here moving to a place of an interpenetration of disciplinary, theoretical and practical concerns within the 'formal voice' of the academy which can only be suggestively alluded to in the space provided here.[8] At the same time, we are working within ecclesial normative theological traditions which – in their catholic expressions – have an established language of "sacred power"[9] (all be it "for service"), which is rooted in some sense of permanent change in the ordained person and transforms their relationship to the rest of the community. For all the language of "service" that accompanies this liturgical and theological language, in both Anglican and Roman Catholic traditions, the practices and rhetoric of 'setting apart', and 'pastoring'[10] carry with them a normativity of both ideas and structures of authority, leadership and 'power over', at least symbolically. At the same time, both modern political philosophy and sociologies of organisation and power, whilst not neglecting the possibilities and realities of 'power over', also make clear the pervasiveness of power and the inevitability of its structural expression as legitimated authority within human communities. To be human and in relationships is to be implicated in 'power dynamics'.[11] In this regard, ecclesiology and the church practices into which it speaks are unavoidably concerned with power, authority and its expression; as ever, the interdisciplinary theological question which demands attention is how to be authentically theological about ecclesial realities whilst avoiding those 'divine blueprints' to which Percy refers, which leave our theology bereft of realistic understandings of human living and communal practice.

Whilst any exhaustive account of ecclesiology and power, understood interdisciplinarily, is clearly beyond the scope of this chapter, a few significant observations may be made from recent literature which inform our discernment of what is learnt from the reflections on our Practices. First of all, the sheer complexity and pervasiveness of power as a theme and as human reality needs to be acknowledged. The contested nature of power is a clear foundation for the sociological argument of Lukes and the theological argument of Sykes; but further thinking, informed, as is Kearsley's, by Arendt and Foucault, enables a closer naming of that contestation, by referring to power over, power to, and power with,[12] accompanied by the realisation that power can be rightly seen as "coming from everywhere",[13] and is therefore best considered in terms of relations and dynamics. This is an important point for ecclesiologists who all too often have considered power and authority in ways polarised by structural ecclesial notions of lay and ordained.

Emerging from this proper complexifying of power and its expressions is the more nuanced notion of *agency*, as descriptive of the variety of ways in which individuals (whether in authority or not), and groups can effect change and/or be effective in their intentions. This highlights the ways in which, as Foucault especially makes clear, ordinary human activity around communication, behaviours and habits can be recognised as more or less intended exercises of power. As Kearsley notes, according to this reading, "handshakes, compliments, hugs and smiles can be rationed out as unintended but meaningful gestures of exclusion"[14] – an observation calling for much reflection from Christian people, especially those in public ministry. Most significantly of all for the ecclesiologist, the naming of agency in relation to power raises a central question of *whose agency?*, and draws us to fundamental questions of what (or who), in the churches' understanding is the root of all power. As Lyndon Shakespeare puts it: "The church … is oriented and ordered; the questions are, to what and by whom?"[15] Whilst not fully agreeing with Shakespeare's (to my mind overly) critical account of management sciences, his work gives us the gift of a clear demonstration of the radical implications of understanding the church not simply as an organisation but as the Body of Christ. This embodiment, which is central to biblical and subsequent understandings of church, draws attention to the Christian community as one which, deeply, intentionally and explicitly, lives life "in the Spirit". It is in the Holy Spirit that the life and power of the church must ultimately rest.

No ecclesiology can be written today which is entirely innocent of these concerns and sensitivities, and there are any number of pastoral realities which add considerable energy to the themes of power, authority and empowerment as we shall see. However, it is arguable that recent theologies of church have overstated the significance of structural expressions of power and authority in church life, formed by and then contributing to the tendency to an *ad intra* focus for ecclesiology. In what follows, informed by more complex and pervasive notions of power and its variety of expression in human communities and relationship, I explore how our disclosed ecclesiology, with its *ad extra* centring in Christian practice in the world might enable us to bring a fresh perspective to this area of church life and thought. In particular, the often-implicit place of the Holy Spirit as agential in the Practices' living of church will come to the fore in our second theme below. First, however, the ways in which power and authority is witnessed to in the ARCS practices is considered.

The reality and complexity of power in the life of the church

Earlier allusion was made to the common-enough paradox – some would say platitude – of describing the 'sacred power' of the ordained as 'service'. This characterising of Christian authority and position as primarily service *rather than* power is frequently observed and can reasonably be critiqued as risking the masking of real power, and so contributing to ecclesial self-deceit.[16] Be that as it may, the paradoxical language persists, in part because of its biblical provenance (e.g., Mark 10: 35–45; John 13: 12–16; I Cor. 1: 18–25), but also because of the felt need to express, however imperfectly, the sense that in ordaining people, and in adopting practical structures of order, leadership and administration, the Christian community is not merely conforming to human practices. Rather, it is, at the same time, seeking to embody something radically different, as human relationships including power relationships, are transformed by the Spirit. This paradox is not, our Accounts of Practice suggest, merely a conceptual one, but one that is also embodied in Christian living as church structures and authorities are experienced as both enabling and disabling, both as of service and as limiting.

It was noted earlier in this book that lay-led initiatives had certain advantages over the more structurally involved practices precisely because there was a certain freedom, and an in-built solidarity with the 'world', and the larger context which mitigated to some extent the '*ad intra* pull'.[17] At the same time, it was clear that such initiatives could also benefit from links with the structures – being empowered, for example, by the engagement and encouragement of the Bishop (F, Opening Narrative), or by being held together through the time and dedicated energy offered by the

Curate (D, Opening Narrative). In the case of LJV, there was also evidence that the stability and continuity provided by the presence of the committed, 'full-time' religious community provided an important and enabling context for the necessarily more fluid community of lay volunteers (A1, Evaluation points concerning the MSJC management team; A2). Such stories challenge any simplified criticism of church life ordered around clergy leadership as negatively 'authoritarian' in principle.

At the same time, however, those more negative readings of the lay-clergy power dynamic can also be recognised. The engaged and collaborative episcopal service experienced in Portsmouth (F) finds something of its shadow in the account and experience of episcopal 'mandate' demonstrated in the work of the Westminster Agency for Evangelisation (B). Here the more managerial delegation of the Agency to carry out the bishop's mandate seemed to leave the Agency in a difficult middle position, located between the theological but largely inoperative authority of the bishop, and the effective but sometimes obstructive power of parish clergy and laity on the ground. The structures were, theologically and theoretically, in place for effective change, formation and renewal; but the bifurcation of the theology of the bishop's authority and the sociological and organisational realities frustrated the effectiveness of the Agency (B1). In subtler ways, too, certain situations of unease around the relative authorities and powers of lay and ordained can be seen in the Practices, as the different ecclesial locations of clergy and the non-ordained made themselves felt: the desire of the parish priest to attend particularly to "the religious side of things" in relation to the guests welcomed by Housing Justice to his parish sits in some tension with the testimonies of the lay volunteers on the ground (E1, Clergy Interview 1); in Portsmouth, the experience of parishes' renewal through the stewardship process was also de-railed by changes of parish clergy, despite the bishop's own engaged support of this work (F2).

One key theme which emerges in these experiences of orders and power is the particular role of parish clergy in ecclesial power dynamics. For both the Portsmouth process (F) and the Westminster Agency (B), the parish priest was experienced as holding a pivotal place in terms of the effectiveness or not of processes of renewal, change and mission. The Westminster workers told of the "frustrations" of trying to work with parishes where, for both clergy and people, there are espoused theologies which are at odds with the Agency's own (B1, Cycle 2, Focus Group 2), and this was also referred to specifically in terms of "my model of church [being] in direct conflict with the model of church of the parish priest" (B3, Agency Team 4, Cycle 2, Focus group 1). For Portsmouth, this crucial placing of the parish clergy in the systems of power in the church community was recognised early on, leading to the appointment of a dedicated team member as Clergy Advisor. Whilst this role was important for bringing parish priests to recognise the liberating gifts of stewardship for their own life and ministry (F2, Parish Priest Interview), it also enabled the tensions, anxieties and possible insecurities around "collaborative ministry" to be surfaced: "Some collaborative ministry has pushed the priest out" (F2, Clergy Advisor).

If it is the case that the Accounts of Practice demonstrate something of how the complexities and dynamics of power are embodied in Christian life, and that, in doing so, they witness both to the effectiveness of lay leadership, and the key position of power held by parish clergy, for service and for obstruction, then they also carry with them witness to experiences of powerlessness. In Portsmouth, the experience of working with clergy better to enable collaboration and shared forms of ministry came up against the established expectations that clergy had concerning their role as, for example, having their 'own' parish (F2). As we have seen, talk of "collaborative ministry" raised the spectre of clergy being "pushed out" – that is, having their position (and, by implication, power) marginalised. Whilst the data may clearly be read in terms of the significance and operative power of clergy, it seems highly likely that these same women and men experienced not power but frustration, lack of agency and powerlessness. This is hardly surprising, as in any complex organisation with highly developed administrative structures, empowerment seems hard to embody, and the existential experience, certainly for those in the organisational 'middle ranks', is often one of lack of agency; indeed, this is illustrated in the Accounts in the experience of CAFOD workers "drowning in paper" (G3, Advocacy Group participant).

Such organisational powerlessness finds a resonance with the more societally contextual powerlessness experienced by those working in more clearly *ad extra*, and FBA settings. Most vividly, the LJVs spoke of being left frustrated and helpless after encountering the need and suffering of those they visited. For Bea, this helplessness even led to her questioning the value of her visits to a man living with mental illness (A4, Participant Observation 3, Bea's Story), a feeling echoed by Isabel in the same data set. Yet, for both these participants, as for the Reflective Writer quoted in A4, this sense of helplessness was linked to reminders that it is in these small acts (exercises of agency) that the power of God was at work: "it is finally God who does these things through [us]" (A4, Isabel's story). Indeed, the stories of the FBA practices abound with witness both to the smallness of lay expressions of agency, and their significance when understood in the context of participations in the mystery of God's own powerful agency: the Messy Church mums beginning to recognise each other in the street (D3 and 4) and the leadership team's hospitality and welcome of mothers (D4, Outsider Feedback Document and Joint Feedback Document); the parishioners' contributions of puddings to the Housing Justice teams (E2, Jonny, Volunteer Focus group 1); the simple friendliness of the shared meal in St. Mary's Alpha meetings (C1, Interview 6); – all these are acts of power in that they are expressions of human agency to effect change. Theologically they can be celebrated further in terms of the power of

God's Spirit at work in the world, mediated, though not limited by, the actions of God's people.

In the power of the Spirit: glimpses of empowerment

This last point draws into a deeper exploration of the theological theme which, I suggest, lies at the heart of all Christian discussions of power – even if it not overtly referred to: the Holy Spirit and pneumatology as that account of the Spirit's work in the world and church. The LJV participants in particular, by relating their perception of the smallness and even hopelessness of their work to effect change to the greater power and work of God in, through and ahead of them, present us with the 'clue' to a theological learning concerning power and its ordering in the church's life and mission. When it is recognised, too, that this articulation of the operant theology of these practitioners also finds correspondence with biblical and contemporary theological notions of "power *through weakness*",[18] particular demand for our attention to this theme can be recognised.

It is, in fact, striking how rarely the questions of authority, ordination and power are explicitly linked with the Holy Spirit in the Accounts of Practice, particularly when we remember how the normative theological sources of scripture and liturgy so often refer Christians to 'the power of the Spirit': Paul's ministry in particular is seen in terms of power and the Spirit (I Thess. 1:5; I Cor. 2:4; Rom. 15: 18–19), and it is, of course, the Holy Spirit that empowers the fearful disciples at Pentecost (Acts 2:1–4). Where the Spirit is mentioned in relation to power and authority in the Practices it seems a difficult theme to handle.[19] So when reference to the 'something bigger' at work in the Westminster Agency's work is interpreted by the Director in terms of the bishop's diocesan plans (B2, exchange between Agency Team 3 and Director), we might reasonably interpret this as a (subconscious) move to identify the power of the Spirit with the ecclesial authority of the Bishop, thereby offering a structurally defined account of pneumatology, at least implicitly. The move among the Messy Church leadership from an anxiety of "Jesus-less community" toward a more positive reading of their work in terms of a "Church of the (as yet) unknown God" (D2), can also be understood in pneumatological terms as the recognition of the expansivity and hiddenness of the Spirit's work among people, as they make the slow journey towards faith in Jesus. Understanding church in pneumatological ways requires a re-examination of how we relate to our structures.

Despite the scarcity of explicit, or even clear implicit reference to the Holy Spirit in the Accounts of Practice, I would suggest that there is, in a number of the Practices, a lived reality of church which can be better understood through the doctrine of the Holy Spirit than through a more incarnational, Christological account of Church, which emphasises the church as, structurally, an embodiment of Christ (Christ's Body).[20] Reference has already been made above to the ways in which the Ignatian spiritual practice of the LJVs enabled them to re-cast their apparently powerless, hopeless efforts to bring about change for the good, through opening these small works up to the greatness of God's own power, working in, but also ahead of them. For the Housing Justice volunteers, too, the 'extending' of the sense of grace beyond liturgical celebration to embrace the feeding and friendship of those in need (E3) speaks of an experience of the Spirit's power beyond the ecclesially structured and 'incarnated', recognising God's activity as Spirit, which, like the wind, "blows where it chooses" (John 3: 8). For CAFOD, as a diverse organisation serving the Gospel, yet made up of a community of different faiths and none, the experience of reflecting together theologically and realising "that we are much more theologically literate than we think" (G2, Feedback Meeting, Asian and Middle East group), also suggests a pneumatological reading of divine presence and power, which is not confined to one church, or even one faith tradition (G2, Outsider feedback Document).

If my interpretation of these Accounts as witnessing to a pneumatological reading of church (even implicitly) is heading in the right direction, then it is significant that one of the places we frequently glimpse this charismatic empowerment of laity in particular is in the places of church-in-the-world. The experience of powerlessness in the face of suffering experienced by LJV volunteers and, to some extent, by Housing Justice workers, is most positively responded to not so much by structural initiatives but by realisations of the gracedness of their own encounters – the activity of the Spirit (God's agency) in these experiences. So, the sense of meeting Christ in these places, and of opening up to a vision which transforms the whole of living and is not ecclesiastically focused, is what enables hope and ongoing action for these lay Christians. It was when the Portsmouth lay person was freed from the notion that renewal was about "the need for the laity to become more involved in the parish" because of the shortage of clergy, that she was empowered to celebrate God's gifts (charisms) in the whole of her life (F3, Questionnaire response). The Spirit's empowerment of lay people for mission may be as much (or more) experienced through the graces and blessings of life in 'the world' than through the initiative of and 'resourcing' from ecclesial structures.

There is, on one level, nothing theologically new or unorthodox in such an account; it is entirely in keeping with a mainstream and biblical account of the Holy Spirit. Indeed, one of the every few attempts to offer a theology of a more collaborative, whole-church practice of ministry and mission in recent times depends on a distinct, but related, notion of relational ontology, and the doctrine of the Trinity, informed by a strong pneumatology.[21] However, the disclosure of this pneumatological reality in the contemporary practices and lived theology of Christians in the world highlights the specifics of this call for churches today. The doctrine of the Spirit, as attested to in the Practices, enables us to reframe our discussions of power, and so of orders, in a way which draws power and agency together, locating human empowerment for action within divine power and agency. A merely organisational account of church power is predominantly read as power over, as office holding and governance, and of who has 'more' power than another – as if power were a limited 'thing' which we are all fighting for a bit of. By contrast the more *ad extra* account of Christian power offered above opens church and mission to the limitlessness of the power of the Spirit in church-and-world, which the organisational structures participate in a limited and specific way, which is – in principle – at the service of this greater and ultimately mysterious activity of the Spirit. As indicated by Sarah Coakley, such a pneumatological emphasis will necessarily privilege the contemplative, and prayer over the simply organisational, managerial and strategic.[22]

Conclusions

What the insights discussed in this chapter argue for is a locating of the theology and practice of church structures, orders and authorities within a practical and deeply theological account of the Holy Spirit – as attested to in the Christian tradition, and lived in Christian experience. The Practices' sense of an empowerment coming from an *ad extra* pneumatological emphasis sits alongside an embodied experience of the paradox of the 'sacred powers' of orders as (at their best) of real service for empowerment. In this way, the traditional Christian language of 'power as service' is somewhat vindicated from any simplistic sense of ecclesial self-deception. At the same time, we can observe particularly in the lay led initiatives such as London Jesuit Volunteers and Housing Justice, a lay agency, or expression of power, which is rooted in a sense of the activity of God's Spirit in and for the world (all be it largely implicit). Here, action is taking place on the basis of volunteering, expressing a certain freedom of discernment and choice in which the Christian disciple opts for self-consciously taking on a certain discipline based on their own sense of vocation and their perceived suitability for the tasks.

The implications of this argument are, practically and theologically, far-reaching. By putting the Spirit's power first, as it were, our disclosed *ad extra* ecclesiology is able to free itself somewhat from any immediate construal of ecclesial power in terms of the lay-ordained difference (even dichotomy). Within such a pneumatological perspective, which privileges the faith of the Christian tradition in the radical freedom, as well as power, of the Holy Spirit, what becomes important is not the relative power and authority of the ordained and lay person, and their 'power relation' in Foucault's sense; rather, the dynamic of power becomes the personal and loving power of the Trinity, in which each participate or share in differentiated, varied and varying (that is, potentially changing, and fluid) ways. This does not eradicate the ordained-lay difference (nor should it, in my view); but it can re-orientate it, by freeing all the baptised, including those ordained to the service of the baptised, to look not so much at each other and their relative powers, but rather toward the one source of all their various empowerments – the Holy Spirit, who "blows where she or he chooses".

An ecclesiology with so much emphasis on the Holy Spirit at work *in the world* does, of course, need to confront the mysterious demands of the discernment of the Spirit. As a final theological theme learnt from our Practices, chapter 11 will turn to consider the ways in which "tradition' plays a crucial, if complex, part in such discernment.

Notes

1 Something of these different locations of the Practices and their implications has been discussed in chapter 6 above.

2 So see, for example, the seminal discussion of Steven Lukes, *Power: A Radical View* (Macmillan, 1974). Lukes has more recently explained this argument very helpfully in relation to current discussion, in a second edition: (Palgrave, 2004). Much contemporary discussion of power and, particularly 'power relations' is rooted in the work of Michel Foucault and – especially politically – that of Hannah Arendt. An ecclesiologically focused discussion of this legacy is clearly and helpfully given in Roy Kearsley, *Church, Community and Power* (Routledge, 2018. Orig. pub. 2008). See especially chapters 3 and 5.

3 A brief and accessible history of these developments, at least in the Catholic tradition, can be found in Joseph Martos, *Doors to the Sacred: A Historical Introduction to Sacraments in the Catholic Church*. Rev. and Updated ed. (Liquori/ Triumph, 2001). From an Anglican perspective see John Macquarrie, *A Guide to the Sacraments* (SCM, 1999).

4 Martyn Percy, *Clergy: The Origin of Species* (Continuum, 2006): 5, 13ff. In response to this, Percy offers an 'evolutionary' account, which takes seriously the importance of environment and context for the shaping of church life, especially in relation to its ordering.

5 Ibid. 180.

6 Stephen Sykes' study of power does much, theologically, to debunk such simplified notions. Stephen Sykes, *Power and Christian Theology* (Continuum, 2006).

7 See Kearsley, op. cit. 38–50.

8 For more detailed accounts, to which this chapter is indebted, the reader is referred not only to the works of Kearsely, Lukes, Percy, Sykes, already cited, but also: Martyn Percy, *Power and the Church: Ecclesiology in an Age of Transition* (Cassell, 1998); Lyndon Shakespeare, *Being the Body of Christ in the Age of Management* (Wipf and Stock, 2016).

9 See *Catechism of the Catholic Church*, 1592. The Church of England liturgy for ordination also has the Bishop: "Through your Spirit, heavenly Father, give these your servants grace and power to proclaim the gospel of your salvation and minister the sacraments of the new covenant." *Common Worship: Ordination Services*.

10 The implicitly hierarchical nature of this language, rooted as it is in the biblical image of the Shepherd and the sheep is sharply brought home by Martyn Percy's observation that "Unlike real life and ministry the shepherd has never been a sheep, and the sheep cannot become a shepherd". Percy, *Clergy*, op. cit. 182.

11 This is especially clearly established in the work of Foucault, which has had a lasting influence of the understanding of power. In terms of a specifically

ecclesiological context, Foucault's significance is well discussed in Kearsley, op. cit. 38–50.

12 Kearsley, op. cit. 25.

13 Ibid. 88.

14 Ibid. 94.

15 Shakespeare, op. cit. 183.

16 See Sykes, op. cit. 115, where the risk of using service language as 'camouflage' in discussions and practices of power is highlighted.

17 See above 122–126.

18 This is especially well explored by Kearsley, op. cit. 159ff. Notably Kearsley develops his understanding through engagement with Jurgen Moltmann's *The Church in the Power of the Spirit* (SCM, 1998), as well as Kyle Pasewark, *A Theology of Power: Being Beyond Domination* (Fortress, 1993) and Lewis Snook, *What in the World Is God Doing: Re-imagining Spirit and Power* (Fortress, 1999).

19 This practical observation resonates with Sara Coakley's account of the development of Trinitairn thought in the early church: Sarah Coakley, *God, Sexuality, and the Self: An Essay 'on the Trinity'* (CUP, 2013). In chapter 3, she draws attention to the ways in which 'praying the Trinity', with its pneumatological significance and emphasis seems to have been sidelined for more technical, philosophical accounts, in the quest for clear orthodoxy. I find her argument compelling, and suggestive of a real human unease about the doctrine and experience of the Spirit, which seems also to be at paly in our Practices.

20 Here, I find I am indebted to my reading of Jurgen Moltmann's criticism of (his understanding of) the Roman Catholic emphasis on the (visible) church as 'the Body of Christ. See Moltmann, op. cit. 68–75.

21 Stephen Pickard, *Theological Foundations for Collaborative Ministry* (Ashgate, 2009).

22 See Coakley, op. cit. 51–52, where theology is rooted in the fundamental human desire for God; and 88–92, where the implications of beginning here and thus privileging contemplation are set out.

Account of practice G

The Catholic Agency for Overseas Development (CAFOD)

Project time frame: September 2009–October 2010

Introductory narrative

The ARCS project was especially concerned to understand church from the perspective of a variety of outreach initiatives. Our work with the Catholic Agency for Overseas Development (CAFOD – https://cafod.org.uk) gave us the opportunity to work with an agency which was, at once, an agency of the Catholic Bishops' Conference of England and Wales, and a development charity employing a wide variety of personnel, and working with more than 5,800 volunteers, largely through Catholic parishes. The development work of CAFOD is focused in more than 40 countries, largely in the global south, and is shaped by working with local partners in the countries in which they operate. As a Catholic charity, CAFOD seeks explicitly to root its work in a normative tradition – specifically, that of Catholic Social Teaching (CST). Its core values – of compassion, hope, dignity and solidarity – are directly related to the central tenets of CST, and form recurrent themes within the organisation's self-articulation.[1] All this presents CAFOD as a particular kind of agency of outreach, with a complex identity comprising a legal charity, a development agency drawing down state funding and a faith-based organisation mandated by the Bishop's Conference and part of the international CARITAS network,[2] with a significant financial and volunteer base within the Catholic community. Its intentional embodiment of a church (normative) tradition is also of particular interest to the ARCS project.

We approached CAFOD on the basis of this particular identity, and also aware that it had a longstanding practice of developing theological work as an accompaniment to its practical development work. As well as a Theological Reference Group, consisting of leading Catholic scholars, the agency also had a Spirituality Team, with a particular remit for the formation of employees (of all faiths and none) in Catholic Social Teaching and its core values. At the time of approaching CAFOD concerning possible research, we found that a member of staff in that team[3] was embarking on doctoral studies in practical theology and so was particularly interested in how the organisation went about theological reflection. Her energy and interest in theological action research as a methodology, and the support of her line manager, gave the initial impetus for the research.

This sense of a common understanding of the project enabled strong ownership from CAFOD from the beginning. After initial meetings, the research questions identified by the CAFOD team focussed on the question of how the traditions of CST were both embodied by, and influenced by, the organisation's practices:

> How do we make use of Catholic Social Teaching to inspire and drive our work in overcoming poverty and injustice?
>
> How does CAFOD contribute to the development of Catholic Social Teaching to make a difference in the world?
>
> (Remit Document)

The aim, as set out in the same document, was to "strengthen the organisational capacity of CAFOD to use Catholic Social Teaching as a resource to overcome poverty and injustice in the world" through deepening staff's knowledge of CST.

The methods of data gathering were particular to CAFOD, and designed by the member of the Spirituality Team who co-ordinated the insider work. A particular challenge was around the structural busyness of the organisation, and finding time for people to reflect and share. In addition, the desire to reach those with experience of working overseas – a core part of the agency's identity – presented logistical geographical problems. The resulting research model brought together groups of staff in the organisation following on from an introductory session held by the inside co-ordinator in her professional capacity. In each of the four subsequent workshops, employees were asked to present material that was 'live' in their work, so that the group might reflect on the questions that arose in the light of CST. The resulting discussions were transcribed, and both the insider team and the ARCS team reflected upon data. In a joint meeting, both sets of reflections were shared and discerned together, following the now-established practices of theological action research.

We were conscious of working here with a professional development agency, which was asking its employees to take time out from extremely demanding schedules to engage in 'theological reflection'. Time pressures continued to be a constraint on the work, but the organisation's commitment to theology and a Spirituality Team as integral to their structures enabled the research to be supported and enabled. Indeed, the staff involved were able to testify that being asked to step away from immediate tasks, and focus on core and foundational ideas that underpinned their work, was enormously helpful – often in ways that they hadn't anticipated.

Four disclosures

1 Catholic Social Teaching: from fig leaf to bay leaf

There were a number of points in the work with CAFOD where it became clear that there was a real desire for CST to be a living tradition within the organisation. Officially, of course, the agency was thoroughly committed to CST as the root of its values and vision. In practice, however, there was a concern that documents of CST were simply mined as sources of quotes that could be used to legitimise actions already decided upon, appealing to the largely Catholic support base, as well as adhering to organisational identity. The tendency toward looking for 'Pope quotes' was recognised – not without humour! More seriously, this raised the issue of how a Catholic agency draws upon normative sources. This disclosure witnesses to the realisation that such an embodiment of a normative tradition need not be a simply passive process, but rather, CAFOD's own theologising was an important source of commentary on CST. This engagement with the tradition through an authentic theologising of the agency's own not only could lead to a greater appropriation of CST but also opened up the possibility that CAFOD had the potential to contribute to the tradition's on-going development. A more dialogical approach to the tradition opened up the possibility of its both challenging and supporting the practices of CAFOD.

The struggle to appropriate the tradition effectively was well witnessed to, as was the experience of its effectiveness when speaking with partners in different parts of the world. One staff member highlighted how, as lay employees, they could struggle to find a common language with the Catholic hierarchies in the global south when they were discussing programmes, and explored the power of CST to bridge gaps between 'development speak' and ecclesial communities:

> Quoting from different popes of course is hugely beneficial when talking to bishops and so, for me, just having a bit more awareness of what people have said and how I could use some of those comments or highlight some of those comments around what Pope Paul VI said about solidarity and working with those who are striving to escape hunger and misery and disease.... I've begun to understand a little bit more about what Catholic Social Teaching is saying, how I might be able to utilise some of those messages, picked out some messages that I think could apply to the situation in Burma and the situation of the church and its response to HIV and AIDS in Burma.... p 4: but I think CST can give the church a framework to enter into discussions with other agencies and articulate the church's response and what is its vision and strategy, and CST runs through all of how the church is trying to articulate its response to HIV and AIDS, but they're perhaps

> not utilising it as much as they could and not necessarily seeing it as a language that could be less threatening than other languages.
>
> (Asia and Middle East Group Participant)

In another group, an Advocacy worker related how CST language and quotes were important in making communication effective in different contexts.

> The way in which I use Catholic social teaching … in terms of a bit of a justification: this is why we work on this; look this is what the Pope said … therefore it is good to work on this. But obviously that comes after we call up "rent-a-quote". There is a bit of "rent-a-quote", but I guess there are two ways in which you use the "rent-a-quote" – and one is kind of reinforce for existing campaigners, oh yes there is a recognition here. … this puts into words something that I feel and links it to an authority I respect. And I guess the other one we use is to kind of help campaigners sell campaigning, I guess, to people who aren't very interested in campaigning – but this will kind of give them a point of reference.
>
> (Advocacy Group Participant)

These Advocacy workers were also prone to that reluctance with regard to explicit faith language that we had noticed in other projects (for example see C3 and E1). This seemed to have led to a somewhat bifurcated use of the tradition, as described by this participant:

> There is also I guess within the team a bit of a feeling of we don't want to be preaching, so we don't want to be coming over too strong, so there is all this talk around using social teaching implicitly using very values based language, picking up on ideas like compassion and hope and solidarity and so there is that element. But I think that just needs more thinking through, because I think at the moment we kind of say either it's the "rent-a-quote" end or it's something that is so implicit that it could be anybody, it's a nice humanist agenda.

What seemed lacking here was a sense of CST as an appropriated language, which could be used fluently with a mature discretion of particular circumstances.

A common experience in doing theology through conversation is that at some point, someone will find a compelling metaphor that encapsulates the point. In this project, it was the participants themselves who generated the language which could give a currency to this idea of a fluent, mature use of CST. This took place in a third session with the Advocacy team, as a participant struggled to convey a hoped for way of working with CST:

> I know they're there [Catholic Social Teachings], that's always the sort of interlocutor in terms of my conceptual ideas. And I think for me

> now, Catholicism is a. . . . because it's a coherent and well developed set of ideas, it's an interesting kind of discursive partner, it's effectively a bay leaf in a big milky stock that sort of infuses the work even if it's not always directly visible.

In later conversations, the bay leaf approach was contrasted with the idea that using 'pope quotes' was like using a fig leaf to cover the essential case being made. Thus, fig leaf versus bay leaf became a short-hand for the dilemmas in how to use the normative resource of CST.

2 *CAFOD staff and the research as formative*

It is widely recognised in action research that the processes of research itself can be transformative, and it was during this project that the pedagogical significance of theological action research processes became increasingly apparent. As the sometimes initially reluctant reflectors in the workshops began to experience the process, they were able to witness to the increasing confidence they felt as they found their own voice in relation their work and CST:

> **Participant 1:** This exercise made me more aware that CST is a living process and local people can help make it. . . . It has made me think, "wow, maybe we are tapping into a layer we don't recognise normally". Another thing that struck me was how much more imaginative the Advocacy team seemed to be that than we were. For this process, you need people with particular reflective and interpretative skills. Advocacy team seem more reflective. Seeing their reflections enriches our experience and enthuses us.
>
> **Participant 2:** This process helped me deal with e-mails from supporters over the Pakistan situation – people wanting their money only to go to Christians – there have been many e-mails about this – what are CAFOD's values in this situation? I was able to explain we don't differentiate or discriminate. One supporter even gave more money when this was explained – she felt guilty for asking. Others refused to give.
>
> (Feedback Meeting Asia and Middle East Group)

Key to this increased confidence was the way in which the Spirituality Team had resourced participants with appropriate materials from CST. The co-ordinator's continued work and her use of the introductory sessions built on the induction session in CST that all CAFOD employees had to attend. Her own experience and expertise in Adult Education brought particular gifts to theological action research process, highlighting its own pedagogical potential:

> The value of the process that [the co-ordinator] did. She fed them documents and resources for them to reflect on and they mostly seemed to

> have got quite rich insights, discovered things in a new way. It allowed staff to digest the material and then reproduce the material in a way that was relevant to their job. This allowed for a pragmatic joining between CST and their practice. Only about half a dozen concepts/principles came up. Surprised at how little people knew about CST. There were clearly some light bulb moments.
>
> (Insider Feedback Meeting Minutes)

This formative value of the project was especially enriched through the inclusion in the conversations of CAFOD colleagues who weren't Roman Catholics. These participants were able to offer different perspectives on CST, often introducing different resources from other religions or literature to help interpret CST. The outsider team identified this in the data and fed it back to the CAFOD team:

> **Valuing the non-Catholic voices in CAFOD**
>
> The team were struck by the richness and diversity of the contributions made by CAFOD staff, and, in particular, the varying degrees of religious literacy. In some instances, those who didn't profess or embody faith tended to think they needed a 'Pope quote' or quote from CST to legitimise their work. In other cases, for example, the Buddhist [in the Advocacy team] knew about CST having studied in the library in preparation for the session. This contrasted with other Catholics who admitted having limited exposure to CST in their own tradition:
>
> > [A Catholic Advocacy Group Participant]: Having grown up in this country, I know bugger all about Catholic Social Teaching and I went to one of those supposedly good comprehensive Catholic schools.... I'm just saying, I'm not convinced the vast majority of Catholics get it.

Again and again the real relevance of CST was disclosed through experiences of living, rather than through an individual's faith affiliation or standing. Take, for example, the bishop's encounters with people with HIV:

> And the Archbishop said, You know, five years ago when we were having these inputs.... I'd never met anybody that was living with HIV. So he said, it was all theory to me. I realised I had a role as a bishop to respond to people in need, but you know it was out there.... now I've met people and it's touched me and I've seen people very sick, I now know personally that I need to be doing something.
>
> (Outsider Feedback Document)

The CAFOD workers were people committed to practice, to the experience of need and practical response, and so might be said to be coming to CST from the opposite position to this Archbishop just referenced. Educationally we might say that their 'process' was already established; and what we were seeing was the effects on this of learning a vocabulary with which to describe it. The richness of this tradition of CST as a source for such language was valued. At the joint feedback meeting, one member of staff commented:

> As a non-Catholic, CST is a really, really useful body of knowledge. Otherwise it becomes pure management speak. CST was not invented by management five years ago. It has a history. People like that, even if they are not Catholic. If we are not careful it can become a mission statement; a fig leaf.
>
> (Joint Feedback Meeting)

Theological reflection using CST had given voice to a rich embodied theology:

> But what came out for me is that we are much more theologically literate than we think. I was astounded by the ability of non-Catholics to reflect theologically.
>
> (Feedback Meeting, Asia and Middle East Group)

Reflecting on this learning after the project, the ARCS team recognised what had been achieved at CAFOD as an opening up of a space, in which the organisation could properly espouse a theology that reflects both its practice and the normative sources it holds to be authoritative. This space for appropriated adult learning gave staff members their voice and built capacity for reflective learning and the embedding of CST within the organisation.

3 Questions of agency, north and south[4]

The particular nature of CAFOD drew us into reflecting more deeply and subtly on questions of agency – issues of how different participants in the Agency's work were able to effect change (or not). CAFOD is engaged in a complex set of principal-agent relationships. It receives funds from Northern donors (from both government and parishes) and needs corporately to act as an agent in ensuring those funds are spent in line with the donors' intentions. It also acts as a principal in allocating funding to Southern partners – often Catholic dioceses or agencies – seeking to understand their needs and match them with the intentions of donors. As the principal in this relationship, CAFOD then has to hold Southern partners to account for the spending of the funds. The language of these conversations was felt by staff to be almost entirely that of professional development work; and, when this language predominated, there was a shift in relationship and conversation with partners, which was not without difficulty:

> I brought up the issue of the burden of programme management and becoming a professional development agency and how that creates

> barriers for us in terms of us as people working with programmes overseas – in terms of showing our solidarity and working in solidarity and feeling that we're in solidarity with our partners. I hope everyone knows what I'm talking about. Everybody knows how many new polices are coming down, how much new paperwork is coming on for our programme stuff. There are whole times of year when you can't even talk to programme staff because they're just drowning in paper and if you go out on trips, I'm sure you've been on trips; a lot of it is just like can we please just fill out this matrix? Can you please get back to us? And it really blocks discussion.
>
> (Advocacy Group Participant)

Members of the group recognised these tensions, and shared something of these frustrations. In response, the outsider team felt they glimpsed a possibility of another way of working that acknowledged the value given CST by both Northern donors, and Southern partners. At the core of this possible way forward was the sense that CAFOD staff might be understood as interpreters both of CST and of the realities of recipients' lives.

The sense of being interpreters was affirmed by the generation of an especially vivid metaphor by one of the Advocacy Group participants – a metaphor greeted with a laugh of recognition:

> I came up with this metaphor when we met and it's the idea that when you look at . . . like London Fashion Week, when you look at fashion shows, do you see clothes that no one would ever wear in real life? But ultimately there is a relationship between those clothes and what you buy in Top Shop or in New Look, and there are designers who translate the stuff that no one would ever wear into the stuff that actually you might buy. So this is like the cat walk! (laughter) I think because we looked at some kind of potential source documents, and I just didn't know what they meant. There was lots of words I didn't understand. . . . there has to be a translation task between theologians talking and real people talking.

The outsider team responded positively to this insight in their Feedback Document:

> **Developing a living espoused theology**
>
> One of the best images emerging in the data was that of the catwalk. The CAFOD staff were seeing themselves as being on the catwalk. For us as a team, that was a cry for an espoused theology. They were seeing themselves on the interface between the normative CST documents (difficult to interpret and hard to put into public documents) and life out in the world. A need is presented by CAFOD staff for

> more space to interpret and articulate these tensions. The CAFOD staff saw themselves as the Top Shop designer who knew what was on the catwalk but who also understood what people would wear and who recognised that they were the people who were best placed to develop it. As practical theologians, we thought this was cleverer than an applicationist approach because it revealed a profound understanding of 'what people would actually wear'. They understood the contexts in which money was being spent, etc. Staff clearly want this process to be informed by a dialogue with CST, but also want it to be informed by the lived realities of the beneficiaries of their organisation.

We might add to this that, organisationally, for such a translation process to be nurtured, appropriate space, time and formation of the kind enabled through the research would be required.

4 The ecclesial nature of CAFOD

The Pope has said that he regards CAFOD and its equivalents around the world (networked through Caritas Internationalis) as being 'part of the church':

> Pope Francis says that Caritas is "an essential part of the Church" and that it "institutionalizes love in the Church". He said Caritas has two dimensions: action and a divine dimension "situated in the heart of the Church".
>
> (www.caritas.org/who-we-are/caritas-is-church/)

Taking this ecclesial nature of CAFOD seriously as a theological reality, expressed through its identity as an agency of the Catholic Bishops' Conference of England and Wales, carrying out the essential mission of love to those in need, the ARCS team were interested to reflect on what this might say ecclesiologically. Our research and learning with this diverse organisation, with its clarity of focus on a particular strand of Catholic normative tradition, raises particular questions about how 'church' is being extended through this kind of ecclesial identification.

On a structural, organisational level, CAFOD is interesting for the ways in which its work crosses some of the normal hierarchies. Its employees – who sit outside the hierarchy and who may not necessarily be Catholic – have the power to challenge proposals and hold to account those in the hierarchy in Southern dioceses. As we have already seen, the vision from the staff members was not so much for these relationships to be based in patterns of management, and the power of the principal funding agency. Rather, what was hoped for was a greater theological content to these ordinary dialogues, based in a common language of CST.

In fact, CAFOD's ecclesial identity was a focus for rich reflection in the outsider team Feedback:

> CAFOD is in a remarkable position ecclesiologically, as both an ecclesial and 'worldly' agency. It can be seen as an *ad extra* agency working with, through and in accordance with *ad intra* ecclesial structures. This placing allows the agency to provide interesting and crucial insights into ecclesiological realities and lived theologies – structures; power; clericalisation.
>
> (Outsider Team Feedback Document)

Indeed, there was some suggestion that the participants' growing confidence in CST was enabling them to raise critical questions about the 'official' church structures with which they worked, often in more conservative social and ecclesial cultures in the global South:

> **Participant 1:** Caritas is normally led by priest.... So I just find that a contradiction. This isn't Catholic Social Teaching.... in the church, the church itself is probably different.... I might be wrong.
>
> **Participant 2:** It's a good point actually. There could be questions about whether this practice of always having priest in charge of Caritas (which isn't universal, because we are a Caritas), but whether that's in accordance with Catholic Social Teaching, because I would argue actually it's not.

As a diverse, 'worldly'-and-ecclesial reality, CAFOD was well placed to speak in fresh and challenging ways into the *ad intra* patterns of church life. The question we were left with, and fed back to the CAFOD team was:

> How might CAFOD be better enabled/become more confident in challenging those ecclesial realities when called to – especially through the shared framework of CST (which, it is supposed, applies *within* Church life as much as anywhere?)
>
> (Outsider Team Feedback Document)

Concluding reflections

The enthusiasm for the theological action research approach led to CAFOD's participating in the final year of the ARCS project – our 'capacity building' projects[5] – in which organisations formed their own 'outsider teams' and worked alongside insiders in investigating issues of shared interest. In proceeding with this additional research, led by the insider co-ordinator of the original project, the question of CAFOD's ecclesial identity and mission was tellingly central:

> What does it mean for CAFOD to be part of Church that is an agent of change? What does it mean in my practice?

> In CAFOD's Strategic framework for the next ten years ("Just One World"), we are focussing on four priorities for the International programme. One of these is, for example: "Increase positive social change through our work with the Catholic Church and communities". The above question is of interest as the data we collect will develop the theological thinking behind the four priorities[6] and will explore fundamental questions about CAFOD and Catholic Identity.
>
> (CAFOD Research Proposal, Capacity Building Project 2010)

This project was once again highly successful in its use of a variety of ways of gathering data and encouraging employees to be creative as to how they learnt, reflected and shared their learning in ways integrating CST and their practice. The pedagogical significance of this work was especially well developed by the co-ordinator in her subsequent doctoral thesis, which specifically explored theological action research as pedagogical practice.[7]

In our earlier work on the ARCS research, *Talking About God in Practice*, we profiled three types of group we worked with: the parish, the diocese and the more 'entrepreneurial' agency – and this three-fold typology has persisted in this book. In many ways, however, CAFOD presents us with another kind of agency, which had, explicitly, both an *ad intra* and *ad extra* ecclesial identity. In fact, subsequent to the ARCS project, some of the most fruitful theological action research has been carried out with such 'church-edge' organisations,[8] contributing not only to the 'edgy ecclesiology' described in chapter 8, but also to the growing literature on faith-based organisations.[9] Our experience with CAFOD has been crucial in our better enabling a variety of forms of theological action research with in complex organisations, and thus engendering significant ecclesiological learning.

Notes

1 For example, see *Just One World*, 2010. Available at: https://cafod.org.uk/content/download/3036/21931/version/1/file/JustOneWorld.pdf.

2 www.caritas.org.

3 Susy Brouard has since successfully completed her professional doctorate, using theological action research within CAFOD. Susanna Brouard, *Abseiling in the Way to Emmaus: Using Theological Action Research to Embed Catholic Social Teaching in a Faith-based Agency*. Unpub. PrD (Anglia Ruskin University, 2015).

4 The use of 'North' and 'South' here refers to the global demographics and disparities, broadly association with northern and southern hemispheres.

5 See chapter 2 above.

6 As set out in *Just One World*, op. cit. note 1 above.

7 See note 3 above.

8 Notably, the *Visions for Educational Leadership Project*, working with Catholic schools in England and Wales; and the *Catholic Marriage Care* project, working with the faith based relationship charity. Details of both these can be found on the Theology and Action Research Network website: www.theologyandactionresearch.net. See also the use of data from the *Listening 2004* project, drawing on the experiences of Catholic families across England and Wales in, Clare Watkins,

"Conversational Methods of Discernment. Learning for Mission from the Domestic Church." Thomas Knieps-Port le Roi and Aldegonde Brenninkmeijer-Werhahn eds. *Authentic Voices, Discerning Hearts: New Resources for the Church on Marriage and Family* (LIT Verlag, 2016): 15–29.

9 See for example the work of Malcolm Torry, *Managing Religion: The Management of Christian Religious and Faith-Based Organizations* (Palgrave Macmillan, 2014).

11 Tradition

Normativity, creativity and faithful treachery

> When I think of Ignatian Spirituality then it's not about going to Feltham [prison] on Sundays. It's about the coffee that I make in the morning and whatever I did before and what I'm doing after, and brushing my teeth, where just all the time, this whole awareness that is not just for when I'm sitting down and thinking that I am aware.
>
> (London Jesuit Volunteers, A2, Joseph)

> And I think for me now, Catholicism is a . . . because it's a coherent and well developed set of ideas, it's an interesting kind of discursive partner, it's effectively a bay leaf in a big milky stock that sort of infuses the work even if it's not visible.
>
> (CAFOD, G1)

The theological learning discussed in chapters 7–10 arose as priorities from the realities of the living of the ARCS Practices themselves. This fifth, and final, theological theme – tradition – has a different relationship with those practices, arising more strongly through the ARCS team's methodological reflections, as they matured through the research. Indeed, a fundamental premise of this project's emerging ecclesiology, working with the four voices in ways which engage practice with normative and formal accounts, concerns the nature of tradition – of what is 'handed on', through words, images and practices of Christian faith. It is the fundamental recognition that the good news is variously 'translated' in tradition, across time, space and contexts, that leads to that characteristic systematisation of theological thinking through the four voices so as better to enable attentiveness to the complex variety of tradition. The exercise has, in turn, suggested something about how Christian tradition is to be understood. Indeed, the four voices framework can be read in terms of a heuristic device for working with a complex notion of tradition, as described in chapter 4 above.[1] In particular, the recognition of the four voices of theology as the fundamental *loci theologici* for our conversations and their learnings drew us into an account of what I have described as a practical fundamental theology, in which 'tradition', as both presently and variously lived and historically discerned, is entered into as a progressing, developing dynamic.[2] The normative voice is there recognised as especially problematic, not only for its often-assumed dominance in the balance of authority but also for the way in which it represents "at least potentially – the whole weight of the long, historically-discerned Christian tradition with its claims around scripture and (for some) church teaching as the privileged places of God's word".[3] The ARCS methodology, epistemology and theological foundation demands a particular kind of attention to the nature of the normative, and the closely related (though not identical) question of 'tradition'.

This is not to say that tradition, as described in what follows, is a purely, or even substantially methodological concern; rather, it is to highlight the way in which our more conceptual methodological thinking about how we did our research and, specifically, the four voices of theology, caused us in the ARCS team to be especially alert to what we were seeing in and learning from the Practices' own, often implicit account of tradition and its place within their work and thought. Of particular and immediate interest is the way in which many of the Practices responded to what we called the normative voice, and to the specific traditions by which – for them – it was mediated; here we saw not so much a living of normativity as corrective, or dominant, in relation to the conversation between the voices, but rather the potential for received and acknowledged traditions, with their peculiar claim to some kind of normativity, to enable and inform contemporary and creative practice and thought. Many of the methodological anxieties, especially felt by practical theologians, concerning any sense of normativity are, I will argue, put into a new perspective by the practical living of, and with, normative traditions on the ground, as will be illustrated in this chapter. In these real-life situations, any simply unquestioned dominance of the normative voice is rarely found, as the visceral and immediate authorities of experience and practice take their place in the living conversations and decision-making. The aim of a four voices, practical fundamental theological approach is to enable lively and mutually formative conversation between these different types of authority – that of the inherited historical tradition and that of the present, yet-to-be-discerned living out of that tradition in contemporary contexts. As we move more deeply into this learning we discover, as a second moment, something of the practised complexity of *traditio*[4] – involving practices of translation, transmission and even, on occasions, a kind of treachery.[5]

Before moving to describe how these insights into tradition were learnt from the Practices, the complexity of thought about 'tradition' in our own time needs to be named. As Yves Congar recognised some 50 years or so ago, the preoccupation with tradition already signifies that its unquestioned living has been dislodged in some way; we need to speak of it because of a sense of its being questioned, or even broken.[6] Certainly, in the Catholic tradition, the movements of *ressourcement*[7] and *aggiornamento*[8] associated with the Second Vatican Council in the 1960s gave rise to renewed consideration of the place of historic traditions and ecclesially authoritative statements within the renewal of theology and church.[9] These debates have widened and intensified as we have moved into a late modern, or what many would describe as a postmodern, context, where the Enlightenment logic of human reason as autonomous and supremely authoritative seems to have culminated in an a-historic, anti-tradition approach to human knowing, living and practice.[10] The highly influential work of Alasdair MacIntyre[11] in particular offers from the field of moral philosophy an account of tradition which has two insights especially pertinent to our reflections. The first is that all thinking takes place in a context of a received tradition, even when that tradition is being questioned or even rejected; the very act of criticising or even deconstructing a tradition requires being versed in it and shaped by it and the use of the skills and methods afforded by it.[12] A second point, which resonates warmly with our reflections on the Practices, is that, according to MacIntyre, tradition as received and lived is necessarily contested – even conflictual – if it is living at all.[13]

Such an understanding of tradition as both received, and as on-going, participatory and necessarily controversial and controversed, is the dominant account given of tradition in much contemporary literature, and confirms this book's commitment to understanding church tradition in and through the complex and controversial realities of faith practices. From the field of literary-historical studies, Stephen Prickett[14] demonstrates the sheer complexity and ambiguity of tradition, as it has been variously understood and engaged with through time and within theology the nuanced account of Lieven Boeve,[15] especially informed by the hyper-pluralism of postmodern contexts, demands that Christian tradition radically re-orientates itself towards the ongoing task of recontextualisation which is at its heart. Such a reading of tradition has profound implications for theology if it is to avoid the 'idolatry' to which Eric Saak refers.[16] Referring to theology's temptation to reify and abstract tradition from the complexities of history, Saak warns that "in the search and desire for, and in the endeavor of establishing, normativity, consciously or otherwise, theologians and Church historians must be very conscious of the structures of evil inherent in systematics and Church history" if they are to avoid such an idolatry of historically conditioned words and practices.[17]

Here the shadow side of tradition in Christian theology begins to emerge – and in more than one way. For Saak, this is about the way theology can be tempted to become so invested in tradition that it moves "from expressing a lived tradition to serving a dying or dead traditionalism", thereby becoming 'infected' with evil.[18] Tran alerts us to another, though related, danger – that of rushing too quickly to 'tradition' whilst forgetting its essential 'humanness', its embeddedness in a history in which Christian traditions demonstrate both good and evil, oppression and injustice. This does not invalidate tradition as an authority, but it does require that it is read and re-read with a continual 'looping back' to rediscover less-heard aspects of that tradition so as to provide critique of more dominant accounts, and a foundation for renewed thinking and practice. In the end, this is about the discernment of the gift of God's revelation of truth within the necessary humanness of historically lived traditions:

> That goodness doesn't always replicate itself (or that sometimes badness yields goodness) is not a strike against the moral significance of tradition ... but only a feature of humanness which theology may ride roughshod over in its rush to tradition.[19]

It is this same caution around an over-enthusiasm for tradition as a kind of solid 'thing' upon which we can draw that leads Rosemann to highlight the importance not only of the continuity of tradition (so emphasised by Joseph Ratzinger[20]), but also its necessary rupture, disturbance and re-reading.[21]

What is emerging from this range of scholarly sources is a contemporary understanding of tradition as something which is complex, ambiguous, but necessary for on-going learning and understanding. What is essential is that tradition is 'living', in the MacIntyrean sense of its being actively engaged with and, as necessary, contested. This sits well with the necessarily eschatological conditioning of the theological task – and, indeed, of all Christian living. This is described by Hovey, who names traditions as "nothing but the confession of middle-creatures whose place in their tradition is determined by a story that is too large to grasp and that is simply still on its way to completion by Jesus and the saints. It is nothing other than the honest reality of good news that still elicits hope".[22] At the same time, it raises a crucial question of *discernment* as it is recognised that tradition is not so much a thing as an ongoing and participatory *practice* or set of practices – a *traditio*. The question is, how are we to determine the good and proper controversy of Christian *traditio*, as distinct from the negatively destructive, sinful arguments which beset ecclesial communities and movements?[23]

An answer to this question – or rather a provisional response to it – will have to wait until the last section of this book. For now, I want to enable the learning of the Practices in this area to speak into the scholarly conversations which have been outlined. In a first look at what we might learn from our Accounts here, I will consider the range of ways in which tradition as normative is variously understood and engaged with in the Practices. This is followed by exploration of a second point of learning: the ways in which the Practices inform us about the complexities and wisdom needed for the translation and transmission of traditions – and the courage needed in risking treachery.

The normativity of 'tradition': responses in practice to that which has been handed on

As already described, much contemporary thinking, in theology and humanities more broadly, recognises the complexity and controverted nature of 'tradition', as that which is both persistently challenged (so as to be 'living'[24] and appropriately eschatologically conditioned[25]), and necessarily received and accepted for the very possibility of language and debate. The 'idolatrous' proffering of tradition as fixed and merely correctional of present life and practice is largely understood in this literature as 'dead' traditionalism. For all that, there remains within Christian communities and conversation assumptions about 'tradition' which all too easily identify the 'traditional' simply with a rigid normativity. Such a misreading of tradition abstracts it from its historical context and, simultaneously, sets it apart from contemporary faith living. Rather than allowing the contemporary understanding of faith tradition to inform how normativity is lived with, many still seem rather to begin with a highly authoritarian sense of ecclesial normativity, which then becomes the lens through which the more complex and debated realities of tradition are perceived. For the Christian practitioner, there continues to be a question about what kind of authority, and normative authority in particular, traditions of various types might properly have. Here, the ARCS Practices can help with deepening our understanding and reflection.

One observation is that a sense of tradition as unquestionable, fixed normativity can lead to different, though equally problematic, responses among practitioners. For example, in the case of the Westminster Agency for Evangelisation, the important ecclesial tradition (for that group) of episcopal mandate and due obedience was received as unquestionable, meaning that the practitioners "don't have that liberty" (B1, Director) that others might have to reinterpret, change or be 'individual' in their responses. As already observed, this Practice group seemed to operate with a highly routinised reading of pneumatology, in which the "something bigger" of their work was repeatedly referred back to the bishop's own plans (B2); what is significant in the present chapter is the way in which this may be seen to result in an implicit sense of they themselves being the holders of 'tradition', in a manner which could contribute to a certain tension between their work and the realities of parish life. A fixed reading of tradition seemed operant, as the Agency staff spoke of being at the place where the 'ideal' and 'real' church met (B1, Agency Team 2), and frequently experiencing how the people of the 'real' church are at odds with the vision and understanding of the Agency team (B1, Agency Team 1; B3, Agency Team 4). Tradition does not seem to be understood here as something which might be going on, or 'making progress'[26] in the church at a parish level, but rather as something into which people have to be educated from elsewhere. For this Agency, it seemed to the ARCS team that tradition seems to have become a particular thing to be handed on to those who lack it in some way – and implicit theology of tradition which has a bearing on the pedagogical methods widely employed by the Agency in its Adult Faith Formation (B5).

There is a different kind of response to this kind of objectifying of tradition which can be seen in the work with St. Mary's parish. Motivated by a desire for welcome to all, and a commitment to inclusivity and hospitality without conditions (C4), this congregation were becoming aware of the difficulties such an all-embracing position presented in relation to conversion, commitment and what they came to understand as the journey needed for the Christian from guest to host (C1). This congregations practical and faith instinct led them to a practice of all-inclusive hospitality in which any requirement for commitment from 'guests' was felt to be *in*hospitable. In this ways they risked becoming "a busy socially active Church" which nonetheless needed to "ask deeper questions about where Jesus was in all that we do" (C3, PCC Member Evaluation Interview). As these studies have shown, this reluctance explicitly to proclaim faith seems an important instinct on the part of the practitioners in response to contemporary culture (for example, in D Messy Church and E Housing Justice), and needs to be received as part of the wisdom from practice. At the same time, it raises the question as to how contemporary, contextual practices, particularly in the late modern West, can more constructively and creatively engage with the particular kind of normativity embodied in tradition as understood in its living, controversial dynamic.

There are some clues here from a number of the ARCS Practices. In different ways, both LJV and the Portsmouth Diocese groups worked fruitfully with different kinds of tradition. In a way parallel to the Westminster Agency for Evangelisation, the Pastoral Renewal of the Portsmouth Diocese was very much a part of the episcopal mandate – a kind of structurally embodied normative tradition. Yet here, the normative played out as *living* tradition, with the bishop's Pastoral Plan engaging conversationally and fluidly with the diocesan teams' experiences, learning about stewardship, and ongoing challenges and blessings. Here, the initial 'normative document' of the bishop became a reference point in a conversation, in which the episcopal authority and vision informed and shaped the work whilst not unquestioningly mandating it. In the case of LJV, the living, adapting engagement with a normative tradition was strikingly fruitful. Their experience demonstrates how highly traditional practices of biblical practice and *examen*, based on the established sixteenth century tradition of St. Ignatius, opened up possibilities for a transformed understanding of highly contemporary, urban experiences. Indeed, this integration of volunteering on the margins of society and Ignatian spiritual practice enabled a transforming of practitioners' lives and outlook which reached beyond the volunteering and reflections themselves:

> When I think of Ignatian Spirituality then it's not about going to Feltham [prison] on Sundays. It's about the coffee that I make in the morning and whatever I did before and what I'm doing after, and brushing my teeth, where just all the time, this whole awareness that is not just for when I'm sitting down and thinking that I am aware.
>
> (A2, Joseph)

It is striking that these very contemporary insights into washing the dishes (A2, Carla's story), teaching science in a twenty-first century classroom (A6), going about ordinary life, seem to be specifically enabled through this established, normative tradition and its practices. Both scripture and Ignatian spirituality are received as proper authorities beyond experience, and shape and test *and grow* the experiences of the volunteers. The significance of living – and so adapting – this tradition and its normative practices is underlined by the volunteers' own sense that the tradition makes all the difference, and that a deeper understanding of it is essential for growing the particular gifts they have received (A2, Sarah).

A particularly clear and intentional example of this living – and so debating – engagement with a normative tradition can be seen in the ARCS work with the CAFOD. In a particular way, not, in principle, that different from the Westminster Agency or the Portsmouth Pastoral Team, CAFOD is clearly under the mandate of the normative and authoritative structures of the church. As an agency of the Catholic Bishops' Conference of England and Wales, CAFOD is bound in particular ways to living the normative traditions of that church. At the same time, it is an international development agency, benefitting from public funds, and employing a wide range of people, from many faiths and none. As such, those ARCS worked with from CAFOD were explicitly aware of what it might mean to live traditions accepted as normative, but in new contexts, demanding new ways of expression. Indeed, this was the focus of CAFOD's research questions, which sought directly to enquire not only about the organisation's living of the traditions of Catholic Social Teaching, but also of its own *contribution to* that normative tradition (G, Introductory Narrative). Here, in a clear way, both normativity and the necessarily controversial and dynamic living of its traditions come together in the real living of a faith practice.

More will be said below about CAFOD's particular and important contribution to this question of normativity and tradition; but here, I want to draw attention to one of the identified learning points which is of particular value for this chapter – that of the move "from fig leaf to bay leaf" in the organisation's understanding of Catholic Social Teaching (G1). This learning refers to the insight from the practitioners themselves that what was required in response to the normative tradition which they worked out of *and* sought to contribute to was a through-going 'immersion' of that tradition within their day-to-day work. The immediate trigger for this insight – and its accompanying vivid description in terms of fig leaf and bay leaf approaches – was the contrast drawn between the more or less superficial use of 'Pope quotes' to illustrate a point (a fig leaf approach), and the deeper appropriation and living of the tradition which allowed Catholic Social Teaching to "infuse the work even if it's not always directly visible", like "a bay leaf in a big milky stock" (G1, final quote). Through the process, the normativity of the tradition of Catholic Social Teaching, never itself questioned, became better understood as what we might call a 'traditioned normativity', into which the real-life work and challenges were drawn in a dynamic of mutual flavouring and enriching. Normativity, read through the lens of living tradition (in MacIntyre's sense), does not require a rigid sense of corrective authority. Far from it! As CAFOD and LJV teach us in their different ways, engaging with the livingness of a normative tradition become a life-giving way of contemporary Christian practice.

Practising *traditio:* faith-full practices of translation and transmission

If CAFOD and LJV have alerted us to the possibility of engaging in a living, dynamic way with received and normative traditions, they also raise for us the question as to what this contemporary living does to what is received. Without doubt, the Ignatian practices of the Volunteers are both continuous with and quite different from those set out by Ignatius himself; and CAFOD, too, recognised that they are involved in a work of 'interpretation', or translation, analogous to the move from the high fashion of the catwalk to the high street fashion store (G3). Engaging in real, practical ways with living traditions not only highlights the necessary conversational dynamic within which all normativity must be held, but also draws attention to the ongoing discernment and reinterpretation of traditions, past and to come, which is the call of all in the church.[27]

The CAFOD naming of their work in terms of 'translating' is helpful in surfacing not only the constructive nature of the practitioner contribution to living tradition but also its risks. "To translate is to betray" (*traduttore, traditore*) as the old Italian saying goes, and if this is true in language, it is as – perhaps even more – true in terms of practised faith traditions. In particular, as highlighted by CAFOD's differentiation of 'fig leaf' and 'bay leaf' approaches, in order for translation to be fluent and truthful, a deep abiding in the realities being translated is required. The task of translation here ran the risk of being reduced to a marketing exercise, of getting the message across. What the reflections of the practitioners brought out was the need for a greater fluency for authentic contemporary and contextual expression of the tradition.

The ARCS research focus on practices which were broadly missionary or evangelising, orientated to the church *ad extra*, at least in principle, meant that we were necessarily working with groups that – explicitly or not – were involved in such processes of translating and interpreting. Indeed, in so far as these processes were themselves activities of 'handing on', they can (and, I think should) be understood as 'traditions' – all be it traditions still in need of discernment. So, for Messy Church, the move was made by a leadership committed to a clear normative tradition, biblically based and broadly evangelical, toward an interpretation or account of church in which play, story-telling and hospitality become church-in-translation for a new population. The use of story-telling, play and craft, as well as the hospitality of active friendship and shared meals is effectively a set of practices embodying *traditio* in its verbal and nonverbal aspects. What the leadership was confronted with in their reading of the data was the way in which this tradition had taken on a life of its own to which the response was that of the 'Jesus less church' anxiety (D2). The 'success' of the translation seemed to be losing a sense of connection of what the translators believed themselves to be translating in the first place. This realisation then required of the Messy Church leaders' discernment as to whether this was a faithful creativity, and so truly *traditio*, or whether it was, in certain aspects, a kind of treachery, or betrayal of the normative tradition they had received and worked out of. The authenticity of the fruits of the resulting reflections in the Messy Church project lies in the reflectors' commitment both to the authority of their experience of grace in their practices of 'translation' and to the normative articulations of tradition to which their community was committed.

This embodiment of a dynamic reading of tradition may well be characteristic of Fresh Expressions of church, and, more generally, of 'edgy-church' life, in that such practices are self-consciously struggling to embody a normative reading of tradition within new contexts. If we want to see what an ecclesiology which embodies a dynamic reading of tradition looks like, we need to move, once again, to the structural 'edges' rather than contenting ourselves with voices from the *ad intra* centre. What we have found in making this move in working with the ARCS Practices is that the 'normative', when lived as part of a complex, controverted 'living tradition', can be a gift to current practices and their discernment. Indeed, in so far as contemporary faith-full practices are themselves bearers of the "tradition which comes to us from the Apostles", enabled by the Holy Spirit, the normative, understood in this way as *traditio*, is an essential gift.

Conclusion

This third section of the book, which has been concerned to engage with the theological learning surfaced through working with these Practices, is ended with this chapter in which the challenge has been to articulate a fundamental theme – that of tradition (*traditio*). In particular, by reflecting on the real-life ways in which faith traditions have worked (and failed to work) for *ad extra* Christian practice, I have sought to illustrate not only the authenticity of those formal theological accounts of tradition with which this chapter began but also a reading of what is 'normative' which is less rigid, fixed, closed than many have assumed it to be. By reading 'normativity' through both practical and formal theological accounts of tradition, a contribution is made not only to the underpinning methodology of theological action research and its related framework of the four voices of theology but also to a wider ecclesiological appreciation of the essential role that normativity as *traditio* holds. We are returned, at this point, to the reflections of section 1, and particularly chapter 4's closing account of the possibilities for a 'practical fundamental theology'. The invitation to all Christians – all people, even – to participate in the mysterious work of the Spirit in continuously unfolding in the world the tradition of Jesus' life, death and resurrection, calls us into particular ways of receiving the traditions of faith (the normative) and living them out into God's future for the world. It calls us into particular ways of church and of theology. It is to a tentative outline of what these ways might be that I now turn in the chapters of the book's final section.

Notes

1 Above pp. 45–51.
2 Above pp. 49–51.
3 Above p. 48.
4 Here, and in what follows, I am drawn to use the Latin verb so as to emphasise and draw attention to the verbal or 'doing' nature of tradition. As this chapter sets out, often a negative account of tradition in Christian theology has been the result of too static or ossified a sense of what this term refers to. For more on this, see my essay: "Texts and Practices," op. cit., 163–178. See also Clare Watkins, "*Traditio* and the Handling of Holy Things. Reflections *de Doctrina Christiana* From an Ecclesiology Ordered to Baptism." *New Blackfriars* (March 2006): 166–183.
5 This refers us to the sense of the *traditor* – the one who 'hands over' – as 'traitor'.
6 Yves Congar, *Tradition & Traditions: The Biblical, Historical, and Theological Evidence for Catholic Teaching on Tradition* (Simon & Schuster, 1998). For all this, as Phillipp Roemann points out, Congar's reading of tradition is that it essentially has conserving and developing functions, rather than any characteristics of rupture or discontinuity. It is this position that Rosemann himself argues powerfully against: Phillipp Rosemann, "Charred Root of Meaning: Rupture and Continuity in Christian Tradition." *Irish Theological Quarterly* 84, no.1 (2019): 3–21. The extended argument can be found in Rosemann's *Charred Root of Meaning: Continuity, Transgression, and the Other in Christian Tradition* (Eerdmans, 2018).
7 A returning to the sources – both biblical and patristic. For the importance of this in Vatican II see: Gabriel Flynn, Paul D. Murray, and Patricia Hardcastle eds., *Ressourcement: A Movement for Renewal in Twentieth-century Catholic Theology* (OUP, 2012).
8 A bringing up to date – the term used by Pope John XXIII in calling the Council.
9 As well as Congar's seminal work see also Henri de Lubac, *Corpus Mysticum: The Eucharist and the Church in the Middle Ages* (SCM, 2006); and *Catholicism: A Study of Dogma in Relation to the Corporate Destiny of Mankind* (Longmans, Green, 1950).
10 This position, argued eloquently and with great scholarship by Alasdair MacIntyre, is well-described by Craig Hovey, "Alasdair MacIntyre's Hermeneutics of Tradition." Craig Hovey and Cyrus P. Olsen eds. *The Hermeneutics of Tradition: Explorations and Examinations* (Wipf and Stock, 2014): 144–169.
11 Key texts for MacIntyre's argument here are Alasdair MacIntyre, *After Virtue* (2nd ed., University of Notre Dame Press, 1984); and *Whose Justice? Which Rationality?* (University of Notre Dame Press, 1984).

12 "All reasoning takes place within the context of some traditional mode of thought, transcending through criticism and invention the limitations of what had hitherto been reasoned in that tradition". *After Virtue* 206.
13 E.g. *Whose Justice? Which Rationality?* 12.
14 Stephen Prickett, *Modernity and the Reinvention of Tradition* (CUP, 2009).
15 Lieven Boeve, *God Interrupts History* (Continuum, 2007).
16 Eric Saak, "Questioning Normativity: Systematic Theology as an Instrument of Evil." Lieven Boeve and Terrence Merrigan eds. *Tradition and the Normativity of History* (Peeters, 2013): 17–47.
17 Ibid. 17.
18 Ibid. 22 n.15.
19 Jonathan Tran "The Wound of Tradition." Craig Hovey and Cyrus P. Olsen eds. *The Hermeneutics of Tradition: Explorations and Examinations* (Wipf and Stock, 2014): 226–252. See 249.
20 For example, see Tracey Rowland, "Joseph Ratzinger and the Hermeneutics of Continuity," Hovey and Olsen, op. cit. 193–225.
21 Phillip Rosemann, see n. 5 above.
22 Hovey, op. cit. 166.
23 Ibid. 149.
24 In MacIntyre's sense referenced above.
25 As Hovey, op. cit.
26 This refers to one translation of the key text in Vatican II Dogmatic Constitution on Divine Revelation, *Dei Verbum*, 8, which speaks of the Apostolic tradition "developing" or "making progress" through the life of the church, as discussed in chapter 4 above. The official Vatican translation now prefers the language of "develop" to translate the Latin *proficit*.
27 See chapter 4's discussion of *Dei Verbum* 8 above 50–51.

Part IV
Conclusions

Rationale for Part IV

The author's claim is that this book demonstrates the possibilities for the renewal of theological and practical approaches to church through an ecclesiology generated from practice. More particularly, the belief is that theological action research, with its reflective framework of the four voices, is making an important contribution to ethnographic approaches to ecclesiology, which can lead us into new ways of studying, theologising and living church for our own time. That being said, all such 'claims' are to be seen as part of the on-going conversations around these questions, and are thus open to change, review and reform. Which is simply to say, I might be wrong!

It is something of this sense of the overall significance of this work that is explored in the last three short chapters of the book. These concluding sections are opportunities to take stock of the adventure that the preceding 11 chapters have taken us on, and reflect on what has been learnt. To this end, they ask three questions: what account of church is given in this work? (chapter 12); what account of theology has been implied? (chapter 13); and what prospects does this ecclesiological approach have for future development? (chapter 14). The responses given to these questions are – in keeping with our conversational commitments – less (or more?) than 'answers' that try to settle matters once and for all. Rather, the end is to seek to go on questioning, keeping open the possibilities of church, its life and its study. This is, after all, a vision of ecclesiology as *epiphanal:* we catch glimpses and keep on journeying.

12 What account of church? Edgelessness, fragility and discernment

In this chapter, reflecting back on what we have learnt in this book, I want to focus on the way in which the large-scale qualitative research project of ARCS has demonstrated how ecclesiology might be differently emphasised and shaped through attention to practices. It is here that I want to name and draw together features of an ecclesiology which takes seriously, as authoritative theological sources, the reflections from the Practices that we've worked with.

Such an exercise is, of course, itself interpretive. Other readers of this same data, and these same chapters, might well identify learning which would differ from what follows, and it is in the spirit of theological action research that I refrain from making too strong a claim for my own interpretation. Reflecting back on where this book started, and the call of Nicholas Healy to resist ecclesiological blueprints, I am conscious of the risk, common to much practice-engaged theology, of concluding with what in the end is simply another blueprint, all be it one drawn from a reading of practices. In order to mitigate such a tendency – although it cannot, I think, be entirely eradicated – I offer not so much a detailed account of church, as reflections on what seem to me to be the essential ingredients for speaking of the Christian community going forward. These ingredients are organised under three headings: edgelessness, fragility and the call to discernment.

In speaking of these things, I am not only encouraged – even compelled – by the Practices and their wisdom themselves but also affirmed by the places in academic ecclesiology where I have found resonances with these themes. In particular, I have been struck by Dan Hardy's sense of the church as called to serve "the movement of human life to its truth",[1] and Pete Ward's recognition of the nature of the church as being continually called into re-making, where (we should note) "making Church is a fluid movement of the Holy Spirit in cultural expression".[2] Nicholas Healy, towards the end of his 2012 chapter, also hints at something like this notion of church in describing it as "the Christian expression of the world".[3] Both in this literature and in our reading of practices in the light of the longer tradition, we seem to be being returned to a sense of church-in-and-for-the-world which, if taken seriously, reshapes ecclesiology in significant ways.

Three key ingredients of disclosed ecclesiology: edgelessness, fragility and the call to discernment

Edgelessness

In chapter 8, I demonstrated the ways in which the ARCS Practices, as distinctly intentional outreach projects, offered a reading of church which was powerfully re-centred at its organisational edges, and, radically, often at the edges or margins of human living. Paradoxically, such a re-centring carried with it an edgeless account of church, as the lay-led FBAs in particular witnessed to encounters with Christ's presence, with the Spirit, in these places of the margins. Whilst this was particularly clear in the LJV and Housing Justice projects, in different ways all the Practices spoke of this energy of 'church beyond church'. There is no need to repeat the learning of chapter 8 here; rather, drawing this basic ecclesiological sense together with other aspects of the ARCS learning, I want to highlight the significance of such a commitment to edgelessness.

Fundamentally, what we are seeing in the Practices is the vivid reality of church lived in and for the world, going out from its centre.[4] This reminds us that the church is 'in the world' because the world is the only place the church can be; and that it is 'for the world' as the Body of Christ[5] and as a "kind of sacrament of salvation"[6] for all humanity. This, in turn, militates against any ecclesial or academic energy which would somehow want to separate 'the church' out from the wider, worldly living of faith, and the wider still human living toward truth, in all its embodied, enculturated and flawed complexity. Any such setting apart of church suggests it can be simply an object, bounded and visible, of study. In their own ways, both systematic theologians' work with 'blueprint ecclesiologies' and many practice-based ecclesiologies risk this 'objectifying' of church. Rather, as Dan Hardy puts it, speaking of his own Anglican tradition's ecclesiology in particular:

> there is no straightforward 'doctrine of the Church' but an ongoing theological formation of the practice of church life. It is a way of theologically and practically renewing the Church that does not necessarily ever become a fixed doctrine. In that sense, thinking 'the Church' is unlike other doctrine: it is more a theological and practical engagement with what Church is and should be.[7]

It is this sort of reflection on the edgelessness of church that has led me to want to see church as a verbal expression as much as, if not more than, in terms of its noun-al reality.[8] This is to return to Barth's call not so much to talk about church as *be* it,[9] but with new insight gained from theological action research with the ARCS Practices. For this is not simply – or even – a refusal to articulate church; rather it is, in accord with Dan Hardy's observations, a call to articulate church as the mysterious and on-going practical-divine reality that it is, by attending to the workings of the Spirit in the world, and Christians' attempts to respond to them. What we encounter there, as distinct (though not separate from) what is seen in the organisational centre of ecclesial structures, is dynamism and life, all be it struggling with sin; we see 'living tradition' in MacIntyre's sense of this term.[10]

There are two more implications of this reading of church which I would particularly name as having especial significance, ecclesiological and practical, for today and into the future. First of all, and perhaps most compellingly, this edgeless understanding of church calls for a reorientation of ecclesiology (and church) away from any assumption that the organisational, structural centre is, in fact, '*the* centre'. What has become clear through this book's reflections is the very limited and particular place of the structures of church – structures which are only truly effective when they serve the church-in-the-world. This prioritising of ecclesial structures as *of service* in this way carries with it an additional imperative: that of becoming an organisation characterised by disciplined and attentive listening if it is truly to be such. After all, we cannot be authentically served by one who already knows what we need before they get to know our daily lived realities.[11] If the ecclesial institution is essential as the holder of tradition and community,[12] it is also to be known as something essential but 'small' in relation to the Christian living in the world, and the wider humanity it exists to serve. It is called, as part of its primary task, to be thoroughly attentive to the real living of Christian faith in all the complexities of the world.

An account of edgeless church also nuances how we might see Christian 'community'. For many, this is construed as a gathered and stable community – a network of relationships and mutual commitment in faith, which is especially (for Anglicans and Roman Catholics) nurtured around the Eucharistic table. The research set out in this book does not undermine this: we need only think of the 'magnetic' community of St. Mary's (C), or the centrality of Eucharist in Portsmouth (F), to be reminded not only of the emphasis on hospitality and relationship but also on the persistent presence and practice of liturgy and sacrament. However, I would suggest that even these moments of affirming community are to be seen in a new light by virtue of what has been learnt. First, from a more *ad intra* ecclesiological perspective, the Practices' learning makes clear that community is not without demand (C); indeed, it might even be demand that really makes someone feel they belong (D4, final quotes). At the same time, as a second point, significant for the church's participation in the *missio Dei* is the witness to more fluid kinds of 'community', appropriate to the world as we find it: communities that do not require a tomorrow (A3, Joseph), community that knows its life primarily through encounters on the street (D3). Such a vision of the Spirit's healing work in the wounded 'skin of humanity'[13] liberates Christian mission from the (self-taught) burden of 'building communities' and frees it to recognise the human and graced community of the chat in the playground, the singing at the children's bath-time and friendship to the stranger. That these things ultimately 'belong' to Christ, and that it is to be desired that they are named and celebrated as such is true; the difference is that, in the expansive working of the Spirit, they are already graced, and do not need to be *made* to belong to Christ by us.

Fragility

One of the unnerving things about an edgeless, in-the-world account of church, which puts the institutional 'in its place' as existing for the service of this unruly, messy reality, is the sense of not being in control. This is an anxiety especially felt by those placed at the institutional centre, as seen in microcosm in the Messy Church project (D), where the leaders of Messy Church had to work to make sense of the (apparent) Jesus-less-ness of the community. Notably, through recourse to scripture and Christian traditions, they were able to hold the reality they encountered through a renewed understanding of church and discipleship. However, it is not simply a managerial anxiety born out of some need to control by those in charge of things. Rather, it is a proper anxiety for all Christians (like the Messy Church leaders) who risk living church 'in the wild'. For the church which re-orientates itself to be centred in the margins, and moves out from itself into a world to follow the Spirit, a level of concern seems quite appropriate. How are we to know the Spirit? How will we know what to do in response? What if we get things wrong (which we will)?

It is in this sense that I want to speak of the fragility of church – not as an essential or ontological attribute of church, which is, after all, Christ's Body and the temple of the Spirit; but rather as a way of referring to what must, it seems to me, be our experience of living church today. We need to become accustomed to our experience of fragility so as to inhabit it as the paradoxical place where we experience of God's power at work in and for the world.

From this perspective, the problem with 'blueprint ecclesiologies' – whether practice-based or otherwise – is that they aim for an improper level of confidence, even certainty, about church. An organisational or purely top-down theological view of church allows us to say grand things about what the church is doing or should be doing, and what its nature and purposes are; and on one level, this can be an important – indeed, essential – part of the ecclesiological conversation. However, when the reading of church becomes more granular, when we look at it in practice, it appears as something much more vulnerable, at least in its particular expressions in particular contexts. It is worth remembering that neither of the diocesan projects that we worked with have been sustainable since we worked with them 10 years ago. On the other hand, a few of the entrepreneurial outreaches are going from strength to strength – Housing Justice, LJV particularly, and of course Mercy Church, which as a nationally established Fresh Expressions, has its own vitality. What is striking is that it is precisely in these places that there was, in the research, a sense of proper fragility, the sense of not being able to grasp entirely or be in control of what was happening – a sense of stepping out into unknown situations and thoughts on a daily basis. Yet these practices of fragility are where the life has continued; they have become accustomed to their experienced fragility and begun to recognise it for what it is – dependence of the Spirit.

It would be a mistake to make too much of this last observation, as if ecclesially structured initiatives are always fated to fail, and lay led entrepreneurial activities always destined to live long; this is clearly not demonstrated in this work. Rather, these reflections provoke a thought that is worth sharing: that the preparedness to live with a proper, Spirit-trusting fragility with regard to our own Christian work is precisely that virtue which is needed for ongoing, developing church life. This calls the churches away from any over-dependence on organisational management and strategy and returns them to the more radical task of taking each step in response to the Spirit without necessarily seeing where exactly we are headed.[14] This brings me to my third characteristic of church: that of discernment.

Discernment

If this disclosed church was simply to be read in terms of edgelessness and fragility (as understood here as 'proper' fragility), this could suggest something of a letting go of institutional church and the traditions it holds altogether. Indeed, there are some aspects of contemporary Pioneer thinking which take us precisely in such a direction.[15] It should be possible for the reader to be clear by this stage that this is not the position taken in this book, which has been at pains to indicate not only the limitations but *the gifts* of the institutional or structured church, as well as of Christian traditions, to the wider church-in-mission in the world.[16] Here, however, it is important to name this relationship of the (small) institution to the edgeless church on the edges in a particular way – as at the service of *discernment*.

The pneumatological, lay and worldly dominate my interpretation of the church we are glimpsing through theological action research with the Practices. Such an account then makes a necessary demand on this largely lay and in-the-world church, that it learns how to discern the Spirit, the following of whom is our only security and remedy for the anxieties of fragility. Such a practice-learnt insight finds resonance with the normative voice articulated by Pope Francis when he repeatedly makes clear the necessity of becoming a church characterised by discernment:

> How can we know if something comes from the Holy Spirit or if it stems from the spirit of the world or the spirit of the devil? The only way is through discernment, which calls for something more than intelligence or common sense. It is a gift which we must implore. If we ask

> with confidence that the Holy Spirit grant us this gift, and then seek to develop it through prayer, reflection, reading and good counsel, then surely we will grow in this spiritual endowment. [167] The gift of discernment has become all the more necessary today, since contemporary life offers immense possibilities for action and distraction, and the world presents all of them as valid and good. All of us, but especially the young, are immersed in a culture of zapping. We can navigate simultaneously on two or more screens and interact at the same time with two or three virtual scenarios. Without the wisdom of discernment, we can easily become prey to every passing trend.[17]

Pope Francis is, of course, speaking as a Jesuit – one deeply formed in Ignatian spirituality with its emphasis on discernment. His account of discernment eloquently expresses this tradition, in naming the complex ways in which insights from human sciences, our own experiences, the guidance of others and church teaching are all involved in *and transcended by* the divine grace of discernment.[18] For Ignatius himself, it is clear that discernment is no easy matter, requiring wise guidance as well as attentiveness to a variety of what we might recognise, in this context, as theological voices. So, in the *Rules for Discernment* which append Ignatius' *Exercises* (probably completed around 1523–1524),[19] much attention is paid to attending to the 'interior movements' within the person who is discerning. Affect, mood, demeanour as well as fruits evidenced in action are to be carefully considered. However, this attentiveness to the interior is not straightforward, as it is clear that both 'the evil spirit' and 'good spirit' act differently on different temperaments, or at different times for people, depending on what might be most effective towards their different ends.[20] Furthermore, rational contemplation of the affective experiences of consolation and desolation – so key to Ignatian discernment – is complicated by the recognition that one might feel consoled though the action of the evil spirit, who often "assumes the appearance of an angel of light".[21] The church called into discernment is called into a place of true difficulty and even apparent confusion as we seek ever more deeply the step to be taken which brings us, and the world, more fully to Christ.

It is important to note that for Ignatius, we are not without guides in this testing and on-going life process of growth. First there he recognises the importance of the wise and experienced accompanier with their qualities of openness, attentiveness and care for the individual discerning; indeed, there is a sense in which there is no really 'individual' discernment for Ignatius, both because of this relationship and as a consequence of the process's engagement with normative authorities as well as that of personal experiences. Then the centrality of the Gospel account of Christ's life and Passion in the *Exercises* holds the discerner close to the Person of Jesus throughout. Added to this, we should also note Ignatius' *Rules for Thinking with the Church*.[22] These are ultimately uncompromising in insisting that "we must put aside all judgment of our own, and keep the mind ever ready and prompt to obey in all things the true Spouse of Christ our Lord, our holy Mother, the hierarchical Church".[23] Ignatian discernment is clearly not about figuring 'our own truth' in matters already established in our faith tradition. A tension is set up here between a clear sense of obedience and the dominant and persistent sense that, *none the less*, the Christian life can be nothing other than a slow, complex way of discernment if we are truly to make progress toward Christ.

Whilst I might prefer a somewhat moderated account of the normative authority of "our holy Mother, the hierarchical Church", there is nonetheless a principle of the struggle to discern in continuity with normative church accounts and traditions in Ignatius which coheres with much of the learning from the Practices. For, at their best, the normative structures and traditions of church were enabling of lay participation in the *missio Dei* in the world.[24] Yet practices of discernment are, it is clear, far from straightforward, and the question is provoked as to how far Christians are enabled for such crucial work today.

Perhaps this is one of the ways in which the normative and formal voices of theology can be re-construed, not as corrective, expert or authoritarian, but as at the service of discernment in the world. By the same account, the small-institutional church approach, which I am proposing, suggests that this institution exists to serve this outreach not only through sacraments, preaching and pastoral care but also through enabling of a culture for discernment, where honesty, the sharing of experience and thought, traditions, and normative practices in free and attended-to conversational living becomes a primary practice of church. In such conversation, in keeping with the traditions of discernment, attention is given with generous openness not only to the normative, the expert, or the experiences of lived faith, but rather, what is attended to primarily is the way in which the Spirit interrupts and opens up these conversations, enabling our discernment of the next step – but perhaps not much more.[25]

Conclusions: outlines for a disclosed ecclesiology

What is emerging here (and it is, by its very nature and in principle a work in progress) is an account of church which is not so much bounded as centred and edgeless. In this, it coheres with Vatican II's account of the church as the People of God, which reaches out from its institutional centre to all the people of the world.[26] However, lest this is diagnosed simply as an effect of what Pete Ward has called the "affective gravitational pull of the church", shaping my thinking and interpretation too uncritically,[27] I would suggest that this book's account of church, in all its intentional messiness, speaks of a church which is simultaneously multi-centred (on its edges, and in encounters with the Spirit in the world) *and* institutionally centred in the essential, yet small embodiment (sacrament?) of church which exists to serve the whole. If the church as described in *Lumen Gentium* can be understood as a centred reality, with concentric 'ripples' of belonging extending out to the whole world, this more multi-layered, multi-centred account of church does not admit of such diagrammatic representation. This is reassuring to me. If the church is the Body of Christ in today's world, the place where the divine agency of the Spirit works with and in, as well as ahead of human activities, we would not expect to find it a matter simply described.

Such an account takes us away from the tension of blueprint ecclesiologies versus practical and historical accounts, and places ecclesiology in a similar place to Dan Hardy's account, discussed above: it is not so much about talking about a 'thing' called 'church', but about processual practices of learning to be church. In such an understanding, the problem is not so much blueprint ecclesiologies as such, but rather, what part they are allowed to play in the process of learning church. As a particular contribution to the wider, four-voiced theology, they can be useful and important, saving us from that congeries of particularities that the later work of Nicholas Healy laments.[28] In a similar way, empirical accounts of church need not be assessed as to whether they can, on their own, substantiate doctrines of church; rather they, too, are invited into a conversation in which their particular insights and gifts might be received.

This is a church necessarily characterised by discernment, and so by such conversation. As such, it challenges in a particular way one common account of church as a 'school',[29] suggesting that some more appropriate language might be found for what is, nonetheless, a properly pedagogical process.[30] Discernment is a kind of learning, but a particular kind. For whilst 'school' intractably refers us to a model where there are teachers and the taught, those who know, and those who need to learn what is known by others (even when ameliorated by the observation that teachers learn from their pupils), it militates against that kind of open conversing for discernment envisaged in this account of church, established in the longer tradition and practised (all be it imperfectly) in the research that underpins this book. The learning and discerning church glimpsed in the Practices is more akin to a kind of household, or family learning, where things are learnt though small practices, mistakes, disagreement and all the complexities of human relationship, illumined, from time to time, by the greater story of which they are a part: the story of Trinity.

What is emerging is a thoroughly lay, in-the-world church, living human life in ordinary, yet with the extraordinary divine gifts of discernment by which the activity and promptings of the Spirit can be responded to. It is a communal human engagement with theology, with faith seeking understanding. To deepen understanding of the implications of this, we need now to consider the kind of theology that is implied.

Notes

1 Dan Hardy, *Finding the Church: The Dynamic Truth of Anglicanism* (SCM, 2001): 129.
2 Pete Ward, *Liquid Ecclesiology: The Gospel and the Church* (Brill, 2017): 68–69.
3 Healy, op. cit. 199.
4 So see chapter 7's account of the *ek*-centricity of church.
5 I Corinthians 12: 12–27. We might also refer to Jesus' own depiction of his disciples as 'salt of the earth', Matt. 5:13; and Paul's referring to the Christian community as 'leaven', Gal. 5:9.
6 Second Vatican Council Dogmatic Constitution on the Church, *Lumen Gentium* 1.
7 Hardy, op. cit. 238.
8 149 above.
9 Karl Barth, *Dogmatics in Outline* (SCM Press. Sixteenth Impression, 1988): 141.
10 See above 229.
11 We might contrast the different ways in which the structures of Portsmouth Diocese (F) and the Westminster Agency for Evangelisation (B) worked to illuminate this.
12 As suggested in chapter 11.
13 An image effectively used by Hardy, op. cit. 84–86 as an image of human interconnectedness and sociality.
14 In this, I have some sympathy with Lyndon Shakespeare's critique of management approaches to the church: Lyndon Shakespeare, *Being the Body of Christ in the Age of Management* (Wipf and Stock, 2016). However, unlike Shakespeare, I would allow for the usefulness of such organisational learning, all be it understood in an ecclesiologically defined way, as the section on 'discernment' in this chapter shows.
15 For literature on Pioneer ministries see: Jonny Baker et al. eds. *Future Present: Embodying a Better World Now* (Proust Publication, 2018); Cathy Ross and Jonny Baker eds., *Pioneering Spirituality* (Canterbury Press, 2015); Cathy Ross and Jonny Baker, *The Pioneer Gift: Explorations in Mission* (Canterbury Press, 2014).
16 For example, see 220–222 above.
17 Pope Francis, Apostolic Exhortation, *Gaudete et Exsultate* (2018): 166–167. Available at: http://w2.vatican.va/content/francesco/en/apost_exhortations/documents/papa-francesco_esortazione-ap_20180319_gaudete-et-exsultate.html#DISCERNMENT.
18 See ibid. 170–172.
19 Reference in what follows are made to the following edition: *The Spiritual Exercises*. Preface by Avery Dulles (Chicago: Loyola Press, 2000).
20 Ibid. 314–315.
21 Ibid. 332.
22 Ibid. 352–370.
23 Ibid. 353.
24 See above 220–222.
25 By making discernment, with its implicit pneumatology, foundational to the ecclesiology envisaged here, I am aware of a certain correspondence with Sarah Coakley's foundational place for contemplation in theology: *God, Sexuality, and the Self: An Essay 'on the Trinity'* (CUP, 2013). The discerning church argued for here is, at first look, a rather more socially and conversationally engaged understanding than that suggested in Coakley's contemplative imperative for theology. However, the resonances here and in the next chapter are striking.
26 Second Vatican Council Dogmatic Constitution on the Church, *Lumen Gentium*, chapter 2.

27 Pete Ward, "Blueprint Ecclesiology and the Lived. Normativity as a Perilous Faithfulness." *Ecclesial Practices* 2, no.1 (2015): 74–90. Ward's basic observation that "ecclesial traditions shape and condition reasoning" (78) when we come to reading church is, it seems to me inevitably the case. The question is: how do we respond to these occasions of coherence between the interpretation of practice and the received tradition – as confirmation of the Spirit's action, or as a failure to think beyond what has been received? Once again, discernment seems required.

28 Nicholas Healy, "Ecclesiology, Ethnography and God: An Interplay of Reality Descriptions." Pete Ward ed. *Perspectives on Ecclesiology and Ethnography* (Eerdmans, 2012): 182–199. See especially 189.

29 For example, Nicholas Lash, "Authors, Authority and Authorization." Bernard Hoose ed. *Authority in the Roman Catholic Church: Theory and Practice* (Ashgate, 2002): 59–71. This language is explicitly questioned by Healy in his 2010 essay "Ecclesiology, Ethnography and God: An Interplay of Reality Descriptions." Pete Ward ed. *Perspectives on Ecclesiology and Ethnography* (Eerdmans, 2012): 182–199.

30 This is illustrated in the Practices, as the importance of lay formation and learning in particular is highlighted: So see B5, G2 and chapter 7's account of F, for example. The pedagogical gifts of theological action research are especially well considered in Susanna Brouard, *Using Theological Action Research to Embed Catholic Social Teaching in a Catholic Development Agency: Abseiling on the Road to Emmaus* (Unpub. Prof. Doc. Anglia Ruskin University, 2015).

13 What account of theology? Practical fundamental theology

Ecclesiology is itself a theological practice of a particular kind; so it is appropriate as we end this book to consider the theological implications of the approach to ecclesiology which has been described. There are two key ways in which this wider theological significance can be understood. The first pertains to the basis of *all* theology in a *practical fundamental theology*, such as outlined at the end of chapter 4, and given particular scholarly depth in the work of Johann Baptist Metz. My second set of reflections are more concerned to speak out of the experiences of composing this book, and working, for nearly 15 years, in theological action research from the basis of this practical fundamental theology. Here, the focus is much more on what is generally understood as practical theology as such, and I argue that the insights of the work described above might helpfully recast this sub-discipline as an authentic 'whole-theology'. The proper impossibility of such a theology, to which my writing here is itself testimony, carries with it certain implications and demands for the Christian theologian today. Above all, it insists that *conversations of discernment* become more and more fundamental to the methods we use in theological practice.

The previous chapter's reflections on ecclesiology ended with reference to the Trinity – God's going out from Godself so as to be with us, and invite us into the divine life – which is the foundation of all Christian theology. As a proper theme of systematic theology, ecclesiology must always refer back to and arise from this trinitarian centre of Christian faith.[1] In a particular way, the church as 'under the heading' of the Holy Spirit in the Creeds, and, especially according to my practice-engaged account as an ongoing creation of the Spirit, draws us through both practices and ecclesiology to a reflection on Christian living which finds its deepest meaning in Trinity. In more recent times, this Trinitarian awareness has shaped theology more explicitly, and a number of writers for whom this awareness is especially clear have been influential in the thoughts that follow: Rowan Williams' account of Christian theology leads the reader from fundamental theological thinking through an understanding of Trinity as "the grammar of God", to return us to the world of faith-full practice.[2] Paul Fiddes' thinking too, as discussed with him and as set out in his book *Participating in God: A*

Pastoral Doctrine of the Trinity,[3] has over a number of years shaped my thinking about the Trinity in relation to Christian life and practice. I am also conscious of some intriguing resonances between what I want to say about practical fundamental theology and Sarah Coakley's account of her systematic theology.[4] In hidden as well as explicit ways, these thinkers have shaped and affirmed the way in which not only the theological *possibility* of a practice-engaged Trinitarian theology, but its *imperative* (even in its 'impossibility'), has been increasingly confirmed as I have sought to learn from faith-full practices.

It is from this fundamental, practical and Trinitarian place that I shall now offer some reflections on what theological action research, and its disclosing of ecclesiology through conversation in and with practices, attending to the 'four voices' of theology, might have to say about theology as such.

Practical fundamental theology: towards a whole-theology

Remembering the impossibility of theology

A preliminary task is to be mindful of the peculiarity, complexity and proper 'impossibility' of theology. Practical theologians, and ethnographic ecclesiologists in particular, are increasingly giving voice to the profound difficulty of doing theology at all, based on the experience of its fluidity, and its necessary embeddedness in cultural contexts and language. So, for Pete Ward, the 'liquidity' of church is closely related to that of theology itself:

> Theology is liquid because if utilizes cultural-conditioned forms of expression: it is construction. . . . It is faith seeking understanding. The theologian builds a world, but the status of this world is not guaranteed, nor does it have any particular claim to apprehend the divine. . . . Theology does not have any special claim to visibility, but neither is it occluded from the vision of God. The point is that what theologians say about God is a contested and contesting field, and to claim anything beyond that is problematic.[5]

In part, this is an especially late modern observation, grown out of the acute sensitivities of secular pluralism, in which not only does faith have no privileged position but where its very claim to having anything worth saying at all is questioned.[6] Such a context, as Boeve clearly argues, re-orientates theology and the speaking of faith toward being one among many voices in the human conversation towards truth and deeper humanity.[7] This, in turn, gives rise to questions concerning theology's basis in faith and so in divine revelation – the very thing that characterises it. If the voices of faith are simply some among many others in this plural conversation of contemporary humanity, it might seem that the claims of Christian faith and the mystery of divine revelation in Jesus have become diminished in the demands of contemporary relativism. If the very basis of Christian theology cannot be recognised beyond the communities of faith, how are we to practice theology as traditionally understood, without its becoming simply a game played by those who believe, and increasingly irrelevant, and even a stumbling block, to those beyond the visible structures of church?

Lieven Boeve offers a robust response to this, in calling the late modern theological and faith communicator to a radical dependence on the Holy Spirit and faith in the 'interruptions' of God in our plural conversations.[8] In his account, the contested nature of theology's basis (revelation) does not lead us to despair of it; rather, its evident fragility in contemporary debate returns us to trust in the Spirit to do the work of interruptive revelation in our multi-voiced and multi-authorised conversations. It is ultimately not up to us to prove God's presences in the world – only to attend to the moments of divine interruption in the conversations in which we are called to participate with the 'knowing' of faith.

These re-visionings of theology in relation to its late modern context, and the empirical turn which is part of its response to that context, is discussed in a slightly different way by Rowan Williams. Most helpfully, Williams describes the perennial nature of this difficulty;[9] this is not simply a contemporary problem of theology but rather the most recent manifestation of a proper difficulty with the theological enterprise itself. Part of his response is to suggest that there is a proper 'negative' aspect to theology which is required for its truthfulness. This is not so much a return to ancient apophaticism, but rather a kind of negativity which insists that theology is always "aware of its location on the 'hermeneutical spiral'", conscious of how this location constrains, shapes and informs what is being said.

> [theology] is 'negative' because obliged to be not only critical of the Church's language and practice but also self-critical, suspicious of its recurring temptation to theoretical resolutions and conceptual neatness.[10]

Williams' *via negativa* is, we should note, in respect of both the incomprehensibility of God, and the surdic, ultimately mute mystery of faith practices as the response of people to the Spirit's agency.[11]

Williams at this point has recourse to Thomas Aquinas, and it is salutary for us to remember that these contemporary reflections on the intractable difficulty of theological and faith speaking can be glimpsed in the longer tradition. Not only that, but we should note also that the 'negativity' (in Williams' sense) of the premodern tradition refers us not only to the impossibility of theology in the face of the mystery of the Trinity, but also – in Aquinas at least – to a proper negativity in relation to the mystery of faith practice. Aquinas, like many before him, propose theology as in principle 'impossible', in so far as it is a *scientia* or way of knowing which seeks to know everything in terms of relation to God[12] – God, who in one sense does not 'exist',[13] and who even in beatitude will only be known as "one unknown".[14] Theology is that very odd *scientia* which is derived from that knowledge which is God's own knowing of all things, in which we may participate in limited ways through faith and God's grace in Word and Spirit. This is the fairly established impossibility of theology as understood as apophatically conditioned. However, Aquinas also speaks of the practical nature of theology, and here too the proper 'impossibility' of theology becomes clear, though in a fresh way especially pertinent to this book's project. It is worth describing this point in a little detail.

Having established that the kind of knowing that theology (*sacra doctrina*) is, is one derived from that *scientia* of God, which is shared through faith, grace and revelation, Aquinas then demonstrates the singlenesss of this discipline by relating it, once again, to the unity of all things as pertaining to God who is their creator.[15] It is at this stage that Aquinas turns to the question as to whether theology is a practical or theoretical *scientia*, or way of knowing, and it may surprise many contemporary readers to discover that his first point asserts that clearly theology is practical as "Christian theology is for action".[16] However, Aquinas cannot settle with this, and his reasons for not stopping here are worth quoting as a chastening challenge to many working in practical theological fields today:

> On the other hand, every practical science is concerned with what men can do and make. Christian theology, however, is about God, who makes men and is not made by them.[17]

To say that theology "is for action" is true, but the nature of this true statement needs probing further if the theologian is to avoid simply being interested in human agency alone. Aquinas' response to this quandary comes through appeal to the nature of *sacra doctrina* as an imperfect participation in God's own knowing:

> Holy teaching (*sacra doctrina*) while remaining single nevertheless embraces things belonging to the different philosophical sciences because of the one formal meaning which is its interest in all manner of things, namely the truth they bear in the light of God. Whereas some among the philosophical sciences are theoretical and some practical, **sacred doctrine takes over both functions, in this being like the single knowledge whereby God knows himself and the things he makes.**[18]

God's knowing is – in keeping with Trinity (although Aquinas does not say this here) – simultaneously practical-and-theoretical. In so far as theology as *sacra doctrina* is a sharing in or mirroring (imperfectly) of God's *scientia,* it is characterised by the holding together of the practical and theoretical in its knowing. This is an aspect of theology's proper impossibility, based not, it should be noted, on any simply technical or even philosophical difficulty in integrating practice and concept, but on the distinctive nature of theology as a partial participation in the Trinity's 'knowing'.

Theology as fundamentally practice-engaged

This last observation from Thomas Aquinas speaks into the central commitment of the theological action research project – the practice of theology as such as fundamentally practice-engaged. This book's early chapters located the methods of theological action research and the four voices of theology that it surfaced, and suggested that this ultimately led to an account not so much of 'practical theology', but of a whole-theology which integratively attended to multiple authorities in theology, including detailed and empirical expressions of faith practices. This whole-theology is based on a reading of fundamental theology – the theological consideration of how we can speak of God at all[19] – which recognises that the theologian's attentiveness to divine revelation insists that attention is given not only to scripture, Christian tradition, and academic disciplines, but also to practices of faith. The basic point that has then been demonstrated is the importance of recognising practice, not for practical theological reasons as ordinarily understood, but for *fundamental* theological reasons: practices are a crucial, living way in which God speaks to us. Aquinas' account of *sacra doctrina* as, uniquely and divinely, a both practical-and-theoretical way of knowing, confirms this as a theological instinct within the longer Christian tradition.

As a preliminary point I note that, in speaking of this sense of a 'whole-theology', there is some resonance with Sarah Coakley's contemplative *théologie totale*[20] which I encountered subsequent to formulating the language of 'whole-theology'. This is not surprising given that Coakley's systematic theological concern overlaps my own ecclesiological instincts, in the common commitment to an integrated theology rooted in practices dependent on the Spirit's action, which takes account of the variety of ways and loci in which faith seeks understanding. There is more to be discussed here, but for now, I would observe that the ways in which the four voices of theology lead us to the idea of a practical fundamental theology with its demand of whole-theology, assumes not only that theology is "uncovered at every level", as with Coakley's *théologie totale*,[21] but that it is lived and 'done' at every level. Whole-theology is necessarily communal and multi-voiced not only conceptually, or in terms of research loci, but in terms of its shared composition among different people occupying different places and expertises in relation to church. Whole-theology is a whole-church practice.

To make a study through practices of the possibilities for a contemporary ecclesiology, and then to arrive at this place of classic theological questions, is both a little disorientating and affirming. It makes clear the ways in which our theological engagement with practice, shaped by attentiveness to the four voices of theology, has been, all along, a practice of theology *as such*: the faith-full endeavour of attending to divine revelation in our own context so as to find understanding and voice for faith. As a theology based on a practical fundamental theology, practices have themselves been significant loci of faith and revelation for this work. Its Trinitarian instinct has been to seek out and learn from the activity of the Spirit in the world, with all the demands of discernment this implies.[22]

This language and practice of 'practical fundamental theology', as observed in chapter 4, can be traced back to the work of the Catholic political theologian Johann Baptist Metz. More than 40 years ago, and approaching this question from a different place, Metz identified the essential importance of recognising fundamental theology as necessarily engaged with praxis.[23] Arguing from a keen sense of the suffering of the late twentieth century world, its economic inequalities, injustices and political oppressions, Metz roots the theological endeavour in *hope* – the call to make real the hope that is within us[24] through Christian faith. But for this to be effective, we cannot simply be interested in hope as an idea, but "rather with the concrete historical and social situation in which subjects are placed, with their experiences, sufferings, struggles ad contradictions".[25] To do theology for the world today makes a particular demand on the theologian to recognise practice as fundamental.

In a footnote at the end of his opening chapter, Metz positions his work with a practical fundamental theology as a necessary critique of the tradition of transcendental theology so much developed by his teacher, Karl Rahner.[26] He comments on how important transcendental approaches have been as a corrective to the neo-Thomist propositional and rigid accounts of theology which dominated Catholicism in the early part of the twentieth century. However, now that this neo-scholastic adversary has "finally collapsed in exhaustion in the strong arms of transcendental theology"[27] the Rahnerian account of theology needs to re-imagine itself in relation not so much to internal theological debates but to the late twentieth century world which is crying out in suffering to God.[28] Metz's own work sets out to respond to this, and in doing so, returns theology to the world, to praxis, and "the faith of Christians in history and society".[29] It is within this tradition, with its passionate care for "the world" – for suffering humanity, and, we are increasingly aware, for suffering creation as a whole – that this book's commitment to a practical fundamental theology finds itself.

Can such a whole-theology be done?

So far in this chapter, I have located the fundamental theological approach that has been at work through the ecclesiological project in relation to both contemporary thinkers and the longer tradition. The risk taken in doing this is not only that this is an inevitably over-brief account but also, and more dangerously for one committed to practices, that it leaves the argument in the place of concept, academic theology and the abstract. To finish these reflections in a way more in keeping with the theology practised in this volume, I will now turn to consider the doing of such a theology as envisaged here.

Learning from the composing of this book: the necessary incompleteness of whole-theology

At the start of this book, I suggested that there was a "proper difficulty" involved in its writing which related especially to the 'writing' of 'practices' in the necessarily complex understanding of theology as disclosed in the conversation between the four voices of theology.[30] On a very straightforward level, I experienced this difficulty as a constant feeling of frustration and dissatisfaction in writing. In particular, as chapters 5–11 sought to take the learnings from practice and relate them to wider thinking in the academy and the longer Christian tradition, I was constantly up against my own limits of expertise, as well as the limits of space. Every time I've written something in these chapters, I have been aware that there will be an expert in missiology, or sacramental theology, or sociology of religion, who will have a better understanding of the themes treated. Indeed, any one of these chapters could have been expanded to a number of extensive in-depth articles on a particular theme. They are, in this sense, not complete. As a result, I've suffered all the way through this writing with a feeling of not quite ever finishing the work in front of me. In order to say anything at all at the level of a disclosed ecclesiology, I have had to be selective, even at the risk of simplifying the arguments of others. It is a proper question to ask, Is such an 'incompleteness' acceptable in a work of academic theology?

Different readers will, no doubt, have differing responses to this question. For myself, the inevitable anxieties of writing in this way have resulted in a more constructive account of the *necessary* incompleteness of *all* theology, relating to what has been said earlier in this chapter about the 'impossibility' of theology. To be sure, such a fundamental 'double negativity'[31] in relation to the theological task cannot be used as an excuse for uninformed thinking, or approaches that lack rigour. However, it may make possible the impossible task of whole-theology – particularly those theologies committed to engagement with practice – by liberating the theologian into a place of realisation that her work is only ever a bit of the larger conversations of faith, to which she may, with some necessary humility, make a more or less helpful, but never finalising, contribution.

The necessarily incomplete form of the kind of practice-engaged theology that this book has worked with can be seen as rooted not only in the human limitations of even the most learned of scholars but also, and more significantly, in the nature of theology itself. Much of this chapter has been given over to considering this 'impossible' way of knowing which is theology, and it is this fundamental truth about the discipline which has made this multi-voiced, necessarily incomplete work of practice-engaged ecclesiology possible. The incompleteness of whole-theology, as presented by theological action research and the four voices of theology, is not such as to render us speechless; rather, it requires us to speak in a particular way. This way is the practice of *conversation.*

The call to conversation as fundamental theological practice[32]

The theme and practice of conversation has been a constant throughout the book. Its presence was especially highlighted in the accounts of theological action research methods[33] and the related theological understanding of the four voices.[34] It surfaces again here, at the end of our account, as having specific theological and epistemological significance. For if it is the case that the practicalities of the whole-theology I have described, with its commitment to practical fundamental theology, is properly impossible as the complete work of any one theologian, it is also the case that the resulting move towards a communal practice of theology carries with it conceptual implications.

The most obvious of these is that theological knowing is of a kind necessarily generated through relationships in which truth is controversed. As such, it can never be a closing-down kind of knowledge – a knowing or expertise which concludes a question as finally answered, and no longer admitting of conversation. Rather, any 'conclusion' exists as a contribution to the next conversation, in which – in keeping with MacIntyre's account of living tradition – it will itself be both acknowledged and contested. This understanding alleviates something of the anxiety surrounding the incompleteness of whole-theology, especially experienced by those of us trying to write from and with practices as fundamental theological loci.

A second implication corresponds with an aspect of Coakley's systematics, in which she identifies as a hallmark of her theology, its nature as being *in via*.[35] This is, of course, not a novel understanding in the tradition, in which, as we have seen, the negativity of theology, in both its facets (toward Divine Mystery, and the mystery of practical living in the Spirit) is understood as compelling theology to ever-new accounts of that revelation with which it is concerned. The whole-theology I am describing is in continuity with such a tradition, in recognising itself as always 'on the way', unfolding in the infinitely varied combinations of faith-full thinking and practices which are its sources for discerning God's revelation. As such, it is properly aligned with the nature of the People of God as themselves pilgrims,[36] who even as a church see things only as if in a mirror and not yet directly.[37] The theology of such a pilgrim people must reflect this sense of not yet having arrived whilst at the same time carrying with it a sure sense of direction as to what – indeed, who – we are journeying towards. Theology in and through conversation is the activity of a people on the road.

In this last observation, we are returned to the central subject of this project: ecclesiology – and, in particular, the theology of church disclosed through thinking with and through practices and their agents. For if theology is most truthfully practised in conversation, then the question is raised: who takes part in the conversation? The position of this book, based on its theology of Spirit and faith-in-the-world answers this question with an adamant (though impossible) 'everyone'. Whilst seemingly ridiculous in its naivety, such a position is, nonetheless, true to the Christian belief in the Holy Spirit and the way God is present to the world. The challenge remains as to how the church, as that part of humanity which explicitly lives toward God who is Trinity and so serves humanity's movement toward truth, can grow more deeply into this kind of conversational practice of theology as a whole community. I believe that the ARCS Practices – and many like them today – suggest that there are many things happening 'on the ground' to which we might turn in order to answer this question more fully and effectively.

Concluding reflections

If this chapter has offered an account of theology which is 'impossible', it has done so in a way which demonstrates that such an impossibility is proper. By indicating the 'double negativity' of theology – in relation both to the mystery of Trinity and in relation to the practicalities of living in the Spirit – it has also suggested a way of bringing systematic and practical theologies together in a circular rather than linear or correlative relationship. There is, rather, a call to a single whole-theology, based on a practical fundamental theological understanding of the proper variety of and coherence between the different loci of divine revelation. As such, it is also a call to a particular way of being – better, practising – church: as a community of discerning conversation, open to the necessarily incomplete and flawed contributions of all who seek what is most true. Our faith tells us that this Truth is found and experienced in the Trinity, but there can be no short cuts in the theological task of articulating this faith, this hope. Rather, the ecclesial conversation itself in and for the world, becomes the expression of the Trinitarian faith and the theology which is its (always provisional) understanding.

Notes

1 This is an especially strong theme in the important World Council of Churches document: *The Church: Towards a Common Vision.* Faith & Order Paper 214 (World Council of Churches Publications, 2013).

2 Rowan Williams, *On Christian Theology* (Blackwell, 2000). See especially 131–180.

3 Paul Fiddes, *Participating in God: A Pastoral Doctrine of the Trinity* (Darton Longman & Todd, 2000).

4 Sarah Coakley, *God, Sexuality, and the Self: An Essay 'on the Trinity'* (CUP, 2013).
5 Pete Ward, *Liquid Ecclesiology* (Brill, 2017): 21.
6 One of the best accounts of this late modern context for Christian theology, and a constructive response to it is given by Lieven Boeve, *Interrupting Tradition: An Essay on Christian Faith in a Postmodern Context* (Peeters, 2003); and *God Interrupts History* (Continuum, 2007).
7 Lieven Boeve, *God Interrupts History* (Continuum, 2007): 41–48.
8 Ibid. This language of 'interruption' in Boeve is explicitly linked to the work of Johann Metz: Boeve, op. cit. 203–204. I am aware, too, of the significance of this language for Sarah Coakley, although with a rather different provenance and suggesting a subtly different reference. For example, see Coakley, op. cit. 56–57; 87, on the interruption of the Spirit.
9 Op. cit. Chapter 9, "Trinity and Revelation." 131–147.
10 Ibid. 146. We are reminded here of Saak's warning about the 'idolatry' of tradition within systematics see p. 217 above.
11 Coakley seems to be suggesting something similar when she describes her work as aiming "to bind questions of theological method, contemplative practice, and desire into a new tether. For they do belong together; and one can see all the more pressingly that they do once one grasps the implications for them of a specifically trinitarian understanding of God". Op. cit. 35.
12 Aquinas *ST I.1.2*. "In this second manner [derived] is Christian theology a science, for it flows from founts recognised in the light of a higher science, namely God's very own which he shares with the blessed". And later: "*Sacra doctrina* does not pronounce on God and creatures as though they were counterbalancing, but on God as principal and on creatures in relation to him, who is their origin and end. Hence its unity as a science (*scientia*) is not hampered." *I.1.3*.
13 Herbert McCabe argues this lucidly in *God and Evil in the Theology of Thomas Aquinas* (Continuum, 2010): 15–33.
14 Aquinas, *ST* 1a.1.9 *responsio*.
15 See note 12 above.
16 See note 14 above.
17 *Summa Theologiae I.1.4*.
18 Ibid. my emphases.
19 Chapter 4, p. 50 above.
20 This is worked out in some detail through chapters 1 and 2 of Coakley's *God, Sexuality, and the Self: An Essay 'on the Trinity'* (CUP, 2013). Summary of the "hallmarks' of *théologie totale* are given 88–92.
21 See Coakley's connecting of *théologie totale* with the *l'historie totale* of the French Annales School, op. cit. 35, n. 2.
22 Here there is another resonance with Coakley, relating to her presentation of the practice of contemplation as fundamental to theology. Op. cit. 88, for example.
23 Johann Baptist Metz, *Faith in History and Society: Toward a Practical Fundamental Theology* (New York, NY: Seabury, 1980).
24 Metz begins his book with a reference to I Pet.3: 15. Op. cit. 3.
25 Ibid. 3.
26 Op. cit. 13, n.15.
27 Ibid.
28 This is a characteristic theme of Metz: *Leiden an Gott* (suffering unto, or toward, God), reminding the comfortable "middle-class" tendencies of theology of the primary orientation of Christian faith toward solidarity with and hope for the suffering world.

29 Ibid. 73.
30 See Preface p. ix above.
31 That is in relation to both the mystery of the Trinity, and in relation to Christian practices in the world and in the Spirit.
32 There is some interesting recent work being done on the place of conversation in theology. In particular I would mention: Jennifer Jackson, *Conversation, Friendship and Transformation: Contemporary and Medieval Voices in a Theology of Discourse* (Routledge, 2016).
33 Chapter 3.
34 Chapter 4.
35 Coakley, op. cit. 88.
36 As significantly recognised by Vatican II's Dogmatic Constitution on the Church *Lumen Gentium* chap. 7.
37 See I Cor. 13:12.

14 Ecclesiology by epiphanies. A prospect

In our paper of 2012, Helen Cameron and I spoke out of the ARCS research about "epiphanic sacramentality".[1] The intention in using this language was to be faithful to our theological action research experience as one in which theological insights were gained through reflection, and real person-to-person conversation, in which 'light-bulb' moments occurred. In these moments of 'epiphany', something was recognised by those in the conversation which was a new way of seeing – an event of revelation-in-miniature. Often, such epiphanies took place through initial disagreements or diverse interpretations of data; other times, they were brought about by the relating of current practices to the longer tradition. In any case, they were – and continue to be in theological action research work – experiences of interruption rather than deduction. They come upon the conversation and its participants rather than our being in control of them.

To say this is not to make any spurious claim either for the lack of real intellectual and personal agency on the part of those taking part in these conversations, or for some paranormal experience! It is simply to draw attention once again to the inductive nature of the theology practised and ecclesiology disclosed in this research, and to the faith-fullness of the researchers regarding the presence of the Spirit in the work and its Practices. What has been learnt has been so not through the setting of a predetermined agenda about the theology of church (although to be sure these existed in our formation and training and will have shaped our understanding to some extent), but rather learning has been discovered, and so ecclesiology disclosed.

One of the characteristics of such an ecclesiology disclosed through epiphanies is that it bears the marks of its necessary incompleteness, its particularity and limited claim to be universal in an especially visible way. However, as the preceding two chapters have argued, this is understood as a part of the distinctive integrity of this disclosed or 'epiphanal' ecclesiology, as it seeks to be shaped by an account of theology as necessarily incomplete, 'doubly negative', and of ecclesiology as concerned with edgeless church of the Spirit's activity in the world. In the end, despite all its limitations, frustrations and openness to expert corrections from all sides, this is a way of doing theology, and ecclesiology in particular, to which I remain more committed than ever having composed the argument of this book.

That I am not alone in this commitment is not only humanly reassuring but also adds strength to the project by enabling just the kind of open, trusting conversation about its prospects as is proper to the overall methodology and its practices. Researchers continue to seek out training in theological action research methods and adapt them for their own work,[2] and growing numbers of doctoral and post-doctoral projects are using the thinking that has been elaborated in this book. As well as the post-ARCS projects outlined in chapter 2, I am currently working with others on two large-scale theological action research projects, on learning within British Methodism and looking at practices of social action involving Roman Catholics and Methodists. All this suggests an on-going future for theological action research and its practices and insights.

This is all very encouraging and suggests that there is something being described in this book which has found a real connection with many researchers in practical theology, and in ecclesiology in particular. However, any future work based on these approaches needs to ask probing questions about the theological epistemology and significance of them, more and more informed by a wider reading of theology of all types; I am especially hopeful for more engagement from biblical studies perspectives. If theological action research and its four voices of theology approach is to be more than simply a method or way of navigating the well-recognised problems of practice-engaged theology, then this more methodological and whole- or fundamental theological questioning must also be continued. For, in the end, as this final section of the book has demonstrated, there is something more being embodied in and claimed by theological action research than a contribution to practical theological method; theological action research presents, I would argue, both a challenge and a hope to theology in the academy. Appropriately enough, the nature and limitations of this 'something more', whilst glimpsed in these later chapters, remains to be discovered through further conversation; but the possibilities of a faith-full, traditioned, and practical whole-theology, which can claim a proper place epistemologically and empirically among the Humanities and Social Sciences are there to be explored.

Above all, as I try to look out over the prospect presented at the end of this exercise of writing up the disclosed ecclesiology of the ARCS project, I found myself drawn to the possibilities for how such accounts of church and of theology as offered here might enable the development of truer and more effective ways of living church today. Not only has this work indicated the disclosed nature of church as edgeless and dependent on the Spirit, it has also argued for a living of church which is primarily conversational in its work of speaking God's hope and love in the world for its healing. As the kind of project described in this book is carried out in more and more locations and by different theologians and practitioners, it is to be hoped that this vision of church can be 'caught' not only by the diverse lay-lived church (which often already instinctively and mutely knows this way of being church), but also, and more problematically, by those at the institutional centre of church. It is only when we are all able to be participant in trusting, prayer-full, person-full and Spirit-full conversation of the kind described in this book and enacted (at best) in its research, that the world will be able to receive church as disclosed to us in epiphanies.

These hopes are not unrealistic, for all their grandiose scope. I can entertain them precisely because of the realities of church I have been privileged to glimpse in the places of the 'ordinary', the edges, the faith-full practices of lay people, in the world today, such as those described in this book. Church is happening. God is with us.

Notes

1 Clare Watkins and Helen Cameron, "Epiphanic Sacramentality: An Example of Practical Ecclesiology Revisioning Theological Understanding." Christian B. Scharen ed. *Explorations in Ecclesiology and Ethnography* (Eerdmans, 2012): 71–89.

2 Periodic training days are offered by TARN: www.theologyandactionresearch.net.

Appendix

An outline of a (typical) cycle of theological action research[1]

The practice of theological action research in each site looks quite different. However, there are five broad stages which can be identified in any theological action research project.

Exploring the opportunities for collaboration

The process begins with some informal conversation around the project between the leaders and the research team to explore whether this will be a good fit for them.

Planning the research

Having agreed to work together on the research, a local team is formed who will take responsibility for the research locally and work directly with the 'outsider', often University-based, team. The main activity is a theological action research training day for the local team, which includes working together on identifying the research question(s). Once a research question is decided a plan is made about how data will be collected.

Gathering the data

Data is collected, by the research assistant on the project, and/or by suitably qualified practitioner co-researchers. The local team are responsible for making initial contact with participants.

Discerning the data

This is the most time consuming but also the most interesting, enjoyable and rewarding part of the process. Transcripts and field notes are distributed to all the members of the teams who then spend time reading and discerning the key themes and insights in relation to their particular research focus. The two reflector teams then meet separately to discuss the themes they observed and each produce a document which summarises the themes. The teams then swap these documents before coming together for a final meeting where a joint 'learning document' is produced, describing what has been learnt.

Naming the learning for action

In the joint reflector team meeting, the conversation is focused around the two teams' documents. The key task of this meeting is to identify and name the joint learning from the research and the ways that this will, or even has already, result in action. Our experience is that learning and action comes naturally throughout the whole process; rather than deciding on learning and action as if this is the final step, the task is to name the learning for action that has arisen through the process.

Note

1 With special thanks to Dr. James Butler, who prepared this text with me for our theological action research training work.

Bibliography

Biblical Quotations are taken from the *New Revised Standard Version*.

All References to the Vatican II Documents are taken from the Vatican Website: www.vatican.va/archive/hist_councils/ii_vatican_council/index.htm

Aquinas, T. *Summa Theologiae*. Vol. 1. Thomas Gilbey ed. London: Eyre & Spottiswoode, 1964.

Aquinas, T. *Summa Theologiae*. Vol. 32. Thomas Gilbey ed. London: Eyre & Spottiswoode, 1975.

Archbishop of Canterbury (Foreword). *Mission-Shaped Church: Church Planting and Fresh Expressions of Church in a Changing Context*. London: Church Publishing, 2005.

Archbishop of Canterbury's Commission on Urban Priority Research Group. *Faith in the City: A Call for Action by Church and Nation*. London: Church House Publishing, 1985.

Ashworth, J. and Farthing, I. *Churchgoing in the UK: A Research Report From Tearfund on Church Attendance in the UK*. London: Tearfund, 2007.

Astley, J. *Ordinary Theology: Looking, Listening and Learning in Theology*. Farnham: Ashgate, 2002.

Astley, J. and Francis, L.J. eds. *Exploring Ordinary Theology: Everyday Christian Believing and the Church*. Farnham: Ashgate, 2013.

Augustine. *City of God*. G.R. Evans ed. and H. Bettenson trans. London: Penguin, 2003.

Avis, P. *The Anglican Understanding of the Church: An Introduction*. 2nd ed. London: SPCK, 2013.

Avis, P. "Ecclesiology and Ethnography: An Unresolved Relationship." *Ecclesiology* 14 (2018): 322–337.

Badcock, G. *The House Where God Lives: Renewing the Doctrine of the Church for Today*. Grand Rapids, MI: Eerdmans, 2009.

Ballard, P. "Can Theology Be Practical." D. Willows and J. Swinton eds. *Spiritual Dimensions of Pastoral Care: Practical Theology in a Multidisciplinary Context*. London: Jessica Kingsley, 2000: 27–35.

Barth, K. *Dogmatics in Outline*. London: SCM Press. 16th Impression 1988. Orig. pub., 1949.

Baumann, Z. *Liquid Modernity*. Cambridge: Polity Press, 2000.

Beaumont, J. "Transcending the Particular in Postsecular Cities." A. Molendijk et al. eds. *Exploring the Postsecular: The Religious, the Political and the Urban*. Leiden: Brill, 2010: 3–17.

Beaumont, J. and Baker, C. eds. *Postsecular Cities: Space, Theory and Practice.* London: Continuum, 2011.

Bennett, Z., Graham, E., Pattison, S., and Walton, H. *Invitation to Research in Practical Theology*. London: Routledge, 2018.

Bevans, S.B. and Schroeder, R.P. *Constants in Context: A Theology of Mission for Today*. Maryknoll, NY: Orbis Books, 2004.

Boeve, L. *God Interrupts History*. London: Continuum, 2007.

Boeve, L. *Interrupting Tradition: An Essay on Christian Faith in a Postmodern Context*. Louvain: Peeters, 2003.

Boeve, L. and Merrigan, T. eds. *Tradition and the Normativity of History*. Leuven: Peeters, 2013.

Boff, L. *Ecclesiogenesis: The Base Communities Reinvent the Church*. London: Collins, 1986.

Booker, M. and Ireland, M. *Evangelism: Which Way Now? An Evaluation of Alpha, Emmaus, Cell Church and Other Contemporary Strategies for Evangelism*. London: Church House Publishing, 2003.

Bosch, D. *Transforming Mission: Paradigm Shifts in Theology of Mission*. Maryknoll, NY: Orbis Books, 1991.

Boyd, J. *The Naked Preacher: Action Research and a Practice of Preaching*. London: SCM, 2018.

Bretherton, L. *Hospitality as Holiness: Christian Witness and Moral Diversity*. Farnham: Ashgate, 2010.

Bria, I. *The Liturgy After the Liturgy*. Geneva: WCC Publications, 1996.

Brierley, P. *London's Churches Are Growing! What the London Church Census Reveals*. Townbridge: ADBC Publishers, 2013.

Brouard, S. *Using Theological Action Research to Embed Catholic Social Teaching in a Catholic Development Agency: Abseiling on the Road to Emmaus*. Unpub. Prof. Doc. Cambridge: Anglia Ruskin University, 2015.

Browning, D. *A Fundamental Practical Theology*. Minneapolis: Augsburg Fortress, 1959.

Brunner, E. *The Misunderstanding of the Church*. Harold Knight trans. London: Lutterworth Press, 2003. Orig. German *Das Missverstaendnis der Kirche*, 1951.

Butler, J. *Exploring the Lived Theology of Small Missional Communities: Uncovering Charismatic Practices and Beliefs to Enable Sustained Engagement in Social Action*. Unpub. PhD, Durham University, 2017. Available at: http://etheses.dur.ac.uk/12849/ Accessed January 2019.

Cameron, H. *Studying Local Churches*. London: SCM, 2005.

Cameron, H. *Resourcing Mission: Practical Theology for Changing Churches*. London: SCM, 2009.

Cameron, H. *Theological Reflection for Human Flourishing: Pastoral Practice and Public Theology*. London: SCM, 2013.

Cameron, H., Bhatti, D., Duce, C., Sweeney, J., and Watkins, C. *Talking About God in Practice: Theological Action Research and Practical Theology*. London: SCM, 2010.

Cameron, H., Richter, P., and Davies, D. *Studying Local Churches: A Handbook*. London: SCM, 2011.

Catholic Bishops' Conference of England and Wales. *Cherishing Life*. London: Catholic Truth Society, 2004.

Catholic Bishops' Conference of England and Wales. *Choosing the Common Good*. Stoke on Trent: Alive Publishing, 2010.

Coakley, S. *God, Sexuality, and the Self: An Essay 'On the Trinity'*. Cambridge: CUP, 2013.

Coakely, S. and Stang, M. eds. *Rethinking Dionysius the Areopagite*. Oxford: Wiley-Blackwell, 2009.

Coghlan, D. *Attending to Experience: Reflections on Engaging in Action Research*, (2003). Available at: www.aral.com.au/whyar/Coghlan.pdf.

Coghlan, D. "Seeking God in All Things: Ignatian Spirituality as Action Research." *The Way* 43, no. 1 (2004): 97–108.

Coghlan, D. "Ignatian Spirituality as Transformational Social Science." *Action Research* 3, no. 1 (2005): 89–107.

Coghlan, D. "Towards a Spirituality of Academic Work: Lessons From Action Research." *Human Development* 27, no. 2 (2006): 38–41.

Coghlan, D. "Authenticity as First Person Practice." *Action Research* 6, no. 3 (2008): 351–366.

Coghlan, D. "Interiority as the Cutting Edge Between Theory and Practice: A First Person Perspective." *International Journal of Action Research* 6, no. 2–3 (2010): 288–307.

Conde Frazier, E. "Participatory Action Research." Bonnie Miller McLemore ed. *The Wiley Blackwell Companion to Practical Theology*. Malden, MA: Wiley-Blackwell, 2013: 234–243.

Congar, Y. *Tradition & Traditions: The Biblical, Historical, and Theological Evidence for Catholic Teaching on Tradition*. San Diego, CA, Needham Heights, MA, and Basilica: Simon & Schuster, 1998.

Congregation for the Doctrine of the Faith. *Letter to the Bishops of the Catholic Church on Some Aspects of the Church Understood as Communion*. Vatican, 1992. Available at: www.vatican.va/roman_curia/congregations/cfaith/documents/rc_con_cfaith_doc_28051992_communionis-notio_en.html.

Croft, S. ed. *Mission-Shaped Questions: Defining Issues for Today's Church*. London: Church House Publishing, 2008.

Davie, G. *Religion in Britain Since 1945: Believing Without Belonging*. Oxford: Blackwell, 1994.

Davison, A. and Milbank, A. *For the Parish: A Critique of Fresh Expressions*. London: SCM, 2010.

De Lubac, H. *Catholicism: A Study of Dogma in Relation to the Corporate Destiny of Mankind*. New York: Longmans, Green, 1950.

De Lubac, H. *Corpus Mysticum: The Eucharist and the Church in the Middle Ages*. Laurence Paul Hemming and Susan Frank Parsons eds. London: SCM, 2006.

Dreyer, J.S. "Knowledge, Subjectivity, (De)Coloniality, and the Conundrum of Reflexivity." Joyce Ann Mercer and Bonnie Miller-McLemore eds. *Conundrums in Practical Theology*. Leiden: Brill, 2016: 90–109.

Duce, C. "Church-Based Work With the Homeless: A Theological Exploration of the Practices of Hospitality." *Practical Theology* 6, no. 1 (2013): 87–103.

Dulles, A. *Models of the Church*. 2nd ed. Dublin: Gill and Macmillan, 1987.

Dunlop, A. *Out of Nothing: A Cross-Shaped Approach to Fresh Expressions*. London: SCM, 2018.

Dunlop, A. and Brooker, A. *Mixed-Economy Mission: Collaborative Ministry for Multi-Church Growth*. Cambridge: Grove Books, 2019.

Faggioli, M. *Sorting Out Catholicism: A Brief History of the New Ecclesial Movements*. Collegeville, MN: Liturgical Press, 2014.

Faggioli, M. *The Rising Laity: Ecclesial Movements Since Vatican II*. Mahwah, NJ: Paulist Press, 2016.

Farley, E. *Theologia: The Fragmentation and Unity of Theological Education*. Philadelphia: Fortress, 1983.

Ferrara, P. "The Concept of Periphery in Pope Francis' Discourse: A Religious Alternative to Globalization?" *Religions* 6 (2015): 42–57.

Fiddes, P.S. *Participating in God: A Pastoral Doctrine of the Trinity*. London: Darton Longman & Todd, 2000.

Fiddes, P.S. "Ecclesiology and Ethnography: Two Disciplines, Two Worlds?" Pete Ward ed. *Perspectives on Ecclesiology and Ethnography*. Grand Rapids, MI: Eerdmans, 2012: 13–35.

Flynn, G., Murray, P.D., and Hardcastle, P. eds. *Ressourcement: A Movement for Renewal in Twentieth-Century Catholic Theology*. Oxford: OUP, 2012.

Francis, L. *Growth or Decline in the Church of England During the Decade of Evangelism: Did the Churchmanship of the Bishop Matter*? Available at: http://wrap.warwick.ac.uk/2877/1/WRAP_Francis_0673558-ie-170210-decade_of_evangelism_mla.pdf. Accessed January 2019.

Gaze, S. *Mission-Shaped and Rural: Growing Churches in the Countryside*. London: Church House Publishing, 2006.

Goodhew, D. ed. *Church Growth in Britain: 1980 to the Present*. Farnham: Ashgate, 2012.

Goodhew, D. and Cooper, A.P. *The Desecularisation of the City: London's Churches, 1980 to the Present*. London: Routledge, 2018.

Gorringe, T. *A Theology of the Built Environment: Justice, Empowerment, Redemption*. Cambridge: CUP, 2002.

Goto, C.T. *Taking on Practical Theology: The Idolization of Context and the Hope of Community*. Leiden: Brill, 2018.

Graham, E. *Transforming Practice: Pastoral Theology in an Age of Uncertainty*. Eugene, OR: Wipf and Stock, 2002.

Graham, E. "Is Practical Theology a Form of 'Action Research'?" *International Journal of Practical Theology* 17, no. 1 (2013): 148–178.

Graham, E. and Lowe, S. *What Makes a Good City? Public Theology and the Urban Church*. London: Darton Longman & Todd, 2009.

Graham, E., Walton, H., and Ward, F. *Theological Reflection: Methods*. London: SCM, 2005.

Graham, E., Walton, H., and Ward, F. *Theological Reflection: Sources*. London: SCM, 2007.

Greenwood, D.J. and Levin, M. *Introduction to Action Research: Social Research for Social Change*. London: Sage, 2007.

Greenwood, R., Oliver, C., Sahlin, K., and Suddaby, R. eds. *The SAGE Handbook of Organizational Institutionalism*. London: SAGE, 2008.

Guder, D. ed. *Missional Church: A Vision for the Sending of the Church in North America*. Grand Rapids, MI: Eerdmans, 1998.

Haight, R. *Christian Community in History Volume 1: Historical Ecclesiology*. New York: Continuum, 2004.

Haight, R. *Ecclesial Existence: Christian Community in History Volume II*. New York: Continuum, 2008.

Hand, C. *Falling Short? The Alpha Course Examined*. Epsom, Surrey: Day One Publications, 1998.

Hardy, D. *Finding the Church: The Dynamic Truth of Anglicanism*. London: SCM, 2001.

Haring, B. *The Sacraments in a Secular Age: A Vision in Depth on Sacramentality and Its Impact on Moral Life*. Slough: St Pauls Publications, 1976.

Hatch, M.J. and Cunliffe, A.L. *Organization Theory: Modern, Symbolic, and Post-modern Perspectives*. 2nd ed. Oxford: OUP, 2006.

Healy, N. *Church, World and the Christian Life: Practical Prophetic Ecclesiology*. Cambridge: CUP, 2000.

Healy, N. "Ecclesiology, Ethnography and God: An Interplay of Reality Descriptions." Pete Ward ed. *Perspectives on Ecclesiology and Ethnography*. Grand Rapids, MI: Eerdmans, 2012: 182–199.

Hegstad, H. *The Real Church: An Ecclesiology of the Visible*. Eugene, OR: Pickwick Publications, 2013.

Hellemans, S. and Wissink, J. eds. *Towards a New Catholic Church in Advanced Modernity: Transformation, Visions and Tensions*. Munster: LIT Verlag, 2012.

Heythrop Institute for Religion, Ethics and Public Life. *On the Way to Life*, 2005. Available at: http://cbcew.org.uk/plain/wp-content/uploads/sites/3/2018/11/on-the-way-to-life-2005.pdf. Accessed August 2019.

Hovey, C. "Alasdair MacIntyre's Hermeneutics of Tradition." Craig Hovey and Cyrus P. Olsen eds. *The Hermeneutics of Tradition: Explorations and Examinations*. Eugene, OR: Wipf and Stock, 2014: 144–169.

Hovey, C. and Olsen, C. eds. *The Hermeneutics of Tradition: Explorations and Examinations*. Eugene, OR: Wipf and Stock, 2014.

Hull, J. *Mission-shaped Church: A Theological Response*. London: SCM, 2015.

Ignatius. *The Spiritual Exercises*. Preface by Avery Dulles. Chicago: Loyola Press, 2000.

Jackson, J. *Conversation, Friendship and Transformation: Contemporary and Medieval Voices in a Theology of Discourse*. London: Routledge, 2016.

Jinkins, M. *The Church Faces Death: Ecclesiology in a Post-Modern Context*. Oxford: OUP, 2002.

Johnson, L.T. *Scripture and Discernment: Decision-Making in the Church*. Abingdon: Abingdon Press, 1996.

Kaufman, T.S. "Normativity as Pitfall or Ally? Reflexivity as an Interpretive Resource in Ecclesiological and Ethnographic Research." *Ecclesial Practices* 2, no. 1 (2015): 91–107.

Kaufman, T.S. "From the Outside, Within, or in Between? Normativity at Work in Empirical Practical Theological Research." Joyce Ann Mercer and Bonnie Miller-McLemore eds. *Conundrums in Practical Theology*. Leiden: Brill, 2016: 134–162.

Kaufman, T.S. and Idestrom, J. "Why Matter Matters in Theological Action Research: Attending to the Voices of Tradition." *International Journal of Practical Theology* 22, no. 1 (2018): 84–102.

Kearsley, R. *Church, Community and Power*. London: Routledge, 2018.

Knights, P. and Murray, A. *Evangelisation in England and Wales: A Report to the Catholic Bishops*. London: Catholic Communications Service, 2002.

Lash, N. "Authors, Authority and Authorization." Bernard Hoose ed. *Authority in the Roman Catholic Church: Theory and Practice*. Farnham: Ashgate, 2002: 59–71.

Lash, N. *Holiness, Speech and Silence: Reflections on the Question of God*. Aldershot: Ashgate, 2006.

Lavallee, H.M. "Practical Theology From the Perspective of Catholic Spirituality: A Hermeneutic of Discernment." *International Journal of Practical Theology* 20, no. 2 (2016): 203–221.

Lenan, R. *Risking the Church: The Challenges of Catholic Faith.* Oxford: OUP, 2004.

Lukes, S. *Power: A Radical View.* 2nd expanded ed. Basingstoke: Palgrave Macmillan, 2005.

MacIntyre, A. *After Virtue.* 2nd ed. Notre Dame, IN: University of Notre Dame Press, 1984.

MacIntyre, A. *Whose Justice? Which Rationality?* Notre Dame, IN: University of Notre Dame Press, 1984.

Macquarrie, J. *A Guide to the Sacraments.* London: SCM, 1999.

Martos, J. *Doors to the Sacred: A Historical Introduction to Sacraments in the Catholic Church.* Rev. and Updated ed. Liquori, MO: Liquori/Triumph, 2001.

McCann, J.F. *Church and Organisation: A Sociological and Theological Enquiry.* London; Toronto: Associated University Press, 1993.

McClintock Fulkerson, M. *Places of Redemption: Theology for a Worldly Church.* Oxford: OUP, 2010.

McDonagh, E. "Fruit of the Earth – Work of Human Hands." Mary Grey ed. *The Candles Are Still Burning: Directions in Sacrament and Spirituality.* London: Geoffrey Chapman, 1995: 22–31.

McDonald, E. *Alpha: The Unofficial Guide. Overview. A Whole New Study on the Alpha Course.* Cambridge: St Matthew, 2001.

Medhurst, K. and Sweeney, J. "Public Theology and Changing Social Values." *Studies in Christian Ethics* 17, no. 2 (2004): 118–133.

Mercer, J.A. and Miller-McLemore, B. *Conundrums in Practical Theology.* Leiden: Brill, 2016.

Metz, J. *Faith in History and Society: Toward a Practical Fundamental Theology.* New York, NY: Seabury, 1980.

Milbank, J., Ward, G., Pickstock, J., and Pickstock, C. *Radical Orthodoxy: A New Theology.* London: Routledge, 1999.

Miller McLemore, B. ed. *The Wiley Blackwell Companion to Practical Theology.* Malden, MA: Wiley-Blackwell, 2013.

Moltmann, J. *The Church in the Power of the Spirit: A Contribution to Messianic Ecclesiology.* London: SCM, 1977.

Newbigin, L. *Trinitarian Faith and Today's Mission.* Richmond: John Knox Press, 1964.

Newbigin. L *The Open Secret: Introduction to the Theology of Mission.* Rev. ed. Grand Rapids, MI: Eerdmans, 1996.

Newlands, G. and Smith, A. *Hospitable God: The Transformative Dream.* Farnham: Ashgate, 2010.

Newman, E. *Untamed Hospitality: Welcoming God and Other Stranger.* Ada, MI: Brazos Press, 2007.

O'Collins, G. *Retrieving Fundamental Theology.* London: Geoffrey Chapman, 1993.

O'Connell Killeen, P. and de Beer, J. *The Art of Theological Reflection.* New York: Crossroad, 1994.

Olin, J.C. ed. *A Reformation Debate: Sadoleto's Letter to the Genevans and Calvin's Reply.* New York: Harper & Row, 1966.

O'Neill, G. and Shercliff, L. *Straw for the Bricks: Theological Reflection in Practice*. London: SCM, 2018.

Ormerod, N. *Re-Visioning the Church: An Experiment in Systematic Historical Ecclesiology*. Philadelphia: Fortress Press, 2014.

Ospina, S., et al. "Taking the Action Turn: Lessons From Bringing Participation to Qualitative Research." Peter Reason and Hilary Bradbury eds. *The Sage Handbook of Action Research*. 2nd ed. London: Sage, 2013: 420–434.

Pasewark, K. *A Theology of Power: Being Beyond Domination*. Minneapolis: Fortress, 1993.

Pattison, P. and Woodward, J. eds. *The Blackwell Reader in Practical and Pastoral Theology*. Malden, MA: Wiley Blackwell, 2008.

Pattison, S. "Some Straw for the Bricks: A Basic Introduction to Theological Reflection." *Contact* 99, no. 1 (1989): 2–9.

Paul, P.J. II (foreword). *Catechism of the Catholic Church: With Modifications From the Editio Typica*. New York: Doubleday, 1995.

Percy, M. *Power and the Church: Ecclesiology in an Age of Transition*. London: Cassell, 1998.

Percy, M. *Engaging With Contemporary Culture: Christianity, Theology, and the Concrete Church*. Aldershot: Ashgate, 2005.

Percy, M. *Clergy: The Origin of Species*. London: Continuum, 2006.

Percy, M. *Shaping the Church: The Promise of Implicit Theology*. Farnham: Ashgate, 2016.

Percy, M. and Nestrop, L. *Evaluating Fresh Expression: Explorations in Emerging Church*. Norwich: Canterbury Press, 2008.

Pickard, S. *Theological Foundations for Collaborative Ministry*. Farnham: Ashgate, 2009.

Pohl, C. *Making Room: Recovering Hospitality as a Christian Tradition*. Grand Rapids, MI: Eerdmans Publishing, 1999.

Pope Benedict XVI Apostolic Exhortation. *Sacramentum Caritatis*. 2007. Available at: http://w2.vatican.va/content/benedict-xvi/en/apost_exhortations/documents/hf_ben-xvi_exh_20070222_sacramentum-caritatis.html

Prickett, S. *Modernity and the Reinvention of Tradition*. Cambridge: CUP, 2009.

Rahner, K. *The Church and the Sacraments*. New York: Herder, 1966.

Rahner, K. *Foundations of Christian Faith: An Introduction to the Idea of Christianity*. New York: Crossroad, 2000.

Reason, P. and Bradbury, H. eds. *The Sage Handbook of Action Research: Participative Inquiry and Practice*. 2nd ed. London: Sage, 2013.

Rich, A. *Discernment in the Desert Fathers: Diakrisis in the Life and Thought of Early Egyptian Monasticism*. Milton Keynes: Paternoster, 2007.

Richard, L. *Living the Hospitality of God*. Mahwah, NJ: Paulist Press, 2000.

Rosemann, P. *Charred Root of Meaning: Continuity, Transgression, and the Other in Christian Tradition*. Grand Rapids, MI: Eerdmans, 2018.

Rosemann, P. "Charred Root of Meaning: Rupture and Continuity in Christian Tradition." *Irish Theological Quarterly* 84, no. 1 (2019): 3–21.

Ross, C. and Baker, J. *The Pioneer Gift: Explorations in Mission*. Norwich: Canterbury Press, 2014.

Ross, C. and Baker, J. *Pioneering Spirituality*. Norwich: Canterbury Press, 2015.

Ross, C. and Bevans, S. eds. *Mission on the Way to Emmaus: Constants, Contexts, and Prophetic Dialogue*. Maryknoll, NY: Orbis Books, 2013.

Ross, C. and Smith, C. eds. *Missional Conversations: A Dialogue Between Theory and Praxis in World Mission*. London: SCM, 2018.

Rowland, T. "Joseph Ratzinger and the Hermeneutics of Continuity." C. Hovey and C. Olsen eds. *The Hermeneutics of Tradition: Explorations and Examinations*. Eugene, OR: Wipf and Stock, 2014: 93–225.

Rudge, P.F. *Ministry and Management: The Study of Ecclesiastical Administration*. London: Tavistock, 1968.

Rudge, P.T. *Management in the Church*. London: McGraw-Hill, 1976.

Saak, E. "Questioning Normativity: Systematic Theology as an Instrument of Evil." Lieven Boeve and Terrence Merrigan eds. *Tradition and the Normativity of History*. Leuven: Peeters, 2013: 17–47.

Sagovsky, N. *Ecumenism, Christian Origins and the Practice of Communion*. Cambridge: CUP, 2000.

Scharen, C. *Explorations in Ecclesiology and Ethnography*. Grand Rapids, MI: Eerdmans, 2012.

Scharen, C. *Fieldwork in Theology: Exploring the Social Context of God's Work in the World*. Grand Rapids, MI: Baker Academic, 2015.

Schillebeeckx, E. *Ministry: A Case for Change*. London: SCM, 1981.

Schillebeeckx, E. *The Church With a Human Face: A New and Expanded Theology of Ministry*. London: SCM, 1985.

Schreiter, R. ed. *Mission in the Third Millennium*. Maryknoll, NY: Orbis Books, 2001.

Segundo, J.L. *Theology for Artisans of a New Humanity (Vol. 4): The Sacraments Today*. Maryknoll, NY: Orbis Books, 1973.

Shakespeare, L. *Being the Body of Christ in the Age of Management*. Eugene, OR: Wipf and Stock, 2016.

Sheldrake, P. *The Spiritual City: Theology, Spirituality and the Urban*. Malden, MA: Wiley Blackwell, 2014.

Shepherd, N. "Action Research as Professional Development." *Journal of Adult Theological Education* 9, no. 2 (2012): 121–138.

Snook, L. *What in the World Is God Doing: Re-Imagining Spirit and Power*. Minneapolis: Fortress, 1999.

Sutherland, A. *I Was a Stranger: A Christian Theology of Hospitality*. Abingdon: Abingdon press, 2006.

Sweeney, J. "Catholicism in Britain: A Church in Search of Its Way." Staf Hellemans and Jozef Wissink eds. *Towards a New Catholic Church in Advanced Modernity: Transformation, Visions and Tensions*. Munster: LIT Verlag, 2012.

Sweeney, J. "Faith in Culture." *New Blackfriars* 94 (2013): 148–159.

Sweeney, J., et al. eds. *Keeping Faith in Practice*. London: SCM, 2010.

Swinton, J. and Mowat, H. *Practical Theology and Qualitative Research*. London: SCM, 2006.

Sykes, S. *Power and Christian Theology*. London and New York: Continuum, 2006.

Tanner, K. *Jesus, Humanity and the Trinity: A Brief Systematic Theology*. Minneapolis, MN: Fortress, 2001.

Thompson, J. *SCM Study Guide to Theological Reflection*. London: SCM, 2008.

Thung, M.A. *The Precarious Organisation: Sociological Explorations of the Church's Mission and Structure*. Berlin; Boston: De Gruyter Mouton, Reprint 2016. Orig. Pub., 1976.

Torry, M. *Managing Religion: The Management of Christian Religious and Faith-Based Organizations*. Basingstoke: Palgrave Macmillan, 2014.

Tracey, P. "Spreading the Word: The Microfoundations of Institutional Persuasion and Conversion." *Informs Science; Organization Science* 27, no. 4 (2016).

Tran, J. "The Wound of Tradition." Craig Hovey and Cyrus P. Olsen eds. *The Hermeneutics of Tradition: Explorations and Examinations*. Eugene, OR: Wipf and Stock, 2014: 226ff.

van der Ven, J.A. *Ecclesiology in Context*. Grand Rapids, MI: Eerdmans, 1996.

Walker, J. *Testing Fresh Expressions: Identity and Transformation*. London: Routledge, 2014.

Walls, A. *The Missionary Movement in Christian History: Studies in the Transmission of Faith*. Maryknoll, NY: Orbis Books, 1996.

Ward, P. ed. *Perspectives on Ecclesiology and Ethnography*. Grand Rapids, MI: Eerdmans, 2012.

Ward, P. *Liquid Church*. Eugene, OR: Wipf and Stock, 2013.

Ward, P. "Blueprint Ecclesiology and the Lived: Normativity as a Perilous Faithfulness." *Ecclesial Practices* 2, no. 1 (2015): 74–90.

Ward, P. *Introducing Practical Theology: Mission, Ministry, and the Life of the Church*. Grand Rapids, MI: Baker Academic, 2017.

Ward, P. *Liquid Ecclesiology: The Gospel and the Church*. Leiden: Brill, 2017.

Watkins, C. "Organizing the People of God: Social Science Theories of Organization in Ecclesiology." *Theological Studies* 52 (1991): 689–711.

Watkins, C. "Collaborators, Informers and Secret Service: Some Thoughts on the Theologies of Laity and Ministry Since Vatican II." *New Blackfriars* 74, no. 871 (May 1993): 263–279.

Watkins, C. "Organization and Management: The Church as a Special Case." *Modern Theology* 9, no. 4 (October 1993): 369–384

Watkins, C. "Objecting to *koinonia*. Why Communion Isn't the Answer." *Louvain Studies* 28 (2003): 326–343.

Watkins, C. "*Traditio* and the Handling of Holy Things. Reflections *de doctrina christiana* From an Ecclesiology Ordered to Baptism." *New Blackfriars* 87, no. 1008 (March 2006): 166–183.

Watkins, C. "Texts and Practices: An Ecclesiology of *Traditio* for Pastoral Theology." James Sweeney et al. eds. *Keeping Faith in Practice*. London: SCM, 2010: 163–178.

Watkins, C. "Practising Ecclesiology: From Product to Process." *Ecclesial Practices* 2 (2015): 23–29.

Watkins, C. "An Argument for *Non-Correlational* Approaches in a Catholic Practical Theology." *Cahiers Internationaux de Theologie Pratique* 8 (March 2016): 141–158. Available at: www.pastoralis.org/CITP-Actes-no-8-Groupe-Santiago

Watkins, C. "Conversational Methods of Discernment: Learning for Mission From the Domestic Church." Thomas Knieps-Port le Roi and Aldegonde Brenninkmeijer-Werhahn eds. *Authentic Voices, Discerning Hearts: New resources for the Church on Marriage and Family*. Munster: LIT Verlag, 2016: 15–29.

Watkins, C. "Ek-Centric Ecclesiology: Innovation, Agency and the Holding of Tradition." *Anvil* 35, no. 3 (2019).

Watkins, C. and Cameron, H. "Epiphanic Sacramentality: An Example of Practical Ecclesiology Revisioning Theological Understanding." Christian B. Scharen ed.

Explorations in Ecclesiology and Ethnography. Grand Rapids, MI: Eerdmans, 2012: 71–89.

Watkins, C. and Shepherd, B. "The Challenge of 'Fresh Expressions' to Ecclesiology: Reflections From the Practice of Messy Church." *Ecclesial Practices* 1 (2014): 92–110.

Weber, M. *The Theory of Social and Economic Organisation*. A.M. Henderson and Talcott Parsons trans. Glencoe, IL: Free & Falcon's Wing, 1947.

Williams, R. *On Christian Theology*. Oxford: Blackwell, 2000.

Willows, D. and Swinton, J. *Spiritual Dimensions of Pastoral Care: Practical Theology in a Multidisciplinary Context*. London: Jessica Kingsley, 2000.

Wolffe, J. and Jackson, B. "Anglican Resurgence: The Church of England in London." David Goodhew ed. *Church Growth in Britain: 1980 to the Present*. Farnham: Ashgate, 2012: 23–40.

World Council of Churches Faith & Order Commission. *The Church: Towards a Common Vision*. Faith & Order Paper 214. Geneva: World Council of Churches Publications, 2013.

Zizioulas, J. *Being as Communion: Studies in Personhood and the Church*. London: Darton, Longman and Todd, 1985.

Index

Printed in Great Britain
by Amazon

37352327R00156